Istanbul households is a social history ὀ   ρορulation
in Istanbul during the turbulent period σι ιιαnsition from the Ottoman Empire
to the Turkish Republic in the late nineteenth and early twentieth centuries.
Istanbul was the first Muslim city to experience a systematic decline in fertility
and major changes in family life, and, as such, set the tone for many social
and cultural changes in Turkey and the Muslim world. Istanbul was the major
focal point for the forces of westernization of Turkish society, processes which
not only transformed political and economic institutions in that country, but
also had a profound and lasting impact on domestic life. This is the first
systematic historical study of the family and population in Turkey or the
Middle East, combining the methods and approaches of social anthropology,
historical demography and social history.

Istanbul households

Cambridge Studies in Population, Economy and
Society in Past Time 15

Series Editors

PETER LASLETT, ROGER SCHOFIELD and
E. A. WRIGLEY
ESRC Cambridge Group for the History of Population and
Social Structure

and DANIEL SCOTT SMITH
University of Illinois at Chicago

Recent work in social, economic and demographic history has revealed much that was previously obscure about societal stability and change in the past. It has also suggested that crossing the conventional boundaries between these branches of history can be very rewarding.

This series will exemplify the value of interdisciplinary work of this kind, and will include books on topics such as family, kinship and neighbourhood; welfare provision and social control; work and leisure; migration; urban growth; and legal structures and procedures, as well as more familiar matters. It will demonstrate that, for example, anthropology and economics have become as close intellectual neighbours to history as have political philosophy or biography.

For a full list of titles in the series, please see end of book.

Istanbul households

Marriage, family and fertility
1880–1940

ALAN DUBEN and CEM BEHAR
Boğaziçi University

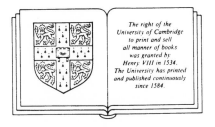

The right of the
University of Cambridge
to print and sell
all manner of books
was granted by
Henry VIII in 1534.
The University has printed
and published continuously
since 1584.

CAMBRIDGE UNIVERSITY PRESS

Cambridge
New York   Port Chester
Melbourne   Sydney

PUBLISHED BY THE PRESS SYNDICATE OF THE UNIVERSITY OF CAMBRIDGE
The Pitt Building, Trumpington Street, Cambridge, United Kingdom

CAMBRIDGE UNIVERSITY PRESS
The Edinburgh Building, Cambridge CB2 2RU, UK
40 West 20th Street, New York NY 10011–4211, USA
477 Williamstown Road, Port Melbourne, VIC 3207, Australia
Ruiz de Alarcón 13, 28014 Madrid, Spain
Dock House, The Waterfront, Cape Town 8001, South Africa

http://www.cambridge.org

First published 1991
First paperback edition 2002

A catalogue record for this book is available from the British Library

Library of Congress Cataloguing in Publication data
Duben, Alan, 1943–
Istanbul households: marriage, family, and fertility, 1880–1940 /
Alan Duben and Cem Behar.
p.   cm. – (Cambridge studies in population, economy, and
society in past time: 15).
Includes bibliographical references.
ISBN 0 521 38375 7
1. Family – Turkey – History – 19th century.   2. Family – Turkey –
History – 20th century.   3. Marriage – Turkey – History – 19th century.
4. Marriage – Turkey – History – 20th century.   I. Behar, Cem, 1946–.
II. Title.   III. Series.
HQ663.4.D83   1991
306.8′09561–dc20   90-33133   CIP

ISBN 0 521 38375 7 hardback
ISBN 0 521 52303 6 paperback

For my wife, İpek Aksüğür Duben
A.D.
For my wife, Büşra Ersanlı Behar
C.B.

and for our parents

Contents

List of Plates

(Those plates which are not attributed belong to Alan Duben)

List of Figures

Note on calendars, weights and currency

CALENDARS

Along with the lunar hegirian calendar, nineteenth-century Ottomans also began to use another hegirian but solar calendar called *rûmî* (Roman) or *mâlî* (financial). After 1840 both calendars were used jointly in legal and financial transactions. From the 1870s on, newspapers and other periodicals also used both calendars. Religious authorities and the *sharia* courts, however, continued to use the classical (lunar) hegirian dates. Towards the end of the nineteenth century the *rûmî* calendar became more popular and, especially after 1908, it superseded the lunar hegirian one in many areas. During the First World War the Gregorian calendar also began to be used. After 1 January 1926 it became the official calendar of the Turkish Republic.

We have, when possible, tried to give both the hegirian and the Gregorian dates in the text and in our references. The hegirian dates given, however, sometimes refer to the lunar and sometimes to the solar hegirian calendars. Census registrations were largely done using the *rûmî* calendar and those are the ones we have used in the text. For printed materials we have made use both of lunar and solar hegirian calendars. In most cases we list the hegirian dates first followed by the Gregorian ones. Conversions were done with the help of the tables found in F. R. Unat, *Hicrî Tarihleri Milâdî Tarihlere Çevirme Kılavuzu* (A Guide to Converting Hegirian to Gregorian Dates), (Ankara, 1974), and a computer program called 'Taqwim: an Islamic calendar convertor', created by Mark Woodworth and John E. Woods, American Research Institute in Turkey, 1988.

WEIGHTS

1 *okka* = 1.283 kilogram

CURRENCY

1 *lira* = 100 *kuruş*

1 *kuruş* = 40 *para*

From the 1840s to the First World War one Ottoman gold *lira* was exchanged for:

0.9 pound sterling

22.8 French francs

8.5 roubles

4.4 US dollars

Note on Turkish pronunciation and spelling

The standard modern Turkish spelling system has been employed in this book except for Turkish words (such as pasha) commonly used in English. The Latin letters in this system are pronounced more or less the same as their English equivalents, with the following exceptions:

Letter	English pronunciation
â	like the *ia* in 'media' if preceeded by a *k* or *g*
c	*j*
ç	*ch*
ğ	*lengthens preceding vowel; thus ağa is pronounced a-a*
ı	like the *a* in 'serial' or *io* in 'cushion'
j	zh
ö	like the German *ö*
ş	sh
ü	like the German *ü*
v	lighter than the English *v*

Arabic terms used in Ottoman or modern Turkish have been given their modern Turkish spellings and pronunciation thus *mehr* and *ümmet* rather than *mahr* and *umma*.

xvi

Acknowledgements

We began the research on which this book is based in 1982 with a grant from Middle East Research Awards in Population and Development. That was followed at later dates by a second grant from the Middle East Research Awards Program, and grants from the National Science Foundation, the Wenner-Gren Foundation for Anthropological Research, Inc. and the Rockefeller Foundation. We are very grateful to those institutions for the support they have given us, without which the project would not have been possible.

We are especially indebted to Frederic C. Shorter of the Population Council, Cairo Office for Southwest Asia and North Africa who, from the very inception of the study, helped focus our efforts and set many of the directions we followed. Perhaps this book would not have existed at all if it were not for him. His own research on the population of Turkey presented us with many of the issues we have elaborated upon in this study. He provided constant encouragement, intellectual stimulation and direction from the early days of project formulation to the writing of the text.

Cem Behar extends his heartfelt thanks to the members of the Cambridge Group for the History of Population and Social Structure, and especially to Roger Schofield and Peter Laslett who, in 1983-4, helped provide him with an ideally stimulating academic environment. Alan Duben is very grateful to Daniel G. Bates and the other members of the Department of Anthropology, Hunter College, City University of New York, for the hospitality and fine scholarly atmosphere with which they provided him in 1985. Discussions with Daniel G. Bates, David D. Gilmore and Bert Pasternak during that year in New York were particularly helpful.

We are very grateful to Zafer Toprak of the Department of History, Boğaziçi University, who discussed the issues of concern with us at

xvii

great length, and provided most generous access to his own personal library and to his vast knowledge of sources for the period. We obtained many of the essential primary and secondary sources used in this book as a result of his help.

We owe special thanks to the following individuals who assisted us at various stages of the research in collecting and organizing the data we used: Nuray Mert, Esen Türay, Hakan Erdem, Nilgün Günaydın, Figen Şatır, Sezen Malta, Ayşe Durakbaşa, Duygu Erdem, Ayse Solon, Aydın Yaşarol and Yunus Yener. We would like to thank Selim Deringil (Department of History, Boğaziçi University) for providing us with certain archival materials, Hayri Mutluçağ for familiarizing us with the various Istanbul archives, and Engin Çizgen for access to her remarkable collection of Ottoman photographs. We thank the elderly Istanbul men and women whom we interviewed for sharing so openly with us their childhood and early adult lives. They provided us with much important information and with a perspective on family life and fertility which we could not have obtained elsewhere.

We are very much indebted to Nevzat Ayaz, former Governor of the Province of Istanbul, for permission to use the Istanbul population archives, to Nurettin Çivi, then Director of the Istanbul Population Department, for facilitating our use of the various archives, and to those who assisted us in each of the district archives. We also thank Abdülaziz Bayındır, Director of the Archive of the Istanbul Religious Courts (*İstanbul Müftülüğü Şeriye Sicilleri Arşivi*) for permission to use the archives and for his assistance, and to Hilmi Şener, former Director of the Istanbul *Darülaceze*, who allowed us to interview a number of the elderly inmates residing there. We also thank Erol Özbilgen, the former Director of the Atatürk Library, for assistance he gave us.

We are especially grateful to a number of individuals who gave generously of their time to read and comment on the text. Faruk Birtek of the Department of Sociology, Boğaziçi University, read the entire text and assisted us greatly with his discerning suggestions. Jale Parla (Department of Western Languages and Literature, Boğaziçi University) and Ferhunde Özbay (Department of Sociology, Boğaziçi University) read parts of the text and provided helpful comments and suggestions. Mary Berkmen read the entire text, and her editorial suggestions were particularly helpful. We also thank the staff of the Cambridge University Press for the meticulousness with which they read and revised the typescript and prepared it for publication. In the end, we alone are responsible for the many deficiencies that remain.

Finally, we thank Kırmızı, always faithfully in our midst.

1

Issues, scope and sources

Our attention was caught a number of years ago by the striking juxta-position of a few demographic figures for Turkey of the 1930s and 1940s which seemed to set Istanbul apart from the rest of the country in a very dramatic way. These figures revealed the rather simple fact that at a time when rural Turkish families were bringing into the world seven children on the average and those in towns and cities over four, the residents of Istanbul were barely replacing themselves biologically. They were giving birth to only slightly over two children.[1] We also soon discovered that this remarkably low fertility was accompanied by a very late age at marriage: twenty-three or twenty-four for women and around thirty for men, as contrasted with official figures of nineteen and twenty-two for rural women and men respectively, no doubt several years higher than was actually the case in Turkish villages.[2]

With fertility rates nearly a third of those in rural areas and marriage ages almost ten years higher, Istanbul had the demographic attributes of many pre-twentieth-century western European societies. How was that possible in the former capital of what was until the 1920s an Islamic empire? Had this been the case for some time? If not, what brought this situation about? And what does all of this mean for our under-standing of Turkish society and the relationship between population and society in a more general sense?

[1] Frederic C. Shorter and Miroslav Macura, *Trends in Fertility and Mortality in Turkey, 1935–1975* (Washington, DC, 1982), 51.
[2] See Samira Berksan, 'Marriage patterns and the effect on fertility in Turkey' in F. C. Shorter and B. Güvenç, eds., *Turkish Demography: Proceedings of a Conference* (Ankara, 1969), for the official figures. Village ethnographies give us earlier marriage dates. See, for example, Niyazi Berkes, *Bazı Ankara Köyleri Üzerine Bir Araştırma* (Research on Some Ankara Villages) (Ankara, 1942), and Paul Stirling, *Turkish Village* (New York, 1965).

These are some of the questions that confronted us as we pondered the population figures we had discovered. We were, at the same time, quite aware of the widely shared view that Istanbul men and women married very young in past times, produced large numbers of children and lived in huge complex households. This was a perspective we also knew to be common to Europeans looking back at their own past, a perspective only recently fractured by the work of John Hajnal, Peter Laslett and a number of other scholars.[3] Might we too look at such conceptions of the Istanbul past with scepticism? If so, what could we expect to find?

We soon came to believe, like Philippe Ariès, that the numbers we had encountered might be taken as signs of social and cultural events not so readily available to the observer; that they might be a kind of surface refraction of substrata of accumulated structures and changes.[4] While, no doubt, late nineteenth- and early twentieth-century Istanbul was in many respects unique in the context of the Ottoman Empire, and even the Turkish Republic, we argue that, in its very extremes, Istanbul of the time dramatized certain basic social and cultural themes then new to Turkish society, some of which were to be central focal points of attention in the years to come.

Istanbul in context

Some time ago Massimo Livi-Bacci observed that, 'The urban population is still a concept in search of application'.[5] That observation is as true today as it was in 1977. We still do not know what we are referring to when we speak of the urban population; we still do not know what it is about urban areas that makes them distinctive, or if indeed they are. This is a long-standing dilemma of urban sociology in general.[6] It is also due to the dearth of urban-based historical demographic or historical anthropological studies dealing with family and fertility, since both fields have, for a variety of methodological and other reasons, a great proclivity to study clearly demarcated,

---

[3] The seminal works are John Hajnal, 'European marriage patterns in perspective' in D. V. Glass and D. E. G. Eversley, eds., *Population in History* (London, 1965), and Peter Laslett, ed., assisted by Richard Wall, *Household and Family in Past Time* (Cambridge, 1972).

[4] Philippe Ariès, 'Two successive motivations for the declining birth rate in the West', *Population and Development Review*, 6 (December, 1980).

[5] *A History of Italian Fertility during the Last Two Centuries* (Princeton, NJ, 1977).

[6] Manuel Cassells, *The Urban Question: A Marxist Approach* (London, 1977); R. E. Pahl, 'Urban social theory and research' in *Whose City? and Further Essays on Urban Society* (London, 1975).

small-scale rural areas and to neglect cities. The in-depth historical study of the family and of the population of cities has been neglected, despite the fact that urban areas have been an especially important locus of family change and fertility decline in various parts of the world, and that metropolises are absorbing increasingly larger proportions of the national population in most Third World societies. The result of this, in addition to our general ignorance of the nature of urban population issues, is that the theories, concepts and methods of the field have largely been dominated by the exigencies of rural societies.

Rural and urban, or rather metropolitan, patterns of fertility were, as we have seen – and still are – strikingly different in Turkey; but we do not really know why that is. The Princeton studies of the decline of fertility in nineteenth- and twentieth-century Europe also concluded that, 'urban fertility [was] lower than rural fertility at virtually every date for which data were collected',[7] though there are cases in the past where it was higher in the city than in the countryside.[8] The Princeton studies also show us that rural-urban fertility differentials can vary by country and by region within a country, though they provide us with no conclusive explanations for why that is so.[9] We also know that household structures were quite different in rural, urban and especially metropolitan areas in the recent past in Turkey. During our period the impact of 'westernization', one of the major forces of change at the time, was limited to the major cities (and to scattered enclaves of people of urban origin in the provinces).

Though rural villagers knew about such ancient birth-control methods as *coitus interruptus*, there is no evidence that they were practising it or any other form of birth limitation in a systematic way. They were what demographers like to call a 'natural fertility' population. That is hardly surprising given a combination of the high infant mortality that prevailed in rural Anatolia, and their own incentives to produce children, particularly sons, to help them run their domestic agricultural enterprises and provide for their old age, and the encouragement they were getting to do so from a pronatalist state anxious to compensate for the huge losses of the First World War.

In Istanbul the situation could not have been more different. Women

---

[7] Allan Sharlin, 'Urban-rural differences in fertility in Europe during the demographic transition' in Ansley J. Coale and Susan Cotts Watkins, *The Decline of Fertility in Europe* (Princeton, NJ, 1986), 236.

[8] Roger P. Finlay, *Population and Metropolis: The Demography of London, 1580–1650* (Cambridge, 1981).

[9] Sharlin, 'Urban-rural differences', 251.

were deliberately cutting short their child-bearing period to about age thirty – fifteen to twenty years before they would have been biologically incapable of reproducing. Clearly, families must have been practising birth control to have stopped bearing children so consistently early, as is evident from the statistical records they have left to posterity. Not only had they been curtailing their fertile years at the upper end for at least fifty or sixty years, but they had also been trimming them at the beginning by marrying later and later, though in all likelihood they were not marrying later in order to do so.

Islam provides the ideological underpinning for child limitation, and the Islamic world a plethora of methods, manuals and devices for carrying this out.[10] Yet rural and small town Turkish Muslims by and large chose not to use them, and kept their fertility high, whereas their big city counterparts did so and achieved the low fertility which caught our attention.

As we shall see, the women of Istanbul were clearly forerunners in Turkey's first transition towards a lower level of fertility. In the last quarter of the nineteenth century the city of Istanbul, with a total fertility rate of about 3.9, fell well below the so-called 'normal' range of total fertility rates of pre-industrial populations. The Muslim population of Istanbul indeed appears to have been the first sizeable Muslim group to have extensively practised family planning. In fact, the high degree of prevalence of parity-oriented family limitation within marriage, combined with a family formation system encouraging late female age at marriage, clearly set Istanbul apart from any discernible 'Muslim' or 'Middle Eastern' pattern. When trying to document the fertility decline in Istanbul in the first four decades of this century, we have, at each step, come across bits of evidence leading to the idea of a much earlier start in the fall of the indices used.

In no other Middle Eastern or Muslim city is there a parallel to these historical trends. In relation to the city of Beirut, for instance – in many respects quite a cosmopolitan place since at least the turn of the century – one reads that, 'on the whole, the census reports offer little evidence that urban educated women of the Levant had, by mid-[twentieth] century begun leading a trend toward smaller families. Only among the highly educated few is any such trend perceptible ... upper class educated Muslims of Beirut began a trend toward smaller families sometime before mid-century'.[11] No predominantly

[10] B. Mussallam, *Sex and Society in Islam* (Cambridge, 1983).

[11] E. T. Prothro and L. N. Diab, *Changing Family Patterns in the Arab East* (Beirut, 1974), 96–8.

Muslim country of the 1980s had as low a total fertility rate or as high a female mean age at first marriage as Istanbul achieved half a century ago.[12]

Istanbul Muslims clearly seem, then, to have stood apart from their coreligionists in the Middle East as pioneers in marriage age and household formation, in family planning practices and in fertility trends. Our perusal of the literature leaves little doubt that there was, and still is, a great variety of patterns of family and fertility in the areas of the world known to be Islamic or Middle Eastern. The unusual situation we have discovered in Istanbul and the present state of our knowledge of the diversity of the fertility and family patterns we have encountered lead us to question, following an argument of Clifford Geertz, in relation to other issues in other places and other times in the Islamic world,[13] whether Islam in itself or the 'Middle East' could constitute an adequate or meaningful frame of reference for grouping or analysing things such as marriage, family formation patterns or fertility.

Fertility was, as we have seen, low in Istanbul even at the beginning of our period, and there are clear indications that families were consistently practising birth control as early as the 1860s or 1870s. This is not surprising given the limited need for a family labour force in a complex urban economy, which even in the pre-modern past could not have been entirely organized as an economy of domestic production and service units. Low fertility was in all likelihood also a response to the probable improved child mortality conditions in the nineteenth century. Theories which connect declining fertility to changing patterns of domestic labour use and intergenerational wealth transfers do not, therefore, have the same relevance in a largely non-domestic urban economy as they do in understanding what happens in the

---

[12] World Bank, *World Development Report (1984)* (Oxford, 1984). See also D. Smith, 'Age at first marriage', *World Fertility Survey Comparative Studies*, 7 (1980). The demographic indicators of two other prominent Middle East metropolises, Cairo and Alexandria, stand in the same relationship to those for early twentieth-century Istanbul as do the indicators for Beirut. In 1960 total fertility rates in the Cairo and Alexandria Governorates of Egypt were 6.0 and 5.8 respectively. In 1976 the figures for the urban areas of Cairo and Alexandria had fallen to 3.9 and 3.7, the level Istanbul had reached around the turn of the century. See *The Estimation of Recent Trends in Fertility and Mortality in Egypt* (Washington, DC, 1982), 64ff. A more recent estimate puts the total fertility rate in Metropolitan Cairo at 4.1 for the year 1980. See Huda Zurayk and Frederic C. Shorter, 'The social composition of households in Arab cities and settlements: Cairo, Beirut, Amman' (Cairo, 1988), 14. A recent study of Beirut calculates its total fertility rate for 1984 at 2.5, again a level which the Muslim population of Istanbul had reached in the 1930s. See H. Zurayk and H. K. Armenian, eds., *Beirut 1984: A Population and Health Profile* (Beirut, 1985).

[13] *Islam Observed* (New Haven, 1968).

transformation of domestic-based rural ones.[14] However, they do perhaps have a limited use in a situation where the organizational weight
of the economy shifts from one in which domestic units are more
prominent, to one in which the balance has tipped to extra-domestic
work locales separate from family life.

Though we are far from having a clear picture of the details of these
important changes, that is what appears to have happened in Istanbul
from roughly the early to mid-nineteenth century onwards. The
increasingly dense commercial connections of Istanbul with the European economy following the westernizing *Tanzimat* reforms of the
1830s not only eventually encouraged the development of a more
widespread wage-labour economy, but even tied ordinary people in
the city into the forces of an increasingly monetarized market. These
developments picked up additional momentum in the 1880s.[15] An
expansion and modernization of the bureaucracy during those years
eventually placed a significant proportion of the population of the
city on a salary or a wage.[16] Unfortunately, it is very difficult to pursue
these very important developments connecting the Istanbul economy
with domestic and demographic structures. The necessary details for
an understanding of the economic and demographic situation in pre-
1880s Istanbul are missing. There are neither detailed social and economic studies which examine the presumed transformation of the Istanbul economy, nor are there demographic data available for the period
from the early nineteenth century to the 1880s. Even for the post-1880s
period, the quality of the economic data available on employment,
wages and cost of living is not adequate for a detailed analysis.

It is not only in economic structure that Istanbul changed during
the nineteenth century. The impact of western ideas and manners
began to have an impact on elite circles in the early years of the century
and became quite widespread by its end. During the first decades
of this century, particularly among the growing proportion of the
population engaged in what we might call modern bureaucratic, com-

[14] J. C. Caldwell, *Theory of Fertility Decline* (New York, 1982); 'Direct economic costs
and benefits of children', in R. A. Bulatao and R. D. Lee, eds., *Determinants of Fertility
in Developing Countries* (New York, 1983); Alan Macfarlane, 'Modes of reproduction'
in G. Hawthorn, ed., *Population and Development* (London, 1978).
[15] Şevket Pamuk, *Osmanlı-Türkiye İktisadi Tarihi, 1500–1914* (An Economic History of
Ottoman–Turkey, 1500–1914) (Istanbul, 1988); Şevket Pamuk, *Osmanlı Ekonomisi ve
Dünya Kapitalizmi, 1820–1913* (The Ottoman Economy and World Capitalism, 1820–1913)
(Ankara, 1984).
[16] Carter Vaughn Findley, *Bureaucratic Reform in the Ottoman Empire: the Sublime Porte,
1789–1922* (Princeton, NJ, 1980); Stanford J. Shaw and Ezel K. Shaw, *History of the
Ottoman Empire and Modern Turkey* (London, 1977), II.

mercial or industrial occupations, the same phenomenon was in evidence. The differences in social and cultural milieux separating Istanbul (and Salonica and Izmir) from most of the other cities in the Empire and from the vast underdeveloped rural areas of Anatolia were enormous. The density of urban life, of communications, education, fashions, and of the social and cultural emulation of the West, as well as the ever-present social mix of Muslim and non-Muslim, created an atmosphere in Istanbul that was quite unique. This flood of ideas, values, manners and aspirations brought with it many issues new to the Ottomans, such as a critique of women's position in society and of arranged marriages, the development of a new family ideal, new domestic manners, new concerns about children's place in society and about child-rearing. The totality of all of these social and cultural elements created an urban chemistry in Istanbul that absorbed and dominated the many newcomers to the city, and produced a unique configuration of personal and domestic life which was to persist until the 1940s.

The literate, bureaucratic classes were quite definitely the ideological forerunners of modern western ideas and institutions which had their impact, albeit indirectly and most often unintentionally, on marriage, family and fertility.[17] Though there is much information about the way of life, values and aspirations of the literate classes, the great masses of artisans, shopkeepers and ordinary labourers have left little which would allow us to delve into the intimacies of their thoughts and family lives. What we do know is either extrapolated indirectly from the statistical records we have in hand, or is related to us through the pens of representatives of the literate classes. The result is that we have not been able to undertake an analysis of class-based patterns of thought and behaviour to the extent we would have liked.

Our study only concerns the Muslim population of Istanbul. At the inception of the research project we had to make a choice about the ethnic-religious boundaries of the population we were going to examine. This was a difficult decision because of the extraordinary ethnic and religious diversity found in the city during our period. A third to a half of the population of Istanbul was non-Muslim at various points during those years, the predominant groups being Greek, Armenian and Jewish. No doubt the non-Muslims shared many features of family and population with Muslims in the city,

---

[17] For a discussion of a related pattern in Europe, see Massimo Livi-Bacci, 'Social group forerunners of fertility control in Europe' in Coale and Watkins, *The Decline of Fertility;* Lawrence Stone, *The Family, Sex and Marriage in England,* 1500–1800 (London, 1977); J. A. Banks, *Prosperity and Parenthood* (London, 1954).

though the Christians and Jews became engaged in the processes of westernization somewhat earlier, which they then helped to diffuse to the population at large.

We decided in the end for a number of methodological and strategic reasons, that it would be necessary to limit our sample to the Muslim population only and, as a consequence, a significant segment of the urban population had to be excluded from our study. Statements we shall make about the whole of Istanbul should, therefore, be taken with this reservation in mind, *cum grano salis.*[18]

Family, fertility and society

The demographic patterns we have isolated were accompanied by a radical reorientation of family life which began during the last three decades of the nineteenth century and which had permeated much of Istanbul society by the 1930s. The Ottomans and their successors the Republican Turks referred to this process as 'Europeanization', and were in most cases quite self-conscious about many of its everyday features, such as changes in dress, manners, speech and gender roles. The Ottoman-Turkish family was in the throes of a civilizational transformation – a thoroughgoing restructuring of fundamental behaviours and attitudes, all of which carried great symbolic value beyond the tiny world of the family. This transformation taking place at home was in many ways a microcosm of processes that were taking hold of society at large.

In the mid-1960s John Hajnal wrote an essay that changed the nature of much thinking in historical demography and that, at the same time, provided the impetus for linking demographic studies with more sociological or anthropological ones which were concerned with families and the formation of households at marriage.[19] In later studies, both theoretical and empirical, Hajnal and many of the members of the Cambridge Group for the History of Population and Social Struc-

---

[18] The specificities of the Istanbul marriage and household formation patterns would be better highlighted with the help of parallel studies on the important non-Muslim segments of the population. The population records of Ottoman Istanbul were kept in separate registers for the various religious communities, and the data for those communities can be found in those registers devoted to them for the 1885 and 1907 censuses. In addition, baptism and burial records may also possibly exist for some sections of the Christian population of the city, and these could supplement such state records.

[19] 'European marriage patterns'; 'Two kinds of preindustrial household formation system', *Population and Development Review*, 8 (1982), also in Richard Wall, ed. in collaboration with Jean Robin and Peter Laslett, *Family Forms in Historic Europe* (Cambridge, 1983).

ture developed and elaborated upon these connections. In the original essay and in his subsequent one, Hajnal contrasted a marriage system which he called European with another one called non-European or joint. Further refinements resulting from a flood of empirical studies in the 1970s and 1980s led to a more narrow delineation of the 'European' pattern to northern and northwestern Europe, with the Mediterranean region exhibiting a distinctive variation on the European structure, and the Balkans largely fitting into the catch-all non-European one that appeared to characterize the rest of the world. All of this did not preclude considerable intra-regional variation. The underdeveloped state of historical demography in the Asian and African world has not enabled us to make other refinements on what, no doubt, will some day be a more differentiated 'non-European' category. Recent work in the Far East[20] has already placed historic Japan in the 'European' category.

While the rural Muslim pattern we find in Anatolia in the past fits Hajnal's non-European or joint system, the urban one we have discovered in Istanbul clearly does not. It is a variation on his European marriage pattern, similar to the one often attributed to the Mediterranean world in the past. Of course, the Mediterranean region is itself not homogeneous, and the more that we learn about it, no doubt the more variation we shall observe. The Istanbul pattern might, for the time being, be called a northeast Mediterranean/Balkan urban one, since we have some evidence that it also characterized Beirut in the thirties and forties and some parts of urban Bulgaria in the late nineteenth and early twentieth centuries.[21] In this regional variation, proportions marrying remained high regardless of the changes in marriage age, such changes in western Europe being associated with significant percentages remaining celibate.

We shall focus considerable attention on the household structures of Ottoman Istanbul families since they are the locus of so many of our concerns. In doing so, however, it is important to take special note of what Ovar Löfgren has observed with respect to historical Swedish society, that is, that one should not give the household 'a far more prominent position in the social landscape than it often

---

[20] Arthur P. Wolf and Susan B. Hanley, 'Introduction' in S. B. Hanley and A. P. Wolf, eds., *Family and Population in East Asian History* (Stanford, Calif., 1985).

[21] Prothro and Diab, *Changing Family Patterns*, 30–47; Maria Todorova, 'Population structure, marriage patterns, family and household (according to Ottoman documentary material from north-eastern Bulgaria in the 60s of the 19th century)', *Etudes Balkaniques*, 1 (1983), 59–72; 'Marriage and nuptiality in Bulgaria during the nineteenth century' (mimeographed, n.d.).

had'.[22] We know, particularly from the contemporary anthropological literature on Turkey and elsewhere, that households are embedded to varying degrees in a large weave of kinship relations and are often fluid and not easily demarcatable social units.[23] Despite their demographic dissimilarities, a joint family cultural system prevailed both in Istanbul and its hinterlands, lending complexity and contradiction to the domestic system of the Ottoman capital. Close-knit familial, particularly intergenerational ties, penetrated the artificial boundaries of the household as a residential unit, creating a much more fluid and flexible system than might be extracted from household records alone.

While dense joint family relations cutting across households characterized Istanbul households and set them apart from their western European equivalents, they were coming in many other ways to resemble them. Certainly the aspirations of Istanbul families were in that direction. Increasingly egalitarian gender relations, a declining role of the parental generation in marriage arrangements, more companionate marriages, a greater focus on children and western manners and dress, all came to separate Istanbul Muslim families from those in the Islamic East – for that matter, even from Muslim western and central Anatolia – and in this sense drew them closer to Europe. The demographic events we shall discuss in some detail provided the substructure and were, at the same time, a kind of sign of those changes.

Studies in Europe for the pre-modern period, particularly in England, have gone to great lengths to link marriage, household formation, fertility and secular trends in wages and prices and have successfully demonstrated the connections between them.[24] Such linkages have not been as clearly developed for the numerous studies of the massive European decline in fertility in the late nineteenth and early twentieth centuries, due to the relatively short time-span within which to observe changes and perhaps because of the aggregate nature

---

[22] 'Family and household, images and reality: cultural change in Swedish society' in Robert McC. Netting *et al.*, eds., *Households: Comparative and Historical Studies of the Domestic Group* (Berkeley, Calif., 1984), 448.

[23] Alan Duben, 'The significance of family and kinship in urban Turkey' in Ç. Kâğıtçıbaşı, ed., *Sex Roles, Family and Community in Turkey* (Bloomington, Ind., 1982); Robert McC. Netting, 'Introduction' in Netting *et al.*, *Households*; S.J. Yamagisako, 'Family and household: the analysis of domestic groups' in *Annual Review of Anthropology*, 8 (Palo Alto, Calif., 1979); Andrejs Plakans, *Kinship in the Past: An Anthropology of European Family Life, 1500–1900* (London, 1984); David I. Kertzer, *Family Life in Central Italy, 1880–1910: Sharecropping, Wage Labor and Coresidence* (New Brunswick, NJ, 1984).

[24] See, for example, E. A. Wrigley and R. Schofield, *The Population History of England, 1541–1871* (London, 1981).

of the data utilized.[25] Where does the Istanbul demographic pattern fit, and how does it connect to the social, economic and cultural changes which we shall discuss?

Demographers of Turkey, and in particular Frederic C. Shorter, who as early as the 1960s began to have some glimmerings of the uniqueness of Istanbul, have speculated as to whether the pattern in Istanbul was due to something peculiar to Istanbul, to western regions of the country in general, or whether it was in some way connected to the exigencies of the economic and social structure of a very large city.[26] Since Istanbul families achieved a low level of fertility as early as the 1920s and 1930s that is still considered a national ideal in Turkey, the underlying causes of this pattern were, and are, of special interest to these demographers. Since post-Second World War fertility decline in Turkey has largely been attributed to birth control, little attention has been placed upon the role of marriage and issues concerning women and the family in the process. Fertility studies of contemporary non-western societies have, in general, de-emphasized what now appears to be a considerable impact of nuptiality upon fertility decline.[27] We have, in many ways, attempted to pick up where the demographers of Turkey have left off. The materials we discovered and our own interests have, however, led us in directions which they might not have followed.

Family history

Our efforts which led to writing this book have been directed by two overriding purposes: to document the changes in marriage patterns, family and household structures and household formation and fertility that characterized Istanbul between the years 1880 and 1940, and to attempt to explain them. In the process of doing so, particularly in our efforts to explain, we have moved away from the typical concerns and quantitative modes of demography into the social and cultural issues more commonly defined by socio-cultural anthropology. In our attempt to explain the demographic structures and changes, we have been led into a study of family and domestic life, the position of men

[25] Coale and Watkins, *The Decline of Fertility*.
[26] Paul Demeny and Frederic C. Shorter, *Estimating Turkish Mortality, Fertility and Age Structure* (Istanbul, 1968); Berksan, 'Marriage patterns'; *Turkey: Report of Mission on Needs Assessment for Population Activities* (New York, 1980); Leila Erder, 'The women of Turkey: a demographic overview' in N. Abadan-Unat, ed., *Women in Turkish Society* (Leiden, 1981); Shorter and Macura, *Trends in Fertility*.
[27] Alan Macfarlane, *Marriage and Love in England*, 1300–1840 (Oxford, 1986), 32.

and women in society, the westernization of family life, the changing bases for marital unions, intergenerational conflict, attitudes towards birth limitation and its methods, as well as many other cultural and social issues in everyday family life.

While we originally selected our topics and concerns with the purpose of contributing to the comparative historical study of family, household and fertility, and were guided by certain theoretical priorities, once we had begun to collect source materials, most of which had never before been used, we also started to follow their dictates. Thus, basing ourselves on them, we began to develop an historical ethnography of family life. While these two goals generally go hand in hand, they did on occasion lead us in somewhat divergent directions.

As we shall see, the decline in fertility during our period was due in equal parts to changing female marriage age and to control of fertility within marriage. Proportions marrying remained very high throughout the period, regardless of the other demographic trends. In attempting to explain the changes in marriage and the effort by married couples to limit the birth of children, we were inevitably led into a study of the Istanbul family system. In the language of demography, the age at which women marry is an intermediate or so-called 'proximate' determinate of fertility, as is the use of various birth-control devices. An analysis of marriage in Istanbul in the past can only make sense within the context of family life, for marriage was not – and to this day largely is not – a purely individual matter, despite a greater degree of individuation than had existed in the past. While the number of children a couple brings into the world would appear to be a more private matter, it too is not an individual decision (if, indeed, it is a deliberate decision at all), but emerges from the complex social aspirations and limitations of the more narrow procreational as well as larger extended family. The age at which men marry has a direct bearing on the household formation system, the system of post-marital residence, on intergenerational relations and on many other factors which may have influenced people's decisions, or affected people's behaviour with regard to their family size. All of these things must in turn be connected to the larger social and economic context within which families operated in Istanbul from 1880 to 1940. It is only in such a setting that they can make sense.

What began as a study of marriage and fertility within a family context then soon evolved into a social history of the family, of which marriage and fertility were only two, though fundamental, parts. The demographic phenomena were our starting-point and a constant grounding. They provided what appears to be an unconscious substructure to the cultural and social changes which people during our period were more aware of. Referring to the demographic phenomena as a substructure does not mean that we attribute to them any sort of causal primacy. We are pointing here to their unconscious nature. The complex interplay of demographic, social, cultural and economic factors does not yield a clear etiology. If anything, however, ideas, values and meanings seem to have been particularly influential as they were transmitted, absorbed, adapted and often distorted in their movement from the West to Ottoman Istanbul.

In common with many studies influenced by anthropological thinking, this one is based on the assumption that the meanings of the actions of individuals are deeply embedded in the social contexts within which they live, and that many of what appear in retrospect to be rational 'decisions' are prospectively rather non-deliberate acts motivated by a complex and even contradictory array of intentions. In a particular study one may choose to place the focus of analytic light on one or more of these so-called intentions, highlighting them quite unnaturally from the context in which they were meaningful to those being studied. One then interprets such actions and their intentions with the project under consideration in mind, often assigning to them a kind of 'rationality', that is, a purposiveness, that they did not in reality have for the actors, but which is constructed by the analyst and made into a 'system'. In this study we shall attempt to piece together the various parts of the social context of marriage, family and fertility in Istanbul and to understand the social forces underlying them, avoiding, as much as possible, however, the temptation to impose a neat system on the data. Even in this limited effort at synthesis and explanation we have been greatly constrained by the paucity of information available about the social, cultural and economic history of the period.

Periodization

This study spans the years approximately 1880 to 1940, from Istanbul during the aftermath of the Ottoman-Russian War of 1877–8 to Istanbul in the decade prior to the Second World War. More significantly, perhaps, it moves from the last period of Ottoman history to the first of the Republic, in a city that bore the brunt of the transformation more than any other place in the region. It was a period of extraordinary change and turmoil – political, social and cultural. In some ways it seems as if the two ends of the period are separated by centuries, not merely sixty years. A periodization which spans such a major political divide is unusual – at least in Turkish history. But for our purposes it makes a great deal of sense, since we are following certain trends and events that began, or at least evolved, during the last years of the Empire and came to fruition during the early ones of the Republic. In demographic, social and cultural terms there were great continuities between 1880 and 1940. Selecting the cut-off point for the study was easy, since we began with the observation that in Istanbul by the 1930s a rather modern demographic and social pattern had set in. Furthermore, in the post-Second World War years Istanbul began a new social and demographic era, the parameters of which were set by the massive immigration to the city from rural Anatolia. Though we have followed certain trends through to the end of the decade, our analyses largely come to a natural end by the early 1930s.

How far back in time to go in order to discover the origins of the phenomena we isolated in the thirties was a much more difficult problem – one which we still have not entirely solved to our satisfaction. To some extent we were limited by the data available. The first Ottoman census which provides data on both the male and female populations of the city in such a way as to make household, nuptiality and fertility analysis possible took place in 1885. Since the modernization of the Istanbul economy and the spread of western ideas and manners to a wide segment of the Istanbul population really only begins after the 1880s, we assumed that the demographic features which we had isolated in the 1930s would begin to be visible at that time. Following our analyses of the 1885 census and of subsequent recordings of vital events in the city, we discovered that although it was to decline consistently throughout the period, fertility was quite low and household structure quite simple even at the beginning of the period. And male marriage age was quite late and even female marriage age surprisingly retarded in the 1880s. It may then be that these trends had begun earlier than we will ever be able to detect, or, alternatively, that they had been that way for a considerable time prior to our entry on the scene. While from a social, economic and cultural perspective the 1880s in Istanbul were in many respects a watershed, from a purely demographic one, they are, perhaps, only the beginning of a heightened trend, one which may have begun somewhat earlier in the century, which we can call 'modern', or which we may choose to label as the first stage of the 'demographic transition' in Turkey. The origins of this pattern remain obscure.

There is at least a thirty-year gap between the completion of the 'first stage' of the transition in Istanbul, and the onset of the more massive one for the rest of Turkey which is still in process. This is in contrast to the urban-rural staging of the decline of fertility in Europe, in which, 'In no instance do urban areas complete their fertility decline before the onset of fertility decline in rural areas'.[28] Why was there such a gap in Turkey? Perhaps the answer lies in an understanding of the very different social, economic and cultural circumstances which separated Istanbul from the rest of Turkish society.

The sources and their limitations

The cross-disciplinary nature of this study is reflected in the choice of sources we have selected, as well as in the methods used to analyse them. Our concern throughout has been to combine the quantitative, often aggregate, data analysis of the demographer with the anthropologist's concern for the institutional context of change and for cultural and historical forces. In order to do this we utilized three different though complementary sources of data: a) census data, records of vital events and other quantitative data bases; b) written sources; and c) retrospective interviews.

Quantitative data

The population censuses and registration schemes developed and utilized in the Ottoman Empire during the second half of the nineteenth century provide a rich source of data for historical studies. The two late Ottoman *de jure* censuses (*tahrir-i nüfus*) of 1885 (1300) and 1907 (1322), and the population registers which were built upon them, comprise a rich and varied array of information on various aspects of Ottoman population and society.[29] These have previously only been utilized in a superficial way. The relevance of the censuses and population registers to the study of marriage, fertility, family and household structure has largely been ignored. Indeed the original main rosters (*esas nüfus kayıt defteris*) have not been used by historians at all.

The 1885 and 1907 censuses were the first Empire-wide censuses undertaken for purposes other than either taxation or military conscription. The system as a whole was made independent of all military, financial and cadastral departments. These censuses have the distinc-

---

[28] Sharlin, 'Urban-rural differences', 259.
[29] The dates we have used to refer to the censuses of 1885 (1300) and 1907 (1322) are the modal dates for registration in the Istanbul rosters. The census itself took several years to be completed in Istanbul.

tion of being the first to record information about females. They were, moreover, the first ones for which precise demographic and social information was collected for each individual included. Great care was taken to assure accuracy of registration. The 1907 census was the more successful of the two in this respect, given the experience gained in 1885 and the resultant stricter regulations imposed both on census officials and the population at large. The data from this census are, without doubt, the most reliable sources for the study of population and the household in late Ottoman society. We have relied almost entirely on the 1907 census for our household data in particular, though we have made use of the one completed in 1885 for comparative purposes. Registration in the Ottoman capital is known to have been quite thorough for both females and males, despite the fact that females over nine years of age could be represented by a male from the same household for the purposes of registration. The rather even male–female ratios obtained from our samples of both censuses lend support to this assertion. Financial penalties were imposed on those who were not registered and strict measures were instituted to ensure that census officials carried out their tasks correctly. Fines were imposed on careless or sloppy scribes. Census officials were required to have certain minimum educational levels and/or a specified number of years of experience in the civil service before appointment. Regular inspections of census-taking procedures were carried out. For the first time, notification periods were set for the declaration of all vital events, with fines for non-compliers. Each individual registered was issued with a population certificate (*nüfus tezkeresi*), a combination of a birth certificate and identification card. The *nüfus tezkeresi* was an essential document for transacting all official and legal business, for buying and selling property, for government employment, school registration or for obtaining travel documents.[30] It is hardly surprising that all of these regulations were most strictly applied in the capital city.

It is likely that registration was more complete for the literate and sophisticated bureaucratic and commercial classes and less so for the *petit bourgeois*, artisanal or wage-labouring classes. Though our data yield the full range of socio-economic strata for Muslim Istanbul during that period, it appears that artisan-shopkeepers and in particular

---

[30] Kemal H. Karpat, 'Ottoman population records and census of 1881/82–1893', *International Journal of Middle East Studies*, 9 (1978), 237–74; Stanford J. Shaw, 'The Ottoman census system and population, 1831–1914', *International Journal of Middle East Studies*, 9 (1978), 325–38.

wage-labourers may have been underrepresented.[31] Since our sample only includes the permanent Muslim population of the city, it clearly underrepresents wage-earners. We know that many of the wage-labourers in Istanbul during the period were single males who resided in special bachelors' hostels (*bekârodaları*). Since all the bachelors' hostels are listed in the registers for non-Istanbul residents (*yabancı defteris*), we did not include them in our sample. Though the percentage of those in the artisan-shopkeeper strata in our sample appears to be low in relation to the bureaucratic and commercial strata, we must remember that more than 35 per cent of the population of the city was non-Muslim and that non-Muslims constituted a significant proportion of the artisanal and shopkeeping professions in Istanbul during the period. Conversely, positions in the state bureaucracy were predominantly in the hands of Muslims.

An impressive amount of demographic data was collected during the censuses and as a result of subsequent registrations of vital events. Individuals are recorded in the rosters as members of residential groups of various types, the most common of which was the household (*hane*).[32] All members of the residential groups, both familial and non-familial, are listed together in the registers by street address. This classification and the street addresses which accompany it are helpful in drawing the social and cultural topography of the city during the late Ottoman period. For each individual name listed, there is information on form of reference and occupation (*şöhret, sıfat, sanat ve hizmeti*), relationship to the head of the household, religion, date and place of birth, date of registration, sex, name of father and mother and marital status, in addition to other information of little sociological

---

[31] Fifty-two per cent of all males in the prime years of working life (between ages thirty and fifty-nine), whose occupations were recorded in 1907, can be classified as belonging to the bureaucratic, professional, military or commercial (*ticarî*) classes, ranging (in the case of the bureaucrats) from very high to quite lowly positions. We classified 37 per cent of all males in our sample as artisan-shopkeepers and 11 per cent as wage-earners. It is perhaps possible that the actual percentages of Muslim artisan-shopkeepers and wage-earners in 1907 were somewhat larger than they appear to be from the census, since the occupations of only 31 per cent of all males between the ages of thirty to fifty-nine in our sample were recorded at the time. It is very likely that there would have been a lesser propensity for (most probably illiterate) wage-earners and for artisan-shopkeepers to have their occupations recorded, than for members of the more literate and sophisticated bureaucratic and commercial occupational groups.

[32] In addition to the *hanes*, we also included certain other units indicated as residences by the Ottoman authorities in our sample, such as *konak* (mansion), *kulübe* (shack) and *oda* (room). The numbers of such units are very small in proportion to those places classified as *hanes*.

value for this study.[33] Since, after the census, the roster was also to function as a permanent population register, space was allocated for the transcription of vital events – births, marriages, divorces and deaths.

The main rosters, where particulars of each individual were recorded – the central focus of the whole registration system – are being utilized for the purpose of historical demographic analysis for the first time in this study. Previously, historians who used the census documents had rested their conclusions almost exclusively upon the local, district and provincial totals. We drew a 5 per cent sample from the surviving rosters concerning the permanent Muslim population of the five central districts of the city. We did not sample the registers (*yabancı defteris*) used for the quite large non-permanent Ottoman population registered elsewhere in the Empire but temporarily resident in Istanbul. Neither did we sample the separate registers utilized for the various non-Muslim populations resident in the city.

The rosters, for our purposes, contain two types of data bases: a) the censuses of 1885 and 1907, which give us data organized by residential units (households) as well as by individuals, and b) recordings of vital events of the household members and their patrilineal descendants subsequent to the two censuses and up to 1940. There is no indication of residence following the censuses, so these data can only be organized by individuals.

The censuses of 1885 and 1907 were, as we have indicated, also designed to function as permanent population registers, probably under the influence of Quételet's Belgian registers. The census totals were to be periodically updated with the help of another series of registers for vital events (*vukuat defteris*) in which births, marriages and deaths were to have been recorded on a day-to-day basis. So far as we know, there was no tradition in Turkey (or in other Islamic lands, for that matter) of recording vital events, be it for religious, legal or political purposes. Before 1885 no centralized birth, death or marriage records existed, except for cases of litigation brought to court – assuredly not a very representative sample. Though vital events were recorded in the main rosters after 1885, the process appears to have been rather haphazard and petered out some years before the turn of the century. No separate registers for vital events exist for

---

[33] By 'form of reference' we mean such terms as bey, *efendi, hanım, ağa, kalfa, devletlû,* etc., often recorded in association with a proper name, which are indicators of the status or position of the individual in society. By 'information of little sociological value' we mean, for example, descriptions of distinctive physical features or markings of an individual.

this period to our knowledge. The first available registers of such type only come onto the scene after 1905, and like the main rosters, have never received the attention of historians or demographers. We drew a 10 per cent systematic sample from the *vukuat defteri*s utilized for marriage registration for the period 1905 to 1940 in the same five central districts of Istanbul, and have largely based our analyses of Istanbul marriage patterns on this source.

It is difficult to be certain about the reliability or exhaustiveness of these marriage data. The registration of vital events is still not universally complied with in contemporary Turkey, and it was probably even less so three-quarters of a century ago, although surely a greater degree of reliability can be expected in Istanbul than in the provinces. There may, however, have been a bias in favour of the upper and middle strata and the artisans and shopkeepers, the more permanent segment of the population, and against the working classes or more recent immigrants from rural areas to the city, whom we can presume would have been less willing or able to keep up with the demands of the registration system.

One of the main shortcomings of the late Ottoman population registration system (as well as of its implementation) is that data on mortality are extremely defective. This is especially so for infant and early childhood mortality. Great emphasis was placed in the Istanbul press and public opinion in the late nineteenth and early twentieth centuries on child health, child-rearing and on the mitigation of what was perceived to be excessive child mortality. The mutual relationship between infant mortality and fertility in contemporary developing societies is the subject of a large body of literature. Although it may be possible to estimate adult mortality patterns indirectly by using orphanhood rates as recorded in the registers,[34] given the limitations of the data, however, a direct insight into infant and child mortality rates and their possible influence on fertility and family formation has proved unfeasible in this study.

Only a limited number of marriage registers kept by certain imams of local mosques in pre-1905 Istanbul have, to our knowledge, survived to the present day. We were able to locate and examine several such registers kept by successive imams at the Kasab İlyas Mosque in central intramural Istanbul. These contain the registration of 654 marriage contracts, spanning a period of forty-two years, from 1864 to 1906. From a purely demographic point of view the registers provide rather

[34] William Brass, *Methods for Estimating Fertility and Mortality from Limited and Defective Data* (Chapel Hill, NC, 1975).

meagre fare. We have used them here only as sources for the study of marriage customs and the financial transactions accompanying Istanbul marriages. To the same end, we have also delved into another source, the Archive of the Istanbul Religious Courts (*İstanbul Müftülüğü Şeriye Sicilleri Arşivi*), and have examined a large number of divorce rulings in Istanbul proper and in the Asian district of Üsküdar between 1885 and 1925.

It would have been very helpful to have been able to compare the results of the censuses of 1885 and 1907 with the two early Republican censuses of our period, conducted in 1927 and 1935. Unfortunately this has not been possible because the original rosters of those censuses do not, to our knowledge, any longer exist. Without the original rosters we are unable to do the kind of household and family analyses we have been fortunate to have been able to undertake for the late Ottoman period. There are also, as far as we have been able to determine, no quantitative surveys of the household or family in Istanbul for the 1920s and 1930s. The result of this is that we have had to base our quantitative statements about the Istanbul household largely on the 1907 census results. That census falls roughly midway in our period and took place at a time of relative stability, so perhaps many of the generalizations we have made from it are applicable to more than just that year. It is very likely that percentages of complex family households, as well as solitary and no family households, declined and that simple ones increased during the twenties and thirties. The interviews we conducted and the written sources we have used, as well as other more impressionistic data, point clearly in that direction. But we cannot be certain, because those sources do not give us large enough numbers to be statistically significant.

Written sources

There are very abundant and rich written sources which one can use to illuminate the cultural and social features of marriage, family and fertility in Istanbul in the late nineteenth and early twentieth centuries. Most of these have not been used for this purpose thus far. Such sources take us beyond the statistical generalizations generated from the censuses and records of vital events, while at the same time providing a setting within which it becomes possible to interpret the statistical data themselves. It is upon such sources that we have constructed a picture of life, especially family life, in late Ottoman Istanbul, as well as obtaining a glimmering of the values, meanings and aspirations which governed people's existence in those days. We have had to piece together the general social and cultural framework ourselves for our inquiry into family and fertility, in the absence of a social history of the late Ottoman period.

Late nineteenth-century Istanbul experienced what we might today call a communications revolution. It was during that time that various media new to Muslim Turkey took hold among broad segments of the growing westernized middle and upper strata. It was a period of a remarkable florescence of popular newspapers, magazines, drama and novels, all modelled after prototypes from Europe, particularly France.[35] These publications began to introduce into Istanbul society a new way of thinking and doing things – to be typified as *'alafranga'* (*alla franca*). The *alafranga* way of life was both the model of modernity as well as the focal point of a growing cultural alienation. Publications of the period, most of which were in the hands of modernists, were often broadsheets for this way of life. Newspapers and popular magazines, increasingly appealing to families and women, were bursting with information on European manners and mores, with critiques of traditional Ottoman family life and the treatment of women and children, and with advice for doing things the 'civilized', that is, 'western' way. But there were also defences of Islamic and/or Turkish tradition, as well as many attempts to accommodate these to European developments. Literature was thought of by many writers during that period as a mass pedagogical device. A major focal point of novels was family life in Istanbul, often written in a modernist mode. Such novels are rich in ethnographic detail about domestic life, descriptive detail which can easily be differentiated and extracted from the frequent moralizing of the authorial voice.[36] It is from the interviews,

---

[35] Şerif Mardin, 'The modernization of social communication' in G. Laswell, D. Lerner and H. Speier, eds., *Propaganda and Communications in World History* (Honolulu, 1979). The Ottoman-Turkish press got off to a very late start. The first newspaper appeared in 1831, but the first really independent daily was only published in the 1850s, and the first periodical appeared in 1862. Given the relatively low literacy rate at the time, their circulation and readership were rather small. The first specialized periodical for women appeared around 1870 and quickly ceased publication. A second was to be published more than twenty years later. The 1890s and 1900s were a period of increasingly strict and heavy political censorship when few papers and periodicals could appear and stay alive for a significant period of time. It was only after the 1908 Young Turk Revolution that Istanbul witnessed a relative abundance of publications.

[36] Andreas Tietze, 'The study of literature as the cultural manifestation of socio-economic changes: achievements and potential of the study of Ottoman literature', *International Journal of Turkish Studies*, 2 (1981); Robert P. Finn, *The Early Turkish Novel, 1872–1900* (Istanbul, 1984); Ahmet Ö. Evin, *Origins and Development of the Turkish Novel* (Minneapolis, Minn., 1983); Berna Moran, *Türk Romanına Eleştirel Bir Bakış* (A Critical Look at the Turkish Novel) (Istanbul, 1983); Orhan Okay, *Batı Medeniyeti Karşısında Ahmed Midhat Efendi* (Ahmed Midhat Efendi Confronting Western Civilization) (Ankara, 1975).

and also from the novels, that we have learned about the dynamics of family and household relations – conjugal, intergenerational and collateral.

We surveyed the major popular newspapers and magazines published in Istanbul between the years 1860 and 1940 for articles on family life and related demographic issues. We selected approximately 700 articles for a thorough perusal, and many of these have been utilized in our analyses. We also read and analysed over thirty novels written during the period from the 1870s to the 1930s. We have also utilized biographies, memoirs and private letters. Though some Ottomans did begin to write (and publish) memoirs starting in the late nineteenth century – those most influenced by the European tradition – they are by and large of a political nature. It is very rare to find memoirs which take up family and private life, and so we are deprived of what in European family history is an important source of data.

Interviews

We conducted thirty-seven in-depth retrospective interviews with elderly men and women born around, or just before, the turn of the century, about their family life and fertility-related issues. Six of these were with men, and focused largely on family life and social issues in the early twentieth century. The rest were with women and were concerned with fertility-related matters in addition to family life. We attempted to obtain informants from as wide a range of social strata as possible, though the difficulties of locating individuals from the lower classes of the requisite age and physical and mental condition to be properly interviewed led us to interview proportionately more women from the middle and upper-middle classes. The names used to refer to our informants are pseudonyms.

The interviews have been particularly valuable in providing us with an alternative perspective on the quantitative data we collected on household and demographic issues. We became aware of the fluidity of household life and of the myriad interconnections between families in different households from the interviews – and to an extent from the novels. We were able to learn about family and household dynamics and population-related issues such as breastfeeding and birth-control methods from the interviews and, in general, to gain insights into the values and aspirations of men and women living in Istanbul in the pre-Second World War period. In addition, the interviews provided us with a check on the nuptiality, fertility and household data we obtained from the census and other registers.

2

City, mahalle, *incomes and subsistence: social and economic framework*

City

So much happened that could have had a direct impact on the lives of ordinary people in Istanbul from the last two or three decades of the nineteenth century to the first several of the twentieth. Perhaps most visible was the extraordinary growth, and then loss, of population. Avalanches of refugees – usually Muslims from the former Ottoman provinces – flooded the city in great waves, as many non-Muslims began in turn to depart for new homelands. The people of Istanbul paid a high price for the nationalistic movements of the nineteenth century, many hundreds of thousands of all faiths being uprooted. As if that were not enough, families were often swept out of their homes and neighbourhoods by devastating fires of major proportions, which destroyed huge sections of the city which was built of wood. The Balkan Wars and the First World War brought economic disaster and increased morbidity, as well as population loss. War was followed by defeat and occupation, and that by revolution and further population loss.

Istanbul was not just defeated in war. Possibly worse was the loss of its 1600-year imperial status and its loss of pride, as the Kemalists moved the capital from its natural cosmopolitan seat to Ankara, only a provincial town in the Anatolian heartland in the early 1920s. The population of the city sank to its lowest in over 100 years. All of these traumatic events were a mere demographic counterpoint to the political cataclysm of transition from Empire to Republic, to the process of westernization – a civilizational revolution which hit Istanbul most directly of all places in the Empire – and to the rapid pace of nineteenth- and early twentieth-century social and economic change. In the midst of this social, economic and cultural storm is our account of marriage, family life and fertility decline.

23

The population of Istanbul was especially fluid throughout the years of this study, as massive numbers of ethnic Turks moved into the city from the collapsing Ottoman provinces of Europe and Asia. The late 1870s and early 1880s, that is the period between the Ottoman-Russian War of 1877–8 and the census of 1885, witnessed the most intense flow and this was repeated again in 1908–9 and especially after the Balkan Wars of 1912–13.[1] As a result of the disruptions caused by the earlier conflict, approximately 1.5 million Muslim refugees had left the Balkan countries alone and settled in Ottoman territories,[2] many passing through Istanbul, the natural funnel for migrants heading east, while no doubt large numbers settled permanently in the capital city. Istanbul was a land of opportunity in the nineteenth century,[3] more so than ever before in the recent past, and the refugees were joined by tens of thousands of single men from the provinces seeking employment in that commercial and industrial entrepôt. Though many of these transients (*bekârs*) were registered in 1885 and again in 1907 in their *bekârodaları* (bachelors' hostels), there were probably many more of them who escaped even the increasingly penetrating gaze of the Ottoman population authorities. We shall never know the full extent of their presence.

In 1885 51 per cent of the permanent Muslim population of Istanbul had been born in the city. Twelve per cent came from Ottoman Europe, 17 per cent from the Middle East, the Crimea, the Caucasus and Central Asia, and 19 per cent from Anatolia. This was the permanent population, and does not include the *bekârs* and others temporarily resident in the capital. In 1907 the percentage of the Istanbul-born was slightly higher – 57 per cent. This must have been due to natural increase in the city, because the percentage of household heads born in Istanbul dropped from 45 to 41 per cent between 1885 and 1907. Fifteen per cent of the 1907 population came from former European Turkey, 7 per cent from the Middle East and Russian territories, and 21 per cent from Anatolia.

Though they were a minority in numbers, the character of turn-of-the-century Istanbul was very much set by those originating in the European, especially the Balkan provinces, and also by many coming

---

[1] Kemal H. Karpat, *Ottoman Population 1830–1914: Demographic and Social Characteristics* (Madison, Wisc., 1985), 75.

[2] Kemal H. Karpat, 'Population movements in the Ottoman state in the nineteenth century: an outline' in J. L. Bacqué-Grammont and P. Dumont, eds., *Contributions à l'histoire économique et sociale de l'Empire Ottoman* (Paris, 1983), 385–428.

[3] Karpat, *Ottoman Population*, 102–3.

from Russia. These people were trendsetters in westernization, in politics and in family life-styles. Many of them came from the middle social strata in the provinces, and they moved quickly into the Hamidian bureaucratic cadres that had expanded very rapidly from the 1880s on, into the newly established professional schools, and for the first time into commercial enterprises that had traditionally been the province of non-Muslims.[4] For Muslims the preferred avenue to mobility, success, wealth and power at that time was not in commerce but through the bureaucracy. Many of the migrants moved rapidly through the educational system, into the middle levels of the bureaucracy and were to become a generation with quite different social and political expectations than their seniors, the *Tanzimat* ruling class.[5] It was such upwardly mobile, provincial-born men, trendsetters as we have said, who provided the cadres for the Young Turk movement, and who later were to become the first Kemalist establishment.[6] Such men and their families were the writers and the readers of a plethora of popular newspapers, journals and plays in the late nineteenth and early twentieth centuries that were a forum for the introduction of many western values, particularly in relation to marriage, family and women.

Istanbul became, at least nominally, more 'Muslim' during our years of focus. The flood of ethnic Turks into the city, especially in the early part of the period, and the departure of non-Muslim minorities towards the end of it, was the cause. The Muslim population of Istanbul rose from 385,000 in 1885 to 560,000 at the outbreak of the First World War in 1914, while the non-Muslim population declined from 489,000 to 350,000 during the same period. The total population of the city jumped from approximately 500,000 in the late 1850s to 874,000 in 1885, and to over a million at the turn of the century, but by the time of the first Republican census in 1927 it had fallen to 691,000, of which 448,000 were Muslims.[7]

Istanbul was the major political, administrative, economic and cultural centre of the Empire. It was also the primary focal point for

[4] *Ibid.*, 60–77.
[5] Şerif Mardin, 'Ideology, student identity, and professional role' (mimeographed, 1972); 'The modernization of social communication'.
[6] Feroz Ahmad, 'Vanguard of a nascent bourgeoisie: the social and economic policy of the Young Turks, 1908–1918' in O. Okyar and H. İnalcik, eds., *Social and Economic History of Turkey* (1071–1920), (Ankara, 1980); Ç. Keyder, 'The political economy of Turkish democracy'. *New Left Review*, 115 (1979), 3–44.
[7] Karpat, *Ottoman Population*, 103, 170–1; İstanbul Şehri Rehberi (Guide to Istanbul) (Istanbul, 1934), 164.

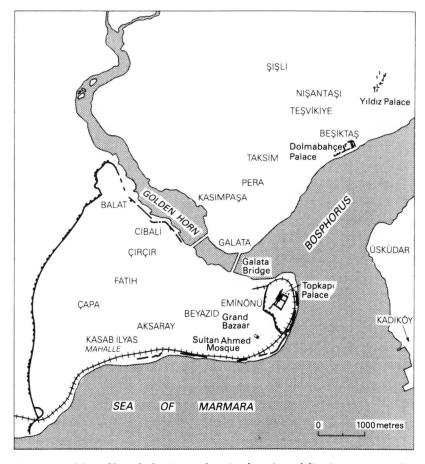

Figure 2.1 Map of Istanbul, *c.* 1900, showing location of districts mentioned.

the processes of westernization which, at the time of the census of 1907, were beginning to penetrate even the lives of middle-class Muslim families in the city. The Young Turk Revolution of 1908 accelerated that process which increasingly set off modern Istanbul from its more inward-looking, parochial hinterlands. It is not an exaggeration to say that the future identity of the country was largely being constructed in Istanbul during those years, not only in its political, educational and economic institutions, but also in its households and families.

The early years of this century probably witnessed the most dramatic changes in the face and in the character of the city. Ahmet Hamdi Tanpınar, poet, resident and passionate observer of Istanbul in transition, put these changes in the following words:

In the fifteen years between 1908 and 1923 [Istanbul] completely lost its old identity. The Young Turk Revolution, three major wars, a whole series of fires large and small, financial crises, the dissolution of the Empire, and finally in 1923 our complete acceptance of a civilization whose doorstep we had been occupying, scratching our heads for a hundred years, completely effaced [Istanbul's] old identity.[8]

A dense weave of wooden houses punctuated with bursts of greenery, covering the ancient hills of the city, was the traditional vista of Istanbul that greeted Mark Twain, a famous nineteenth-century traveller. He wrote, recalling the view from the sea: 'Constantinople makes a noble picture, but its attractiveness begins and ends with its picturesqueness'.[9] Up close it was a maze of dirty, narrow, densely packed streets and cul-de-sacs, many of which would not even permit the passage of a wheeled vehicle. The westernized Turks of the period had no less of an antipathy for such a display of urban settlement than did many foreign visitors. They were disturbed by its health implications and its vulnerability to fires, and considered it most unscientific, uncivilized and backward.

Many of the neighbourhoods burnt out by the frequent fires of the nineteenth century became the sites for a more regularized grid of streets and houses following western urban-planning principles.[10] These were, however, disconnected pockets set in the older organic urban fabric and determined solely by the extent of the fires. Though the model was Haussmann's Paris or the Ringstrasse of Vienna, the reality was more modest. The physical pattern of many streets and neighbourhoods changed quite dramatically as a result of these innovations, but their social composition was not radically affected. Traditional low-income groups were not displaced to peripheral districts as was the case in the nineteenth-century restructuring of Paris.[11] A number of main arteries were cut through the old city easing transportation from neighbourhood to neighbourhood, but it does not seem that life at the *mahalle* (neighbourhood community) level for most inhabitants changed radically.

---

[8] *Beş Şehir* (Five Cities) (Istanbul, 1969), 146.
[9] *The Innocents Abroad or the New Pilgrim's Progress* (New York, 1911), 66.
[10] Zeynep Çelik, *The Remaking of Istanbul: Portrait of an Ottoman City in the Nineteenth Century* (Seattle, 1986), 49.
[11] *Ibid.*, 80.

Plate 2.1 Looking across the Golden Horn, Istanbul, *c.* 1900. The dense weave
of wooden houses is visible in the foreground.

Although many writers speak of increasingly high population
densities in many of the traditional neighbourhoods in the nineteenth
century, especially in intramural Istanbul, we do not have precise
indicators of the dimensions of this development or of its impact on
the supply of housing in the city at the time. It seems that population
expansion and the residential density in the old city began to push
some segments of the Muslim population out to the suburbs along
the Bosphorus and to the Asian side of the city, and in the late nineteenth century to the hills beyond Taksim Square and above Beşiktaş.
The construction of the new Galata Bridge crossing the Golden Horn,
and the initiation of regularized ferry services along the Bosphorus
and in the Sea of Marmara, facilitated movement to neighbourhoods
that more often than not reflected the principles of nineteenth-century
'scientific' urban design.

'Mahalle'

The most striking social divisions in the residential patterns of nineteenth-century Istanbul were those of ethnicity and religion, not social class. The traditional Muslim *mahalles* of Istanbul, like those of other Islamic cities, were segmental structures if viewed within the total urban framework, and they resembled each other in their heterogeneous class composition.[12] Such *mahalles* were generally not very large in population; nor did they cover a large geographical area. Ten or fifteen streets at most, sometimes grouped around a small *meydan (piazza)*, a mosque, one or two public fountains, a *hamam* (public bath), a school and a few shops were the ordinary extent of most of the city quarters of Istanbul. Most took their names from those of the founder of the local mosque, the benefactor of the local school or fountain, a past or present celebrity living in the area, a Roman or Byzantine monument and even, in a few cases, the province or town from which most of the inhabitants originated.

The old *mahalles* in the past were, as we have observed, very mixed in terms of social class and status. In describing his *mahalle* just after the turn of the century, Kâzım Bey, an old Istanbul resident of the labouring class says:

In those days the middle [*sic*] class used to live there, and amidst them were found high government officials. For example, Derviş Pasha lived in Çapa, so did the Minister of Finance. I mean, in those days Istanbul was not divided up into classes. In the midst of the ordinary folk there were the bigshots.

Nemlizade Tahsin Pasha and his family lived in a huge *konak* (mansion) across from Kâzım Bey's simple two-storey wooden house. He and his mother – but never his father – would occasionally visit with the pasha's wife in the evenings. Tanpınar writes: 'In old Istanbul, even in my childhood, rich and poor, all classes, would entertain together.'[13]

From the notebooks of the imam of Kasab İlyas *mahalle*, along the Sea of Marmara in the centre of the intramural city, we get a detailed portrait, street by street, house by house, of a typical Muslim neighbourhood in 1885. The occasional occupations listed, and the forms of reference associated with the names of the homeowners or tenants – bey, *efendi*, *çavuş*, pasha, *ağa*, and *hanım* – are dispersed in what appears to be a random fashion throughout the 150 residences on the twelve streets for which we have records. Among the

---

[12] İlber Ortaylı, *İstanbul'dan Sayfalar* (Pages from Istanbul) (Istanbul, 1986), 199.
[13] *Beş Şehir*, 157.

homeowners, the pashas and beys or the porters (*hammal*) and pudding-makers (*muhallebici*) are not clustered in separate parts of the neighbourhood. Even the tenants range from a night-watchman to the Director of the Treasury Department.

The *mahalle* of Şenlikdede situated within the extensive district of Beşiktaş had, according to the 1907 census, a total of 833 inhabitants (413 male and 420 female) residing in 206 houses. There were, in addition, in the same *mahalle*, nineteen shops, two primary schools, two mosques, one fountain, one *bostan* (vegetable garden), twenty-one stables, five gardens, seven *bekârodaları*, one bakery and five vacant lots.

In 1885 Kasab İlyas *mahalle* contained around 150 houses, two mosques, three public fountains, three stables, five *bekârodaları*, five *bostans*, a *hamam*, two bakeries, a school, a police station, a *tekke* (dervish convent) with a small cemetery next to it, five gardens, thirty-seven shops, twenty-four *mağaza* (storehouses) and thirty-one vacant lots.

We have counted a total of 147 *mahalles* in the 1907 census in intramural Istanbul (comprising the present districts of Fatih and Eminönü). In 1914 intramural Istanbul had a population of 240,528.[14] Each *mahalle*, therefore, had an average population of only around 1,600. Some, assuredly, were much larger. A considerable number, however, on the eve of the First World War, consisted of two or three streets and a number of vacant lots. Fires and the higher mobility of the population during the war years created the necessity of restructuring these *mahalles*. Nevertheless, their average size was not to change very much after reorganization and regrouping. In 1928, an administrative reorganization reduced the number of intramural Istanbul *mahalles* to 114,[15] each having then an average population of around 1,800. A new cadastral plan was implemented in Istanbul, many *mahalles* disappeared, and new boundaries were drawn for those which remained.

The *mahalles* were the centres of economic and social life. Largely divided along ethnic – not class – lines, they were communities with a certain degree of autonomous control over their day-to-day affairs and a degree of communal solidarity, with a myriad of informal mech-

---

[14] See *Memâlik-i Osmaniyenin 1330 Senesi Nüfus İstatistiği* (Ottoman Population Statistics from the Year 1330/1914) (Istanbul, 1330/1914). The results of the 1907 census for Istanbul were never published in full detail.
[15] See 'Mahalle mıntıka ve daire teşkilâtı' (Neighbourhood, district and borough organization), *Şehremaneti Mecmuası*, 43, 45, 48, 49 and 51 (March, May, August, September and November 1928). For the population of Istanbul in the 1920s, see Zafer Toprak, 'La population d'Istanbul dans les premières années de la République', in *Travaux et recherches en Turquie, 1982* (Louvain, 1983), 63–70.

anisms for monitoring and regulating public morality. Until the nineteenth century there was no local authority at the *mahalle* level and urban administrative duties were the responsibility of the urban *kadıs* (religious judges). The *mahalles* were, nevertheless, well entrenched as the basic community at the local level, and the authority of the *kadı* was mediated by the religious leader (imam, priest or rabbi) located in the *mahalle*. His most important duty was to apportion and to collect from each inhabitant of the community the lump-sum tax imposed by the Ottoman State. He also acted as a guarantor for every single individual. For instance, any newcomer who wanted to set up house in the *mahalle* had to have the imam's approval (and also produce proof of his potential solvency). The local leader's influence rested on the performance of this duty. It cannot be said, however, that it was always fulfilled with justice or with equanimity.

With the administrative reforms of the *Tanzimat* period, all administrative powers were taken away from the religious judges, and the imams lost many of their responsibilities and powers as representatives of the local urban communities.[16] The *mahalles* remained, however, the basic building-blocks of the urban fabric of the city. After 1827 laymen were for the first time appointed as local headmen (*muhtars*) for each *mahalle*, and they acquired some of the prerogatives which had previously belonged to the religious leaders.

The class-based differentiation of the urban fabric was a phenomenon that had to wait for the twentieth century, and especially for the post-Second World War period, though one does observe the beginnings of the socio-economic stratification of neighbourhoods in the years before and after the First World War. During the Young Turk period, a small number of wealthy, modern-minded Muslim families began to leave the traditional enclaves of those of their faith in intramural Istanbul for 'apartment life' (*apartman hayatı*), in the new neighbourhoods of Nişantaşı and Şişli, which lay north of traditional non-Muslim Pera. This flow continued through the war years and into the 1920s and 1930s. The war years were in many respects a watershed for segments of the old elite.

Increasing construction of modern apartment buildings, particularly in the late 1920s and 1930s,[17] provided for the needs of those who chose to reject the traditional *mahalle* life of their fathers. A pervasive theme in many homes during the last years of the nineteenth century

[16] İlber Ortaylı, *Tanzimattan Cumhuriyete Yerel Yönetim Geleneği* (The Tradition of Local Administration from the *Tanzimat* to the Republic) (Istanbul, 1985), 100–4.

[17] *İstanbul Şehri Rehberi*, 166–7.

was intergenerational conflict – the old traditional Ottoman-Islamic values of the senior generation versus a rejection of these and the predictable infatuation with everything western of the juniors. A consequence of this was often a move, spatial – and very symbolic. In the well-known novel *Kiralık Konak* (A Mansion for Rent), Servet Bey, the *alafranga* uxorilocal son-in-law of a wealthy but old-fashioned Istanbul gentleman, desperately wants to get out of his father-in-law's quite adequate residence. The period is just prior to the First World War. He complains: 'I can't understand why we have to live here like nomads when there are such perfect modern apartment flats available in Şişli.'[18]

For most, such a move was not even contemplatable. Muslim life in the city continued on in its traditional neighbourhoods until the post-Second World War years. But the fracture had begun in the Young Turk period and was hastened by the crises of the First World War.

What sorts of houses did people live in? Could an average family easily have found housing for themselves and what was the market like? Did it fluctuate considerably? Were there shortages? And what, in any case, did people consider to be adequate housing? The first question is easy to answer, the others considerably more difficult. We know very little about the supply of housing in pre-Republican Istanbul other than the most general of statements.

Residences were typically divided into three categories: *süflî*, or inferior – usually meaning run-down and single-storey; *fevkânî*, two-storey; and *mükellef* or luxurious.[19] Halide Edip [Adıvar] describes the early twentieth-century district of 'Sinekli Bakkal' in the novel of the same name: 'The houses were always made of wood and two-storey, with dilapidated roofs and old-style eaves stretched out over the street almost resting on each other.'[20] From the little that remains of the old *mahalle*s in Istanbul today, one does get the distinct impression, like Halide Edip, that the two-storey *fevkânî* type of residence was the most common one. These houses typically have about fifty or sixty square metres of interior space per storey, usually divided between two rooms separated by a large vestibule (*sofa*) on each floor. There must have been population pressure on the existing stock

[18] Yakup Kadri Karaosmanoğlu, *Kiralık Konak* (A Mansion for Rent) (Istanbul, 1981 [1922]), 167.
[19] Ortaylı, *İstanbul*, 200.
[20] *Sinekli Bakkal* (published in English as *The Clown and His Daughter*, London, 1935) (Istanbul, 1980).

Plate 2.2 A street in an Istanbul Muslim *mahalle* of the 1870s, showing a variety of houses, the majority being the two-storey *fevkânî* kind.

of housing in the late nineteenth century, because Serim Denel[21] in discussing the changes in ordinary residential architecture after the fires, refers, in addition to a move away from wood, to increased building height and to a shrinking or elimination of the little gardens that had been such an integral part of the old-style homes – the bursts of green that Mark Twain had liked so much in the Istanbul vista. Such a sacrifice of time-worn patterns and domestic pleasures could only take place out of necessity. There were, as we have seen, large numbers of people flooding into the city throughout the late nineteenth and early twentieth centuries, and when the human flows were at their greatest, the pressures on housing must have been considerable.

In addition, thousands at a time were left homeless by the fires that struck down whole districts at rather regular intervals, further diminishing the housing stock. The destruction caused by some of the fires is quite well documented. For instance, to take only the devastation that occurred just after the turn of the century within intramural

Plate 2.3 Houses of the Istanbul wage-labouring class, 1906.

Istanbul, the fire in the quarter of Çırçır (1908) destroyed 1,500 houses, that in Aksaray (1911) 2,400, in Balat (1911) 350 and the famous fire of Cibali, which occurred in 1918, more than 7,000 houses. The Aksaray fire, which broke out on 23 July 1911 and lasted for a whole day, according to the accounts published in the press, also destroyed about 3,000 shops, fifteen bakeries, sixteen mosques, three public baths and two schools, in addition to the 2,400 houses.[22]

Some of the pressure on housing was met by increased density, and some by urban expansion, by a population shift to the newer districts on the periphery. Crowding was, no doubt, the response of the least privileged elements of society. The Pathfinder Survey of Istanbul in the aftermath of the First World War bears witness to such crowding at that time. In focusing on the homes of the many women left widowed with children after the war, the researchers note that:

The lack of homes for any class may be responsible for this crowding. It

[22] Reşat Ekrem Koçu, 'Aksaray yangınları' (The fires of Aksaray) in *İstanbul Ansiklopedisi* (Istanbul, 1958), I, 539–42.

is certain that the fact that large areas of the city are lying in ruins from fires must cause terrible pressure on the poorest members of society.[23]

Such crowding must also have existed after the earlier fires.

Fifteen per cent of all residences in Kasab İlyas *mahalle* contained one or more tenants in place of or in addition to the landlord. Many of the widows referred to in the Pathfinder Survey were also no doubt tenants, given their destitution. A well-informed writer and journalist, Ahmed Midhat Efendi, estimates that around 1890, about ten per cent of Istanbul's 'local' population lived in rented lodgings,[24] though it is difficult to substantiate this. It would not be unreasonable to say that 10 to 15 per cent of the permanent population of the city around the turn of the century was living as tenants. Although there are no first-hand data, we can surmise from what we know of the population movements within the city of Istanbul in the last quarter of the nineteenth and the first quarter of the twentieth centuries, that this proportion must have been much higher in the new settlements on the Asian side of the Bosphorus and in the new quarters to the north beyond old Pera (roughly the present-day districts of Taksim, Nişantaşı, Şişli and Teşvikiye).

Standards of living

Before we can discuss the degree to which economic factors influenced family life in Istanbul, we must have some idea of household well-being during the years of this study. What was the nature of the local economy in which families operated at that time? Did it change in any way over the years of concern? To what extent was subsistence a problem for families in the city? These are some of the questions which we shall try to answer in this section. We can only do so, however, in a tentative way using the available figures on individual wages and the cost of living, since detailed studies of household subsistence and levels of living do not yet exist for the period we have selected. Surprisingly, even less is known about the 1920s in this respect.

The price–wage scissors cut through the daily life of a significant portion of the population of the Ottoman capital. Shaw and Shaw tell us that, in 1886, 11.4 per cent of all adult Muslim men in Istanbul

---

[23] C. R. Johnson, *Constantinople To-day; or, The Pathfinder Survey of Constantinople* (New York, 1922), 291.
[24] Okay, *Batı*, 163.

were working for the government[25] and were at least in part dependent on a salary for a living. We have calculated that in 1885, around 40 per cent of all Muslim household heads permanently settled in the city were dependent upon fixed monthly or daily remunerations for a living, in occupations ranging from unskilled construction worker to high-ranking military officer or upper echelon bureaucrat. Among these, 31.4 per cent were either military officers or government employees of various ranks and 8 per cent wage-earners in non-governmental concerns of various kinds.

The period was one of rapid numerical expansion for both the bureaucracy and the wage-earners in general. The total number of civil servants being remunerated from the state budget rose from around 150,000 in 1895–6 to more than 180,000 in 1909–10.[26] The proportion of wage- and salary-earners among Muslim heads of household in Istanbul rose to more than 50 per cent in 1907 – 38.4 per cent for military and government employees and over 10 per cent for other wage-earners. An increasing proportion of the Muslim population of Istanbul was undoubtedly being integrated into a wage and market economy; wages as an income type and wage-earners as an economic group were gradually acquiring predominance. This explains the importance one must increasingly place on wages and cost-of-living indicators, real and nominal wages, as evidence of the well-being and standard of living of people in the city during this period.

Wages and cost of living, 1880–1918

It is possible to put together a tentative picture of wages in nineteenth-century Istanbul and its environs from the various sources available.[27] To give an example, in the 1860s an agricultural labourer in the vicinity of Istanbul was earning a daily wage of six to seven *kuruş*, at a time when a kilo of flour cost one *kuruş* and a kilo of beef around two. In the 1870s a skilled textile factory worker earned four to five *kuruş* a day. Towards the turn of the century in Istanbul a craftsman was earning from seven to thirteen *kuruş*, and in 1906 from nine to eighteen *kuruş* a day. A tannery worker earned a daily wage of about twelve *kuruş* in the years after the turn of the century. Daily wages in Istanbul

---

[25] *Ottoman Empire*, II, 244.
[26] Vedat Eldem, *Osmanlı İmparatorluğunun İktisadî Şartları Hakkında bir Tetkik* (A Study of the Economic Conditions of the Ottoman Empire) (Istanbul, 1977), 211.
[27] Charles Issawi, *The Economic History of Turkey: 1800–1914* (Chicago, 1980), 37–51, 333–8.

were about 20 per cent higher than they were in the provinces.[28] It is estimated that at the turn of the century 'money wages of unskilled labour were about twice as high as around 1850 indicating a distinct rise in real wages'.[29]

In calculating wages, one must take into account the strong segmentation of the Istanbul labour market along age and sex lines. At a time when ordinary male textile workers earned nine to fourteen *kuruş* a week in the 1870s, women were earning only three to five *kuruş*, and children one or two.[30] Similar cases have also been reported in both Istanbul and Anatolia for various other industries.[31] The availability of extra household income through the work of women and children, exploitative as it was, certainly constituted both a degree of compensation and an element of flexibility in times of depression or economic crisis.

Nominal wages were, it seems, on a rising trend during the quarter of a century up to the First World War.[32] Civil servants were always in an advantageous position throughout our period, earning average salaries much higher than the monthly wages of labourers. Ever since the *Tanzimat* period, the state bureaucracy constituted what was perhaps the most important single factor segmenting the labour market within the Empire. Until the post-First World War period, the civil service was in fact considered by Muslims as the most desirable area of employment for a young man. To give a single example of the wage differentials in the city at that time, let us take the average daily wage (14.1 *kuruş*) of an Istanbul labourer in 1913.[33] This was the equivalent of a monthly income of around 350 *kuruş*. The mean monthly salary of Ottoman Foreign Ministry officials in Istanbul at that time was 1,177 *kuruş*, more than three times the wage of the

---

[28] *Ibid.*, 42–4. The prices of flour and beef are those of Bursa, a city 130 miles from Istanbul. Eldem's implicit estimates of the wage differential between Istanbul and the provinces is even greater than Issawi's estimate of 20 per cent. For the years immediately preceding the First World War, Eldem's figures point to a difference of sometimes greater than 50 per cent between Istanbul and the mean wage in various industries in the provinces, with a significant difference between the provinces themselves. Eldem calculates, for instance, that the average *industrial* daily wage in 1913 was 14.1 *kuruş* in Istanbul and 12.5 *kuruş* in the provinces (*Osmanlı İmparatorluğu*, 209–12).

[29] Issawi, *Economic History*, 37.

[30] *Ibid.*, 43

[31] D. Quataert, 'Ottoman households, Ottoman manufacturing and international markets'. Paper presented to the Workshop on Turkish Family and Household Organization, City University of New York, New York, April 23–5, 1986.

[32] Eldem, *Osmanlı İmparatorluğu*.

[33] *Ibid.*, 212.

labourer.[34] The average wage paid to Ottoman civil servants in Istanbul in 1913 was surprisingly close to that – 1,166 *kuruş*.

What was considered as a decent living wage is another matter. It is very important to know the ways in which the recipients of these wages and salaries, or the public at large, perceived the existing wage-scale and the economic hierarchy, and what they thought it would take to support a family, since this would constitute a point of reference for what was to happen later during the First World War. Around the turn of the century, a salary of 540 *kuruş* was deemed sufficient to support a small family. In 1897 a petitioner asserted that a monthly salary of 600 *kuruş* was not adequate to support his (probably larger) family.[35] Findley estimates that a government official in the mid-1890s would have considered a monthly salary of 1,000 *kuruş* adequate to support a family.

Two other calculations of the minimum salary necessary for an 'average' family in Istanbul produce somewhat lower figures. Based on the quantities of goods and services consumed by a family of middle standing in 1914, one of these figures is 945 *kuruş*,[36] well under the mean monthly salary of civil servants in Istanbul for the same date. Zafer Toprak puts the monthly budget of a mid-level government official in July 1914 at a low of 235 *kuruş*.[37] His estimated basket of necessary goods and services is, however, quite spare and does not include rent and transportation. Nevertheless, these last two estimates are done for the year 1914, when both wages and the average level of prices were higher than in either the 1890s or the first years of this century. One is tempted to conclude that in the decade or two before the First World War there is every indication of a rise in the level of living for families in Istanbul.[38]

The prices of staple consumption goods in various cities of the Empire in the nineteenth century and up to 1914 show a surprisingly high degree of variability and fluctuation. For instance, in 1844, one *okka* of wheat bread cost 1.05 *kuruş* in the city of Salonica and only 0.35 *kuruş* in Edirne just about 150 miles away. In 1853 one *okka* of flour cost 1.5 *kuruş* in Izmir and 2.4 in Istanbul, both major Ottoman port cities. An *okka* of wheat flour cost 4.0 *kuruş* in Izmir in 1855

[34] Carter Vaughn Findley, 'Economic bases of revolution and repression in the late Ottoman Empire', *Comparative Studies in Society and History*, 28 (1987), 81–106.

[35] Cited by Findley in *ibid.*, 87.

[36] Eldem, *Osmanlı İmparatorluğu*, 214–15.

[37] *Türkiye'de Millî İktisat*, 1908–1918 (Nationalist Economics in Turkey, 1908–1918) (Ankara, 1982), 333.

[38] Issawi, *Economic History*, 8.

and only 2.5 kuruş in the same city in 1856.[39] This as yet incompletely unified internal market, and the apparently random price fluctuations it gave rise to, were also strongly felt in the capital city.

Avoiding any sweeping judgements about prices and the cost of living, Issawi considers the last quarter of the nineteenth century to be a time when agricultural prices and those of basic foodstuffs showed a decline. He writes: 'This trend was reversed in the first years of this century and accelerated after 1908, and all indications point to a sharp increase in the price of foodstuffs and the cost of living right up to the outbreak of the war.'[40]

Wage and price figures relate to each other and give us a tentative picture of real wages and living standards. Both Eldem and Issawi are, as a result, only able to provide us with an impressionistic picture of costs and living standards in the late Ottoman Empire. Eldem states, for instance, that, 'Before the First World War, mean wages and salaries in the Ottoman Empire were slightly higher than in neighbouring countries'. He goes on to argue that, 'as prices were also lower, and the purchasing power of money higher, we can say that the purchasing power of wages and salaries was greater in the Ottoman Empire'.[41] Issawi also concludes that 'it is very probable that per capita output and income rose significantly between the 1870s and the First World War'.[42]

Other studies generally confirm these conclusions. In their study of Ottoman wages from 1839 to 1913, Boratav, Ökçün and Pamuk calculate detailed long-term and medium-term trend equations for Ottoman nominal wages, excluding the bureaucracy.[43] The authors estimate that nominal wages in urban areas rose at an average rate of 1.1 per cent a year from 1839 to 1913. This corresponds to a total rise of 118 per cent over the seventy-four years covered. The authors distinguish four main sub-periods within this wide time-span. In the period running from 1839 to 1854 no significant trend is perceptible. Then, after a sudden increase of more than 40 per cent due to the Crimean War, a new trend is discernible from 1858 to 1873. In this period, the wage-index is estimated to have increased at a rate of 0.5 per cent per annum. In a third period running from 1879 to 1896 money wages declined at an average rate of 1.0 per cent per year. With the 'world economic

---

[39] For all these figures and many others, see *ibid.*, 334–6.
[40] *Ibid.*, 334.
[41] *Osmanlı İmparatorluğu*, 212.
[42] *Economic History*, 6.
[43] 'Ottoman wages and the world economy, 1839–1913', *Review*, 8 (1985), 379–406.

upswing' after 1896, Ottoman nominal wages rose once again at an annual rate of 1.1 per cent until 1908. Money wages made another jump of more than 20 per cent in the aftermath of the 1908 Young Turk Revolution. Thereafter, strikes and the legalization of trade unionism, together with the relative scarcity of industrial labour that arose from the series of wars after 1912, ensured a continuously rising trend in nominal wages until the outbreak of the First World War.[44]

The doubling of real wages within the seventy-five years preceding the First World War is hailed as an 'impressive achievement' for a pre-industrial economy. Ottoman wages fared quite well when compared to English wages of the same period. The ratio of Ottoman to English wages varied within a fairly narrow range in the nineteenth century, and up to 1914 – between 32 and 46 per cent. Given that the cost of living was higher in England, 'the difference in the levels of living between the working classes of the two countries appears to be even smaller than the figures on wages reveal'.[45]

Of course, wages and the cost of living only take on their full meaning within the context of people's demands. One must in some way be able to chart demands over the same period as wages and living costs, in order to determine whether families were truly satisfied with their material lives. The increasing penetration into everyday life in Istanbul of capitalist market relations and the beginnings of consumerism that followed it, starting in the second half of the nineteenth century, must have left their mark at least on the better-off families in the city, though no doubt even the poor were beginning to become aware of a world of new material objects and desires developing in their midst. In the years following the Crimean War Istanbul shops began to feature the newly imported consumer goods of Europe – clothing, home furnishings, foods and various luxury items. Starting in the last few decades of the century, popular newspapers and magazines began to advertise these goods on a regular basis and by the turn of the century popular publications were full of such advertisements, which must have influenced people's thinking and, as a result, their demands.

Did the demands of households double in the seventy-five years preceding the First World War as did wages? No doubt they increased, since middle- and upper-class families were clearly beginning to redo their dress and their homes and to reorganize many other aspects of their domestic consumption in the European fashion. But we do

[44] *Ibid.*, 390–1.
[45] *Ibid.*, 393.

not know how demand related to supply, and as a result, how levels of satisfaction or discontent varied during the period. This is an area, like so many in Ottoman social history, that has yet to be investigated systematically. We are, therefore, unable to answer this most crucial question for the understanding of households and families during the period we have selected.

War shock

The rather optimistic picture of wages and levels of living we have portrayed suddenly begins to be shattered with the outbreak of hostilities in 1914. Within a few years the wage–price scissors had begun to cut unsparingly against all public or private sector workers and civil servants who lived on fixed incomes. Unprecedented rates of inflation, as well as various shortages hitherto unknown even during either the 1854–6 Crimean War or the 1877–8 Ottoman-Russian War, wrought havoc on both the slowly but surely improving purchasing power of the wages of the labouring classes and the privileged salaries of the state bureaucrats.

The first price movements in Istanbul after the beginning of the war were of a speculative sort.[46] As early as 1914 the government and the local authorities in Istanbul had decreed a price freeze on all basic necessities such as flour, bread, salt, sugar and petroleum, and had taken over the task of provisioning and distributing such goods in the capital. Disorganization and panic immediately created a black market, and prices rocketed as a result. The difference between the official and the black-market price of basic necessities continued to widen throughout the war. The public had difficulty in understanding the existence of two sets of prices, the government price often being much above both the cost and the pre-war price of these goods. A sample of these two sets of prices is shown in table 2.1.

Transportation and various means of communication were disrupted, supplies were sometimes insufficient, the already tenuous link between various markets throughout the country further weakened, psychological and speculative increases and decreases in demand became frequent, while real or imaginary news from the front or overoptimistic or overpessimistic expectations often led to sudden jumps in the market prices of most basic necessities.

In the midst of such unprecedented changes in prices and market

[46] The economic data contained in this section derive mainly from the following two books: Ahmet Emin [Yalman], *Turkey in the World War* (New Haven, Conn., 1930), 144–56; and Toprak, *Millî İktisat*.

Table 2.1. *Official (O) and black-market (B) prices of some basic necessities
in Istanbul (yearly average in* kuruş).

Year	Bread O	Bread B	Sugar O	Sugar B	Beans O	Beans B	Mutton O	Mutton B
1915		1.65		7.5		7		8.5
1916	1.6	9.5		30		15		16
1917	2.5	18	20	112	10	40	30	35
1918	2.5	34	30	195	15	65	50	125

Source: Zafer Toprak, *Türkiye'de Millî İktisat, 1908–1918* (Ankara, 1982), 327.

Table 2.2 *Istanbul cost-of-living index (1914 = 100).*

Date		Index	Date		Index
January	1917	405	January	1919	2130
July	1917	790	July	1919	1225
December	1917	1465	December	1919	1260
January	1918	1645	January	1920	1440
July	1918	1905	July	1920	1420
December	1918	2205	December	1920	1440

Source: Ahmet Emin [Yalman], *Turkey in the World War* (New Haven, Conn.,
1930), 144–56; Toprak, *Millî İktisat,* 331–2.

structures, the Ottomans began, for the first time, to calculate price
indexes. A semi-public organization, the Administration of the Ottoman Debt (*Düyûn-u Umumiye İdaresi*), began to record the retail prices
of all basic consumer goods in Istanbul in order to give certain bonus
payments to its employees. From 1 January 1917 a statistical record
of retail prices was kept by this Administration from which a cost-of-
living index was then computed (see table 2.2).[47]
    Ottoman society was facing inflationary pressure of such dimen-
sions for the first time in its history. Some of the basic necessities

[47] The *Düyûn-u Umumiye* cost-of-living index was discontinued after 1920. It seems,
however, that the 1920s was a period of relative price stability, followed by a decline
after 1929. Taking the year 1923 as a base, the Istanbul consumer price index stood
at 127.7 in 1926, and dropped to 111.7 in 1928. Thereafter, it reached 75.9 in 1933, following
a quite regular downward movement. Between 1929 and 1933 the wholesale price
index for Turkey fell by about 50 per cent (see F. Ergin, 'Birinci dünya savaşında
ve Atatürk döneminde fiyatlar ve gelirler' [Prices and incomes in the First World
War and in Atatürk's time], *Atatürk Araştırma Merkezi Dergisi,* 3 (1986), 59–84).

underwent price increases even greater than the already extraordinarily high rate of inflation. An *okka* of sugar which cost 3 *kuruş* in July 1914, cost 250 *kuruş* by September 1918. The price of an *okka* of rice went from 3 to 90 *kuruş*, that of potatoes from 1 to 27 *kuruş*, the price of olive oil from 8 to 180 *kuruş*, and the price of kerosene from 1.5 to 160 *kuruş* during these few years. Toprak's monthly basket of necessary goods calculated for a mid-level official in July 1914 at 235 *kuruş* cost 4,594.25 *kuruş* in September 1918.[48] If the 1914 price is taken as a base of 100, the index had jumped to 1,953 four years later.

Throughout this period the press persistently bemoaned the extraordinarily high cost of living. The fact is that the Ottomans had to confront the greatest increase in cost of living amongst all of the belligerent countries. Taking 1914 as a base year, the cost-of-living index in 1918 was 203 in England, 206 in France, 293 in Germany, 268 in Italy, 380 in Greece, 633 in Finland, 165 in the Netherlands and 1,163 in Austria. The corresponding index for the city of Istanbul was 1,920.[49]

The Istanbul press of the war years devoted a remarkable amount of space to social and economic questions. In spite of the war – or perhaps precisely because of it – commercial, agricultural and industrial questions were in the forefront of the news. It is perhaps not a coincidence that the *Journal of Economics (İktisadiyat Mecmuası)* began publication in February 1915. The provisioning of cities, prices, food production and agricultural problems of various sorts (in particular productivity, transportation and distribution) received at least as great an amount of attention as direct news from the war fronts. In order to improve agricultural productivity and the provisioning of cities and to eliminate food shortages, agricultural machinery was imported from Germany for the first time.

Wages, on the other hand, were very far from catching up with these astronomical rates of inflation. Immediately after the onset of the hostilities, the Government made it clear that it expected some sacrifice from its civil servants by decreeing a uniform cut of 50 per cent in the salaries of all public officials. Later, in 1915, when the wartime inflation had begun to be more severely felt, salaries were restored to their pre-war level, but the Ministry of Finance refused to reimburse the 50 per cent cuts for the one-year period preceding November 1915. In September 1916, a cost-of-living bonus of 20 per cent was awarded to officials with monthly salaries below 1,000 *kuruş*,

---

[48] Toprak, *Millî İktisat*, 333.
[49] Eldem, *Osmanlı İmparatorluğu*.

and a bonus of 15 per cent to those having a salary above that figure. In March 1918 a similar bonus was again awarded and lower salaries were exempted from taxes.

Toprak estimates that the purchasing power of the salaries of civil servants fell by about 60 to 80 per cent during the war,[50] and the situation was probably even worse for lower echelon officials. Many of the lower grade military were also in a very difficult position. To take the case of the Ottoman Navy as an example, only the Admirals were earning a salary more than sufficient to cover the bare cost-of-living expenses in 1918.

In August 1916 the Society for the Employment of Muslim Women (*Kadınları Çalıştırma Cemiyet-i İslamiyesi*) was founded under the auspices of Enver Pasha, Minister of War, and Naile Sultan, a daughter of Sultan Abdülhamid II. The objective of the Society was clear: to try and alleviate some of the labour shortages caused by the war, by encouraging Muslim women to work outside the home.

This was quite a remarkable occurrence in an urban Islamic social and cultural environment where the work of women outside the home was virtually unknown. The reaction to the Society's appeal, however, was extraordinary and quite surprising. Within four months, the distressing economic conditions had pushed almost 14,000 Muslim women of Istanbul to apply to the Society for a job. The Society's headquarters were flooded with letters of application, and literally besieged by masses of women who wanted to supplement their husbands' salaries, much eroded by wartime inflation. The Society, faced with so many pleas, had to establish soup kitchens for these women in distress – a step far removed from its initial aims.[51]

It was to a certain extent due to the activities of the Society that female work outside the home started to become a reality in Istanbul. Many Muslim women, thanks to the official patronage of the authorities, began to work in offices, factories, telephone exchanges, etc., all posts previously occupied almost exclusively by their non-Muslim Istanbul counterparts. On 12 August 1916 the newspaper *Tanin* proudly noted that many lower- and even middle-class Muslim women of Istanbul were, like their non-Muslim counterparts, contributing to the imperial war effort and participating more fully in the social and economic life of the capital city. If 'liberation' be the right term to use, one can say that the circumstances of the war provided a major

---

[50] *Ibid.*, 334.
[51] 'Kadınları çalıştırma teşebbüsü' (The attempt at employing women), *Vakit*, 111 (9 Şubat 1918/9 February 1918), 1.

push towards the 'liberation' of Muslim women in the Ottoman capital.

The desperate situation of government employees led to considerable debate in Parliament in November 1917. The deputies observed that officials were not able to shift the burden of a higher cost of living to anyone else. The wage and occupational hierarchy of the city had been inverted; a top level civil servant was in a worse position than a common porter. By 1918 an ordinary street porter was earning from 7,500 to 9,000 *kuruş* a month, that is, just as much as a major-general within the Ottoman army, while a ministerial director's salary did not exceed 7,200 *kuruş*. Parliament agreed that the impartiality of judges and the general dignity of public service was in jeopardy. However, it was impossible at the time to increase salaries, and the only positive step taken was to exempt officials from paying a special tax which had been levied on those excused from military service.

A flurry of articles appeared in the Istanbul press during the war years on household economics and budgets and on the necessity of avoiding extravagance. The motto of the feminist journal *Kadınlar Dünyası*, 'A family is like a company' (*Her aile bir şirkettir*) was used to extol the virtues of co-operative and frugal family life. An article in *Sabah* of 7 July 1916 stresses the need for each household to budget its expenses, especially in times of distress. Small wonder then that the idea of marriage as an economic association received increasing attention during this period. In an article published in 1920 entitled 'Marriage and Subsistence', the well-known journalist Ahmed Emin [Yalman] writes that:

Marriage is first and foremost a matter of subsistence. Some statisticians say that there is a very close relationship between the price of bread and the number of marriages. If the economic situation does not improve and if the dangers of the crisis are not eliminated, the encouragements to matrimony will have no effect.[52]

We find many traces in the press during the war years, and those immediately following it, of the (we now know misplaced) perception that the economic hardships of the period had caused a decrease in the number of marriages and an increase in the divorce rates in Istanbul, something clearly on the mind of Ahmet Emin. Cries of alarm were raised to uphold the 'religious and moral sanctity of marriage'.[53]

---

[52] 'İzdivaç ve maişet' (Marriage and subsistence), *Vakit*, 828 (26 Şubat 1920/26 February 1920), 1.

[53] 'İzdivaç ve talâk' (Marriage and divorce), *İnci*, 1 (1 Şubat 1919/1 February 1919), 1.

As a result of the wartime inflation, the traditional income distribution pattern of the city was completely disrupted. A large portion of the population, the military and bureaucratic cadres, pensioners and other people living on fixed incomes had to face hitherto unimaginable hardship and sudden poverty. Social, cultural and occupational hierarchies within the city were set on end, and the bureaucratic elitism which had so dominated the Empire ever since the *Tanzimat* period was all but destroyed. Many officials found secondary work or engaged in some sort of business, in spite of the official interdiction, and the gap between a low salary and the high cost of living was increasingly met by corruption. Under such circumstances it is hardly surprising that long-established economic and social values were profoundly shaken.

This temporary reversal of the traditional economic, cultural and social values is reflected in anecdotal form in an article which appeared in 1923 in the women's magazine *İnci*. The story, as told by a friend, begins with two brothers of modest origin, both in primary school. The elder brother, diligent and hard-working, pursues his studies at the *rüşdiye* (middle school) and ends up as a school teacher. The other leaves school and becomes a porter at the Galata customs house. The friend meets them again twenty years later. While the street porter owns three houses, the teacher has difficulty in paying his own rent, and is dependent on his younger brother for a decent living.[54] There is no doubt that the brunt of wartime inflation in the city was largely borne by those on a fixed salary or wage. The exorbitant prices that families of this sort had to pay for daily necessities filled the pockets of tradesmen and speculators, many of whom were later disparagingly typified as 'the 1332 (1916) merchants' or 'war rich'.

In the midst of the crisis which its traditional bureaucratic and salaried classes were undergoing, Istanbul witnessed the birth of a completely new commercially oriented Muslim 'middle class'. Young Turk governments, inspired by Turkish nationalist ideas, had, since the revolution of 1908, been encouraging the development of such a Muslim Turkish business and industrial class to replace the Greek, Armenian, Jewish or Levantine merchants and manufacturers who had traditionally been performing that role in Istanbul. The abolition of the Capitulations, the many centuries-old privileges and tax exemptions given to foreign and Levantine merchants, was only one of the important steps taken in that direction during the war years. The

---

[54] 'Oğlum, tahsil-i ilm et, yoksa hammal olursun' (Study hard, my son, or else you shall be a street porter!), *İnci*, NS 8 (Mart 1923/March 1923), 2.

exceptional circumstances of war, and the decade of turmoil and social transformation which followed, were important impetuses to the emergence of this new Turkish bourgeoisie which joined the old bureaucratic elite in its aspirations for a western style of life.[55] There is little doubt that the economic crises of the 1910s were a watershed in Istanbul social and cultural life, opening the door to the diffusion of western values and styles of life to the middle- and lower-middle classes in the city.

Though traditional *mahalle* life survived most of the demographic and social changes that confronted Istanbul in the late nineteenth and early twentieth centuries, such inward-turning segmental structures increasingly became anomalies within the highly differentiated social and economic life of the city. Capitalist market relations penetrated the local community and home lives of ordinary people in Istanbul, in a way and to a degree they had not done so before. While this separation of home and work brought great opportunities for some and was a liberating force for many, it also meant an increasing dependency and vulnerability to economic processes beyond people's control. The inflation and economic instability of the war years created a great sense of shock and disorientation in many people, and this, combined with the many other changes of those times, no doubt made more palatable the social and cultural changes they were then experiencing and were yet to experience. By the 1930s the class structure of the city on the ground had also begun to show signs of change as the districts of Istanbul came to be more clearly associated with one, rather than a mix of classes. This process really only came to fruition, however, after the Second World War. These were the physical and economic co-ordinates of the world in which we found households and families during those years.

---

[55] Feroz Ahmad, 'War and society in the Young Turk period', *Review*, 11 (1988), 265–86.

3

Households and families: structure and flux

Households and families

Kâzım Bey, the son of a horsetrader who had emigrated to Istanbul from the Balkans along with hundreds of thousands of fellow-Muslims after the disastrous Ottoman defeat in the war with Russia of 1877–8, is, perhaps, as typical a Turk of late Ottoman Istanbul as one can find. He was trained as a typesetter before the First World War, in the days when Turkish was printed with the Arabic script, and spent the rest of his life in that trade, working for some of the best-known newspapers in the city. Kâzım Bey was born in 1893 and grew up in the heart of the Muslim world of the city, in its most densely populated district, Fatih, in what he described as a very average (*mutavassıt*) family. His childhood household was a far cry from the numerical grandeur that is often attributed to Istanbul households of the past. The family was sheltered in a two-storey wooden structure, and it consisted of his mother, father and two younger brothers. Even as such, it was a little larger than the mean for the census of 1907 which was conducted when Kâzım was fourteen years old, and upon which we shall rely for our statistical account of the Istanbul household.[1] The mean was 4.2 and that included both family and non-family members, such as servants (see table 3.1.). That number does not tell us that there were many households in the city consisting of only one person and that that there were also some very populous ones, the largest in 1907 containing twenty-seven persons. In general, however, the population of the old Ottoman capital was composed of the sum

---

[1] Much of our household analysis rests on the census of 1907; not, however, because we claim it was a typical year in this period of great changes. We have selected that census because it falls roughly midpoint in our period, because it portrays a relatively stable population, and because it is the most accurate census of the period for which local level registers are available.

Table 3.1. *Households in Istanbul 1907, numbers and proportions of types and of residents by type and mean numbers of residents per household*

Household type	Number of type	%	Number of residents	%	Mean household size	Mean number of family residents	Mean number of non-family residents
Solitaries	152	12.9	168	3.4	1.0	1.0	–
No family	95	8.0	288	5.8	3.0	1.6	1.4
Simple family	470	40.0	1671	33.8	3.6	3.4	0.2
Extended family	188	16.1	984	20.0	5.2	4.7	0.5
Multiple family	141	12.0	1082	21.9	7.7	6.9	0.8
Unclassifiable	130	11.1	739	15.0	5.7	3.1	2.6
All households	1176	100.1	4932	99.9	4.2	3.6	0.6

Source: Istanbul population rosters, 1907.

of quite small domestic units. Forty-six per cent of all households had three or fewer persons in them, and over 60 per cent of the population lived in such demographically modest circumstances. The significant number of solitaries in the city no doubt brought down the mean somewhat, but not very much. The combined mean for family households at that time was only slightly higher: 4.7 people. The small average size of Istanbul households just after the turn of the century is not really surprising given what we know about the average rural household of the period, which, considering the benefits of family labour in the domestic agricultural economy of the time, was itself quite moderate in size, containing anywhere between 5.3 and 6.5 members.[2]

The home of a person of modest means in Istanbul at that time, such as Kâzım Bey's father, would ordinarily have consisted only of family members; it would not have contained live-in servants. Only 8 per cent of all households in the city in 1907 had the luxury of having servants registered with them as residents, and most of these were found in the homes of the upper crust of society, as might be expected. Kâzım Bey's childhood household was simple in structure; that is, it only sheltered one conjugal unit and offspring, with no additional relatives. It did not even contain his grandparents, who lived a fifteen-minute walk away in the same expansive district. The modal household type in Istanbul in 1907 was the simple family household (see table 3.1). Forty per cent of all households were of that type, and they contained 34 per cent of the permanent Muslim population. Such households were typically not very large, with 3.6 residents on the average who were usually family members.

While Kâzım's childhood household size and structure were indeed modest in a purely demographic sense, the connections between his home and those of others related to his immediate family were complex. His grandmother, his mother's mother to be precise, walked the fifteen minutes and visited them on a daily basis to look after her grandsons. Perhaps she was there especially frequently because her son-in-law was often travelling in Anatolia, buying and selling horses. In a sense, in terms of her help in child-rearing, she was an important part of the household. Kâzım Bey told us that he 'grew up in her hands'. In another sense, she was not part of it at all since

---

[2] Alan Duben, 'Turkish families and households in historical perspective', *Journal of Family History*, 10 (1985), 89. There are no reliable data on rural household size and structure for the late Ottoman period. The figures presented here are based on very few cases and must be taken as rough approximations only.

Plate 3.1 An Istanbul family of modest means, 1919. Husband and wife (dressed in rather modern clothes) appear to be close to each other in age and, from their position in the photograph, perhaps in status. Their son may be thirteen or fourteen and their daughter five or six years old, indicating a birth interval of about eight years. As far as we know, they have no other children. The elderly woman is either the mother of the husband or the wife.

she did not reside there, and would not have been recorded there in the census.

Plate 3.2 A military family in the early Republican years, 1920s. Though the mother is wearing the traditional *çarşaf*, her near pubescent daughter is modern in attire.

If we now move to an elite household in pre-First World War Istanbul as described in the novel, *İbrahim Efendi Konağı* (The Mansion of İbrahim Efendi), we see a similar interpenetration of households. 'There

Plate 3.3 An early Republican family, 1920s. The symmetry of the pose is striking. There are only two children.

was always a coming and going, communication, movement between the two homes', the author Sâmiha Ayverdi observes,[3] referring to the homes of İbrahim Efendi and his brother Hilmi Bey. İbrahim

[3] *İbrahim Efendi Konağı* (The Mansion of İbrahim Efendi) (Istanbul, 1982), 6.

Plate 3.4 An Istanbul family of average means, 1922.

Efendi was a widower, and his sister-in-law, Hâlet Hanım, who lived
nearby, was constantly in their *konak* (mansion) and took the responsibility for raising his two daughters when they were young. She is
a person who is described as having had an influence over the most
minute details of her brother-in-law's domestic life. However, there

was also a certain ambiguity in her role: 'She was never entirely a part of the household, nor entirely separate from it.'[4]

Functional connections of these sorts between family households were quite common in pre-Republican Istanbul, since we have come across them in relation to households of all social strata. They are not uncommon even today in Istanbul or other major Turkish cities, where intergenerational, interhousehold, extended family ties are particularly strong, even in a situation where nuclear family households overwhelmingly predominate as the statistical norm.[5] These vital ties still provide, and appear to have then provided, services, often for child care, that the demographically modest circumstances of most households could not otherwise afford. The nuclear family pattern, which was very common as least as early as the beginning of this century in Istanbul, did not seem to have increased the costs of children to parents as Macfarlane argues it did in England.[6] Even when the family was living apart from relatives, their services were in most cases readily available if needed. In Istanbul, and throughout Turkey for that matter, the costs of children have, to our knowledge, always been spread between generations. When they coresided, given traditional Turkish patterns of seniority and authority, the senior generation not only helped out, they also had overriding rights of intervention in the upbringing of any juniors in the household.[7] When they did not live together, the same pattern in a somewhat more diluted form persisted between households.

Sixteen per cent of all Istanbul Muslim households in 1907 were extended in structure, containing, that is, an additional non-conjugal relative or relatives who might help out with domestic tasks (see table 3.1). Such households were larger on the average than simple family households (consisting of 5.2 persons), sheltering 20 per cent of the permanent Muslim population of the city. In most cases the extension from the nuclear family core was a parent: in 82 per cent of such cases, the mother either of the husband or wife, usually of the husband. She was typically a widow and a dependent of her son, and would play an important role in rearing his children. Invariably the

---

[4] *Ibid.*, 11.

[5] Serim Timur, *Türkiye'de Aile Yapısı* (Family Structure in Turkey) (Ankara, 1972); Duben, 'The significance of family'; Emre Kongar, *İzmir'de Kentsel Aile* (The Urban Family in Izmir) (Ankara, 1972).

[6] *Marriage and Love*, 69–70.

[7] This has emerged from a number of the retrospective interviews we conducted, as well as from our observations of many contemporary Istanbul families. It seems also to have characterized rural Turkey in the past. See, for example, Berkes, *Bazı Ankara Köyleri.*

mother would be listed after her son in the census register, a clear sign that authority rested with him and not with her. Without her husband, the senior male, her son if she had one, would take over the headship of the household. Given this pattern of authority and the fluid boundaries between households, it may be that there is little sense in making a distinction between nuclear and extended family households. It does not appear that such a distinction would in any case have been very meaningful for early twentieth-century Ottomans. Extended households had a greater number of non-family members than did simple family households (see table 3.1). Only 12 per cent of all Muslim households in the city supported two or more couples, though given the greater average size of such arrangements (7.7 persons), 22 per cent of the population lived that way. Nearly three-quarters of these households contained two generations, equally divided residentially between those organized uxorilocally and those patrilocally. Almost one person on the average in such households was a non-relative, typically a servant. Coresidential patterns in the Ottoman capital were considerably less complex than in rural areas, where approximately 20 to 30 per cent of all households were of the multiple family type.[8] Most households in Istanbul in the middle of our period of study had to look outside themselves for additional help with domestic tasks if they needed it, because they had neither relatives nor servants living with them.

Dumont and Georgeon describe the household of an upper echelon bureaucrat in the same period, just after the turn of the century, based on a diary that the master of the house, Said Bey, wrote.[9] His household, though larger than that of Kâzım Bey's, contained for the years 1902, when we intercept them, to 1908, six family members and an average of three or four servants. The family members were his wife and four children. Said Bey's mother, who was alive then, and we presume a widow, was living separately, though her son was paying her monthly rent. Her life, though demographically simple, was socially and economically complex. These are surprising domestic arrangements for Ottoman times, and Dumont and Georgeon explain them as the result of Said Bey's adoption of, along with a proficiency in the French language, a '*modèle familial occidental*' that he acquired from his exposure to *alafranga* culture via novels and the theatre. The

[8] Duben, 'Turkish families', 91.
[9] Paul Dumont and François Georgeon, 'Un bourgeois d'Istanbul au début du XXe siècle', *Turcica*, 17 (1985), 127–82; François Georgeon, 'XX. yüzyıl başlarında bir Osmanlı ailesinin bütçesi üzerine notlar' (Notes on the budget of an Ottoman family at the beginning of the twentieth century), *Tarih ve Toplum*, 23 (1985), 43–6.

household becomes more 'Turkish' in 1908, when his daughter Semiramis marries and brings in her husband to a uxorilocal residential
arrangement that, though not common, was considered highly desirable at the time. Only 3.4 per cent of all Muslim households in the
city were of this type in 1907. But, then, only 3.6 per cent were the
patrilocal stem family household that many have thought of as the
typical residential arrangement of the Ottoman past.

One of the most striking features we find of the distribution of Muslim households by structure in early twentieth-century Istanbul is the
very high percentage of individuals, mostly men, but also a large
number of women (perhaps like Said Bey's mother) living alone or
in what we call no family households: 'The city [even the Islamic
city, it seems] favors solitude.'[10] In 1907, 21 per cent of all households
were of these two types combined. Thirteen per cent of all households
were what are known as solitaries, and nearly half of these were
young unmarried men under the age of thirty. We should remember
that this figure is for the permanently registered part of the population.
There were also large numbers of single men living in *bekârodaları*
(bachelors' hostels) in the city at the time whom we did not include
in our survey because they were considered transients, though they
might have been living in the city for years. In other words, our figures
tend to underrepresent the actual numbers of solitaries in the city
at that time. Another note of caution in relation to these statistics
should be introduced at this point. Classifying households by percentages of types as we have done is a form of analysis remote from
the domestic experiences of the individuals being studied. While 13
per cent of all households were solitaries only 3.4 per cent of all Muslims at the time lived alone (see table 3.1, p. 49). Only slightly less
than 6 per cent lived in no family households. If we are concerned
about the experiences of individuals, then the latter figures are the
important ones. If we are interested in the more experientially distant
array of household types, then we should look at the former ones.

The swollen numbers of solitaries and no family households in the
1885 census reflect the large numbers of dislocated individuals who
flocked into Istanbul after the Ottoman-Russian War of the prior
decade. The population of Istanbul was in great flux during our period,
particularly in the years between the Ottoman-Russian War and the
census of 1885. By the time of the 1907 census the inflow of migrants
had levelled off, and large numbers of those living alone or out of

[10] David Herlihy and Christiane Klapisch-Zuber, *Tuscans and Their Families: A Study
of the Florentine Catasto of 1427* (New Haven, Conn., 1985), 311.

families had married or were absorbed into existing family households. Many of those living by themselves were young men, who
presumably had migrated alone or ahead of their families, and naturally set up their own households only after they had established themselves in the city and were in a position to provide for a family. While
the flow of migrants to Istanbul dropped off after the 1877–8 war,
it did not stop, and the significant numbers of households and persons
that we catch living alone or without their families in 1907 probably
reflect the continuing drama of dislocation and resettlement. Nearly
two-thirds of all Muslim household heads in Istanbul in 1907 were
born outside the Ottoman capital, and that is a low figure, for if we
were to add in the impermanent population of the city it would be
even higher.

The differences between the two censuses, and in particular the
lower percentages of solitaries and no family households in general,
and the decreasing frequency with which we find women living alone
by 1907, may be interpreted as a sign of the increased normalization
of Muslim residential life in the city, following the shock of the massive
inflow of refugees in the late seventies and eighties. One sign of this
normalization is that certain indicators of household life of the non-
Istanbul born tend to more closely resemble those of the Istanbul
born in 1907 than in 1885. This does not necessarily reflect an 'Istanbul-
ization' of those patterns, though that is certainly possible. It might
also reflect a gradual return to a prior residential pattern that had
been disrupted by war and migration and which took a generation
to begin to be re-established, a pattern that may not have been so
different from that found among older Istanbul families. For example,
the combined percentage of those household heads born in Istanbul
either living alone or in no family households was only 16 in 1885,
whereas for all heads it was double that (30 per cent). By 1907 the
gap between the Istanbul born and the non-Istanbul born had dimi-
nished considerably. The same percentage of Istanbul born was living
alone or without family as had done so twenty-two years earlier. But
by 1907 only 20 per cent of the non-Istanbul born were living alone
or in no family households. In 1885 the mean household size of those
born in Istanbul was 4.8 persons, but for those born in the Balkans
it was 3.5. In 1907 households with Istanbul-born heads averaged 4.5
persons, with those headed by emigrants from the Balkans containing
4.4 persons.

Fourteen per cent of all households in 1907 were headed by females
(see table 3.2.). What is striking is that 32 per cent of all female household heads lived alone, and 14 per cent were in no family households,

Table 3.2. *Household types by sex of heads, Istanbul, 1885 and 1907*

Household types	1885					1907				
	Male-headed Number	%	Female-headed Number	%	Female-headed (row %)	Male-headed Number	%	Female-headed Number	%	Female-headed (row %)
Solitaries	96	13.7	63	36.4	40.0	97	9.6	53	31.9	35.0
No family	74	10.6	43	24.8	37.0	71	7.1	24	14.4	25.0
Simple family (total)	250	35.7	32	18.6	11.0	420	41.7	50	30.1	11.0
Couples with-out offspring	77	11.0	2	1.2	3.0	93	9.2	1	0.6	1.0
Couples with offspring	138	19.7	2	1.2	1.4	253	25.1	3.0	1.8	1.0
Widowers with offspring	35	5.0	0	0	0	74	7.4	0	0	0
Widows with offspring	0	0	28	16.2	100.0	0	0	46	27.7	100.0
Extended family	122	17.4	20	11.6	14.0	171	17.1	77	10.2	9.0
Multiple family	94	13.4	5	2.9	5.0	133	13.2	8	4.8	6.0
Unclassifiable	62	8.9	10	5.8	14.0	115	11.4	14	8.4	11.0
Total	698		173	19.8		1007		166	14.1	

Source: Istanbul population rosters, 1885 and 1907.

Table 3.3. *Household size by occupation of head, Istanbul, 1907*

Occupation	Number of households	Number of residents	Mean number of residents	Mean number of family residents	Mean number of non-family residents
Elite	54	306	5.7	4.6	1.1
Civil servants/ military	127	603	4.8	3.9	0.9
Artisans/ shopkeepers	115	528	4.6	4.1	0.5
Labourers/ wage-earners	32	131	4.1	3.3	0.8

Source: Istanbul population rosters, 1907.

usually sharing their domestic quarters with another woman or women. More than half of the women living alone were under the age of forty-five, that is, most likely still in their fecund years. These figures were even higher in 1885 when 20 per cent of all household heads were women, 36 per cent of whom were living alone at the time. These surprisingly high figures are a bit deceptive, because we must remember that they indicate percentages of households and not percentages of the women living in them. When we examine the experiences of the adult female population we get a different picture. The percentage of women fifteen years of age or older living alone was 5 in 1885 and 3 in 1907. Though lower, these are rather high figures for the Muslim population of a city in which norms for female behaviour were still quite restrictive, and where living outside family life was looked upon with considerable disfavour.

We are not surprised to learn that large and complex households were most likely to be found attached to those with elite professions. The average household of upper crust turn-of-the-century Istanbul Muslim society contained 5.7 members (see table 3.3). Most of the heads of these households were high level civil servants and military people, a distinction between which was not often easy to make at that time. Since their average age of forty-nine was six years higher than that for household heads in general, it may be that their above average size is attributable, at least in part, to the demographic advantages of a later stage in the domestic cycle. For middle level civil servants and military, as well as other what we today would call white-collar workers, the mean was slightly lower at 4.8. For the households of the traditional artisans and shopkeepers of the city the mean was 4.6.

Table 3.4. *Household type by occupation of household head, Istanbul, 1907*

| Household type | Occupational classes | | | | | | | |
| | Elite | | Civil servants/ military | | Artisans/ shopkeepers | | Labourers/ wage-earners | |
	Number	%	Number	%	Number	%	Number	%
Solitaries	4	7.4	12	9.4	8	7.0	4	12.5
No family	–	–	4	3.2	7	6.1	5	15.6
Simple family	26	48.1	47	37.0	61	53.0	8	25.0
Extended family	8	14.8	30	23.6	18	15.7	11	34.4
Multiple family	10	20.8	18	14.2	15	13.0	2	6.3
Unclassifiable	6	11.1	16	12.6	6	5.2	2	6.3
Total	54	16.2	127	38.1	115	34.5	32	9.6

Source: Istanbul population rosters, 1907.

And for the lowest level of society with which we have contact, ordinary workers, and others who only had their labour to sell for a wage, the mean was 4.1.

It is also not surprising that of the non-family household members who could clearly be distinguished as such 60 per cent were servants among the elite, only 28 per cent among the civil servants, 15 per cent among the craftsmen and shopkeepers, and 5 per cent among the labourers. Twenty-eight per cent of the households of Muslim labourers permanently settled in Istanbul at the time contained one or more non-conjugally related persons (solitaries and no-family households), whereas only 13 per cent of the artisan-shopkeepers did so (see table 3.4). Twenty-one per cent of the elite households were multi-family as were only 6 per cent of those whose head was a labourer. Even the civil servants and artisan-shopkeepers could not match the elite in the complexity of their domestic arrangements, with 14 and 13 per cent respectively having two or more conjugal units living under the same roof. Complex households were clearly something largely for the rich and the elderly, because age, occupational status and wealth went hand in hand, particularly in a society where the most prestigious and the most desirable occupations for Muslims were in the civil or military bureaucracies.[11] Such complex households

[11] Findley, *Bureaucratic Reform.*

were also a project that the Istanbul born had a comparative advantage in obtaining, no doubt due to the higher probability of several generations being together in one place among more settled families. Seventeen per cent of the households of Istanbul-born heads were multiple family, whereas only 10 per cent of those whose heads were born elsewhere attained such domestic complexity. Both elite and artisan-shopkeeper households had high percentages of simple family households (48 and 53 per cent respectively), and correspondingly moderate percentages of extended family households. For the civil servants, the balance between the two was more evenly distributed. Thirty-seven per cent were simple, and 24 per cent were sharing their lives with an additional relative or relatives. Even fewer labouring class families lived without an additional relative. Twenty-five per cent were simple in structure, and 34 per cent extended. Put somewhat differently, when labourers lived in family households they would more commonly have an additional relative with them than not.

Household types and the domestic cycle

The size and composition of households in late Ottoman Istanbul, as elsewhere, were not fixed matters. It was common for individuals to experience living in different types of households at different stages of their lives. The procession from one type of household to another as one moves through the various stages of life generally fits into a standardized pattern that varies from society to society, depending upon a complex variety of social, economic and cultural factors. We can learn something about the pattern for Istanbul by examining the ages of household heads for the various types of domestic units. If we take the 1907 census as our norm, a clear age-specific pattern of headship emerges. The modal age for solitary and no family household heads was between twenty and twenty-nine, for simple and extended family household heads between thirty and forty-nine, and for heads of multiple family households was over sixty years of age (see fig. 3.1). In other words, living alone or without a proper family was more likely something that young adults would have experienced in those days. The middle ages were the prime ones for headship of simple and extended family households. Members of the most senior cohorts were more likely to head multiple family households. The average ages of the other household members, such as spouses and offspring, would, naturally, vary with the age of the head of the household.

The domestic experiences of most individuals changed as they grew up and aged. In 1907, 25 per cent of all household heads between

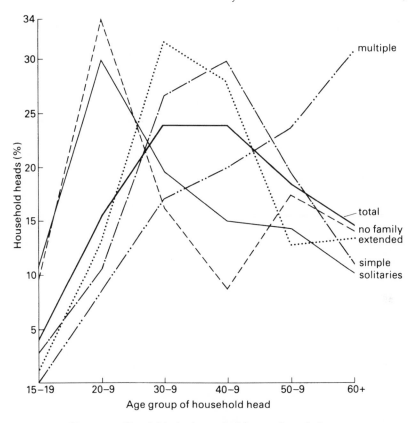

Figure 3.1 Headship by household type, Istanbul, 1907

the ages of twenty and twenty-nine lived alone, whereas only 11 per cent of those between thirty and thirty-nine and 9 per cent of those sixty or over did so (see table 3.5). Only 28 per cent of the twenty to twenty-nine-year-old age cohort headed simple family households, whereas 45 per cent of the thirty to thirty-nine year olds did so. This dropped to 30 per cent for the cohort sixty or over. However, 25 per cent of those in the eldest age group headed multiple family households, while only 16 per cent of the next youngest cohort, the fifty to fifty-nine year olds, did so.

These figures represent the experiences of household heads, most of whom were male. The sequences of types over time would emerge most clearly in separate analyses of the life courses of males and females, an approach which would also account for (that part of their) lives not spent as heads of households. We could in that way learn

Table 3.5 *Residential patterns of household heads by age group, Istanbul, 1907*

Age groups of household heads	Solitaries		No family		Simple family		Extended family		Multiple family		Unclassifiable		Total	
	Number	%	Number	%	Number	%	Number	%	Number	%	Number	%	Number	%
15–19	16	34.8	9	19.6	13	28.3	2	4.4	0	0	6	13.0	46	100.0
20–9	44	24.9	31	17.5	49	27.7	25	14.1	12	6.8	16	9.0	177	100.0
30–9	29	10.5	15	5.4	123	44.6	59	21.4	24	8.7	26	9.4	276	100.0
40–9	22	8.0	8	2.9	138	50.4	52	19.0	28	10.2	26	9.5	274	100.0
50–9	21	9.9	16	7.5	90	42.5	24	11.3	33	15.6	28	13.2	212	100.0
60+	15	8.9	13	7.7	51	30.2	25	14.8	43	25.4	21	12.4	168	100.0

Source: Istanbul population rosters, 1907.

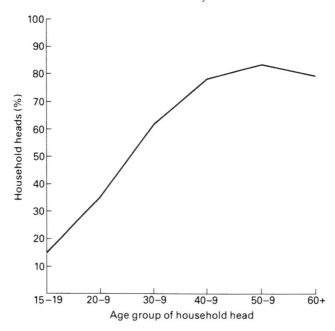

Figure 3.2 Male headship rates, Istanbul, 1907 (male household heads aged 15+ as a proportion of all males 15+)

of the percentages of individuals who at various points in their lives experienced living in different types of households. Unfortunately, such data are not available for our population, though an examination of headship rates for the two censuses gives us certain clues as to the differing age-specific sequences for the total population of males and females and not just for heads of households. The patterns were quite similar in both 1885 and 1907. For males, the curve is one very much like that found in pre-twentieth-century western Europe: a significant percentage of individuals attaining headship at a relatively young age. Just about 60 per cent of all males became heads of households by their thirties. From that age on approximately 80 per cent of all males in the population headed their own households (see fig. 3.2). As would be expected, the headship rates are much lower for females (see fig. 3.3). A maximum of 16 per cent of women in 1907 in any particular age group headed their own households at any one time, and that was when they were between fifty and fifty-nine years of age, when, that is, presumably as widows in their prime, they would most likely have been household heads.

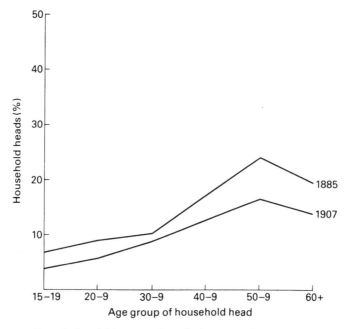

Figure 3.3 Female headship rates, Istanbul, 1885 and 1907 (female household
heads aged 15+ as a proportion of all females 15+)

Even the households of the solitaries or of those who did not live
as families were quite fluid. In our analysis of the registers, we
observed that in many cases individuals (relatives or others) were
subsequently registered in households that had appeared as solitary
or no family units during the census periods. Often this was the result
of solitaries marrying subsequent to the census, or their being joined
by other relatives, all of these events leading to a change in the composition of their households. Registrations of individuals following the
two census periods of 1885 and 1907 cannot be used as indicators of
household composition, since, after the censuses, individuals –
usually from the same patriline – were attached to the household
groupings set up during the census, regardless of where they resided.
Henceforth, the census registers were used as devices for permanent
population registration. Our data on headship rates lead us to believe
that living as a solitary or in a no family household was a brief
stage through which the individual passed, until he or she was able
to get married or to provide for or otherwise attract familial coresi-
dents. A significant percentage of solitaries and heads of no family

Table 3.6. *Servants resident in Istanbul households*
by age group, 1885 and 1907

Age groups	1885		1907	
	Number	%	Number	%
< 15	59	23.9	24	24.0
15–19	51	20.6	19	19.0
20–9	62	25.1	17	17.0
30–9	36	14.6	18	18.0
40–9	25	10.1	7	7.0
50–9	11	4.5	8	8.0
60+	5	2.0	7	7.0
Total female	212	85.3	80	80.0
Total male	35	14.2	20	20.0
Total	247	100.0	100	100.0

Source: Istanbul population rosters, 1885 and 1907.

households were young and also single. Forty-three per cent of those who lived alone were under thirty in 1907; 45 per cent of the heads of no family households were also that young. We must remember, however, that this was not a permanent way of life for most.

Households also changed their composition over time, for those who could afford it, with the coming and going of servants. Such helpers were predominantly young and female. In 1885, 85 per cent and in 1907, 80 per cent, of those discernible as servants in our sample were female (see table 3.6). Seventy per cent of the total servants of both sexes in the earlier census, and 60 per cent in the later one, were under the age of thirty. Service in late Ottoman Istanbul had a very clear life-cycle pattern, with girls entering at a very young age and a significant number departing for marriage. The place of departing servants was filled with those from a lower age cohort, who in turn followed a similar pattern of departure.[12] Nezahat Hanım, whose pre-First World War childhood years were spent in a comfortable Istanbul house filled with such servants, tells us that, 'there was always one coming and one going; they'd be raised up in the house, given a dowry (*çeyiz*) . . . and then leave'. In 1885 only 7 per cent of all servants were over fifty years of age. In 1907 the figure, though higher, was only 15 per cent.

There are many indications that in addition to the movement through the stages of the domestic cycle, household size and compo-

---

[12] Fatma Aliye, *Nisvan-ı İslam* (Muslim Women) (Istanbul, 1309/1891).

sition in late Ottoman Istanbul were very fluid, much more so than our census data can by their very nature reveal. Since the censuses only record permanent household members, we cannot learn about what seems to have been a rather common tradition of very long-term visitation between members of extended families. Perhaps a glance at the household of Naci Bey – an elderly Istanbul gentleman – when he was eight years of age, more or less at the time of the 1907 census, will fill in the gaps that the census data cannot.

Naci Bey's father was an officer in the Ottoman army. The household he describes, resident in a large *konak,* appears to be typical of many elite households of the time in Istanbul and elsewhere in the Empire. Naci Bey listed the members of his large multiple family household in the following order: father, mother, mother's sister and her son, two elder brothers, father's sister and her daughters, mother's mother, and six servants. 'We were a very large family (*aile*), indeed,' he added. Later in the interview, however, it emerged that his two aunts, one divorced, the other a widow, whom he considered part of his household were also described as long-term guests. His mother's sister stayed for two years and then returned to her own house. His father's sister stayed for six months. They returned to their 'own *ailes*', as he put it, including them as part of two families, or rather households (which is what he really means, even though he uses the word *aile*). The common blur between family and house-hold is convenient, because he can use the word to mean a coresiden-tial domestic unit and a non-residentially bounded family. It is not clear for how long his aunts' residences overlapped in the house since he may have compressed certain events. What is clear, is that they were an integral part of his household for a considerable period of time, though they would most likely not have been registered there during the census, and therefore do not figure in our calculations of household types.

Naci Bey's childhood household swelled with such guests and changed structure from an extended to a multiple family household, and then decreased in size and complexity when they finally left. Should we count his aunts and their children, who stayed so long and who participated in household activities on a regular basis during that time, as part of his household as he did? Such intermittent house-hold members or long-term guests, as it may be, were relatively easily absorbed into existing households in late Ottoman society, because there were not very rigid social boundaries separating one potential household of close relatives from another at that time. The same is true in Istanbul today, though various physical and social conditions make very long-term coresidence unacceptable. The physical structure of the home, size permitting, was merely a vehicle for this ebb and flow of family members who would constitute a natural part of the family household when they were there.

The Istanbul household formation system

The fall in total fertility in Istanbul between the census of 1907 and the year 1945 was due in equal parts to a decline in marital fertility and to changes in nuptiality (see chapter 6 for a discussion of this). This is very important, because in the post-Second World War period changes in nuptiality have played only a small part in the drama of fertility decline for Turkey as a whole. In order to understand patterns of nuptiality in Istanbul during those years we must, therefore, look carefully at the timing of marriage and the social, economic and cultural circumstances that underlay what quite naturally to those joining in wedlock appeared to be purely family or private sorts of decisions. There seems to have been a rather distinctive Istanbul pattern of marriage and household formation, one that bears little relation to that found in Anatolian Turkey, but that resembles in certain respects patterns found in some of Turkey's Mediterranean neighbours to the west.

We now know that the pattern is not at all what it seems to have been to many Turks or to most European observers of Turkey. Ahmed Midhat Efendi, one of the most popular Turkish writers of the late nineteenth century, portrays Muslim marriage patterns in Istanbul in his novels and essays in the terms in which many people have commonly perceived them: girls in particular – like the proverbial European child brides of the past – were described as marrying very young, not long after puberty 'at thirteen or fourteen, or fifteen at the latest'.[13] In his well-known novel *Felâtun Bey ile Râkım Efendi* (1875), Mustafa Merakî Efendi, the father of the protagonist Felâtun Bey 'was married . . . at the age of sixteen . . . to a girl of twelve'.[14] Generally speaking, however, men were portrayed as marrying much later than that. In the same novel Râkım Efendi married at the age of twenty-seven. But many people believed, and still believe, that men in Istanbul also married very young in the past. Perhaps they believe that because it fits in with the way they conceive households

---

[13] *Bahtiyarlık* (Happiness) in *Letaif-i Rivayat* (Finest Tales) (Istanbul, 1302/1885), 123–4.
[14] *Felâtun Bey ile Râkım Efendi* (Felâtun Bey and Râkım Efendi) (Istanbul, n.d. [1875]).

as having been set up at marriage in the past. We shall discuss this important matter in some detail.

Charles White, writing about Ottoman families in Istanbul in 1844, articulates what was certainly the most common view held by Europeans at that time, and also, interestingly enough, by most Turks even today about marriage age in the past. He tells us that:

The majority of Osmanlis attach so much importance to the early marriage of their children, that they sometimes discuss and arrange these matters before the birth of the destined spouses. Mothers, whose sons have scarcely attained their fifteenth year, can neither sleep nor eat until the latter are suitably disposed of; and the same anxiety is felt by those who have marriageable daughters.[15]

There are no reliable statistics available on marriage age for Istanbul of that period, so we cannot comment with certainty upon White's observations. We do know that the mean marriage age for males just after the turn of the century was nearly thirty and for females almost twenty. It is rather unlikely that only about fifty years prior to that time marriage ages could have been so much lower.

Lucy Garnett, an astute observer who wrote a number of books about Ottoman family life around the turn of the century, appears to perpetuate the same myth, but then hesitates in the face of evidence of change. She explains, in what almost appears to be a paraphrase of White, that, 'Early marriages are ... the rule among Osmanlis'.[16] Most interestingly, however rudimentary it may have been, she moves beyond a description of marriage age to the beginnings of an analysis of the components of the household formation system of the time, telling us that, 'the patriarchal customs alluded to ... mak[e] it unnecessary for a youth to wait until he has a home of his own before taking a wife'.[17] Finally, perpetuating the apparent myth of early marriage, she takes cognizance of change: 'Formerly, youths of eighteen were married to girls of from twelve to fifteen; but nowadays [the year is 1909, just after the Young Turk Revolution] such very youthful couples are seldom met with.'[18] Exactly how old were they then? And under what sorts of constraints and arrangements did they get married? If we are to understand the circumstances underlying marriage patterns, we must adopt Lucy Garnett's model, her concern,

[15] *Three Years in Constantinople; or Domestic Manners of the Turks in 1844* (London, 1846), III, 198.
[16] *Home Life in Turkey* (New York, 1909), 237.
[17] *Ibid.*
[18] *Ibid.*

that is, to explain the relationship between setting up a home and getting married, and examine the late Ottoman household formation system in Istanbul. We must, however, be cautious about accepting her statements, which often represent the ethos of family life rather than the frequency of occurrence of certain patterns, without a critical sensibility, given what we now know about the actual living arrangements of Ottomans in Istanbul.

The implication of Lucy Garnett's analysis is that Ottoman young men were not burdened with the expenses of setting up their own homes at marriage, as she knew was the expectation of those getting married in England and in parts of Europe at the time. They had little choice, she felt, given the strong patriarchal tradition in Turkey, other than to include the bride in their father's household, forming what we now call a two-generation multiple family household. Since, the argument goes, young men in Turkey in the past did not have to spend their youth accumulating sufficient resources to support a wife and future family, they could get married at a young age. It seemed clear to Garnett and other observers that pressures, both cultural and economic, were pulling in the direction of early marriage and multiple family households, creating a system very much like that which Hajnal describes as characterizing most of the non-European world,[19] and which he calls the joint household system. Ziya Gökalp, the Durkheimian sociologist and ideologue of the Young Turk and Kemalist Revolutions, called this patriarchal multiple family household, which he said typified the period, the *konak* type family.[20] Though it was not his intention, his choice of the term *konak* (urban mansion) clearly points to households of the elite or, rather, generalizes about a historical period on that basis. How typical were such large complex multi-generational households? Were there great differences between Istanbul and its hinterlands? Can we build the Ottoman household formation systems of Istanbul and its hinterlands on the common foundation of the multiple family household? It appears that there is some confusion in this area that must be clarified before we can decide.

Quite a lot has been written in recent years about household formation patterns in Europe and, in particular, about what are believed to be the distinctive features of the (western) European family and household. The impetus for many of these efforts may be attributed

---

[19] 'Two kinds'.
[20] 'Aile ahlâkı-' 3 (Family morality), *Yeni Mecmua*, 17 (1 Teşrin-i sâni 1917/1 November 1917), 321–4.

to John Hajnal's now classic essay on European marriage patterns in past times. The evidence Hajnal collected led him to draw a rough line from Leningrad to Trieste as the eastern frontier of the pattern that he and others have claimed as a possible feature of the West or of western civilization.[21]

In Hajnal's joint household system, men and women marry early and start life in a household in which an older couple, usually the man's parents, is in charge. The senior generation, and that means the father when he is alive, remains in charge until his death. The system accounts for fission in which several married couples may split to form two or more households, each containing one or more couples. The timing of the split is especially important, and has a crucial effect on the size and composition of households, Hajnal tells us.[22] Laslett has recently elaborated upon Hajnal's model utilizing current research on the European family and household, and has presented us with a more differentiated set of patterns, or tendencies as he calls them, as to the composition of the family household.[23] These are largely geographically based distinctions, which he notes often belie considerable intraregional variation. France is notable in this respect in the western region. Laslett's regions are: 'west and northwest'; 'west/central or middle'; 'Mediterranean'; and 'east'. How does early twentieth-century Istanbul fit into this scheme? It would be helpful in locating Istanbul in this way not only to view it in relation to Europe, with which it had a geographic, and if only belatedly, nevertheless increasingly pervasive, cultural connection. It is also important to view it from the perspective of the rural Anatolian Turkish heartland with which it shared deep rooted cultural and social traditions, but from which, as we shall see, it differed in many important ways.

There is little doubt that the Muslim household formation system in rural Anatolian Turkey in past times was non-European, resembling in many respects Hajnal's joint household system. It also appears to share certain tendencies with the 'east' (European) type that Laslett distinguished. Residence was patrilocal, authority remained in the hands of the patriarch, and the young married couple had no control

---

[21] 'European marriage patterns'; Peter Laslett, 'Characteristics of the western family considered over time' in P. Laslett, ed., *Family Life and Illicit Love in Earlier Generations* (London, 1977), 12–24; E. A. Wrigley, 'Population history in the 1980s', *Journal of Interdisciplinary History*, 12 (1981), 218–19.

[22] 'Two kinds'.

[23] Wall, *Family Forms*, ch. 17.

over the factors of production, as inheritance was delayed until the death of the paterfamilias.

Marriage did not have the significance in the rural Turkish household formation system that it had in western Europe. Mortality rather than nuptiality appears to have been the engine pulling the system. In the ideal Turkish system, marriage meant the entrance into the husband's household of a bride (*gelin*), the formation of a new conjugal unit (*aile*) in the household, and the beginning of legitimate sexual relations and biological reproduction. It did not change the residence of the husband, nor did it have any significance in terms of the transfer of rights to property. Neither did it change the structure of the household (*hane*) as a production and consumption unit.

As an economic entity the *hane* was not constructed by the sum of conjugal units. Rather, the division of labour for production fell along lines of sex and age, which meant that husbands and wives spent much of their time in work groups composed of members of their own sex, and when they entered the household conceived as a production unit, they did so in the role of adult male and female labourers. The system of residence was, as we have seen, clearly patrilocal, and the patriarch had the responsibility for providing residential quarters for the new *aile*, either under the same roof or in close proximity. The residential quarters of the couple were furnished either by the parents of the groom or of the bride, with variations from region to region. Marriage also involved the transfer of wealth, either to the bride herself as *mehr*, a practice in accordance with Islamic law and more commonly found in cities or in areas under their influence,[24] or to the father of the bride as *başlık*, a very widespread customary practice in Anatolia contravening Islamic precepts.

The rule for rural Turkish households was, as we have seen, that fission should not take place until the death of the patriarch. In theory, this might mean that Anatolian Turks in the past lived in large and complex households composed of married offspring and their children before the split. In reality, as we shall see, a significant number of them did not live that way, although, it seems, through no choice

---

[24] Halil Cin, *İslâm ve Osmanlı Hukukunda Evlenme* (Marriage in Islamic and Ottoman Law) (Ankara, 1974), 210–51; Peter Benedict 'Hukuk reformu açısından başlık parası ve mehr' (Brideprice and *mehr* from the perspective of legal reform) in A. Güriz and P. Benedict, eds., *Türk Hukuku ve Toplumu Üzerine İncelemeler* (Ankara, 1974), 8; Ronald Jennings, 'Sakaltutan four centuries ago', *International Journal of Middle East Studies*, 9 (1978), 89–98; Haim Gerber, 'Social and economic position of women in an Ottoman city, Bursa, 1600–1700', *International Journal of Middle East Studies*, 12 (1980), 231–44.

of their own. The estate would be divided at the death of the father, with offspring receiving their customary shares. Married brothers might live together for a short period after that, but it would be unusual for them to continue doing so for long. As a result, the division of the estate almost inevitably meant the breakup of the *hane*. All of this is assuming that the household had two sons and they were married at the time of their father's death. What proportion of fathers would have been so lucky as to have had two sons who survived to marry and to have been alive to witness those happy events? The household or households emerging after the father's death would have been nuclear in structure and small in size. Very likely they would also have contained the widowed wife of the patriarch, whom her son or sons would look after until her death. Households in rural Turkey in the past went through a series of phases as their members aged. In only one of these phases were they large and complex structures. They appear to have followed a cycle virtually identical to that of southern Transdanubian households in Hungary during the eighteenth and early nineteenth centuries.[25]

Like neighbouring pre-twentieth-century Christian Russia and the Balkans, early age at first marriage was the rule in rural Turkey for both men and women. Though Anatolia borders on the northern Mediterranean, its marriage system seems to have been as impenetrable to the traditions of the region as the Taurus Mountains are to Mediterranean ecology. For men, marriage probably took place no later than twenty or twenty-two; for women, it occurred between fourteen and eighteen. In a society such as Turkey of the recent past, where the control of female sexuality was so intimately linked to the honour (*namus*) of the family,[26] a daughter's early marriage was a safe strategy to follow. Since marriage was not linked to the devolution of property, and since there was no need to be self-supporting upon marriage, a relatively young age at first marriage for men was a reasonable alternative. The age differential between husbands and wives was low in contrast to the northern Mediterranean pattern that Richard Smith, largely following Herlihy and Klapisch-Zuber, describes.[27]

The rural Turkish household formation system in the past can be

---

[25] Rudolf Andorka and Tamás Faragó, 'Pre-industrial household structure in Hungary' in Wall, *Family Forms*, 296–9.

[26] Michael Meeker, 'Meaning and society in the Near East: examples from the Black Sea Turks and the Levantine Arabs (II)', *International Journal of Middle East Studies*, 7 (1976), 390.

[27] 'The people of Tuscany and their families in the fifteenth century: medieval or Mediterranean?', *Journal of Family History*, 6 (1981), 107–28; Herlihy and Klapisch-Zuber, *Tuscans*, 211.

called a joint household system, because the rules of the system call for the joint residence of senior and junior generations at the marriage of the latter, and because of the young age at which people married. The rules, however, do not describe the ways families actually lived, because there were often barriers – social, economic or demographic – to the realization of those rules. At any one time, it appears that between 17 and 34 per cent of all households were composed of two or more couples. Nearly 60 per cent were simple in structure.[28] Under ideal conditions, ideal that is in terms of what we know about rural Turkish cultural preferences in the past, most individuals would have experienced all the household types at some point in life. The existence of a large percentage of simple family households at any one time is, among other things, merely the result of the percentage of households that are in the early stages of development after splitting, households, that is, headed by younger men whose children have not yet married. The ideal conditions were, however, very difficult to live up to in the past. We have calculated on the basis of estimated life expectancies for the period, that only about 35 per cent of all fathers lived long enough to see the marriage of their first-born son.[29] Most fathers would have been dead for some years before that time, and thus most sons would have come into their inheritance early in life, and might have lived in a simple family household once their siblings had grown up and married. The demographic constraints on the household formation rule in the past in Turkey were formidable indeed. Given plentiful land in most parts of Anatolia until the 1950s, the ecological or economic limitations to supporting large numbers of people in complex households that existed in many parts of western Europe in the past were not very great. Demographic forces were, however, very powerful in the past in Turkey.

The contrast between rural Anatolia and Ottoman Istanbul in marriage patterns and household formation was as great as it was in so many other aspects of the social and economic life of this dichotomous society. Not long after the turn of the century, the mean marriage age for men in Istanbul was thirty and for women twenty-one, a pattern, which if we take into account an elevation in age of a few years, more closely resembles the Mediterranean one that we know about in particular from urban Italy in the past,[30] than that of the Anatolian hinterlands of the Ottoman Empire which we have just described.

[28] Duben, 'Turkish families', 88–91.
[29] See *ibid.*, 92–3, for an explanation of the calculations used.
[30] Smith, 'People of Tuscany'; Herlihy and Klapisch-Zuber, *Tuscans*.

As in urban Tuscany, nearly 500 years earlier, 'the city discouraged males . . . from assuming the burden of matrimony early'.[31] It is hardly surprising that Istanbul, the cosmopolitan capital of the Ottoman Empire and a major port city with dense maritime connections with the whole Mediterranean basin, would differ from the rural, land-locked hinterlands of the Anatolian plateau. It is also not surprising that family and household formation patterns in an urban economy increasingly slipping away from the traditional primordial, if not kin-ship-based production arrangements of its pre-modern past, would differ from those of a rural society in which small family farms using rather simple technology were the norm.

The age at which people marry is the key to so many other aspects of their domestic life and demographic behaviour. Schofield, Wrigley and Smith, in a number of recent studies, have examined the complex connections between age at marriage, the economy and fertility pat-terns in pre-nineteenth-century England, and have come to the conclu-sion that the age at which women married was the major fertility regulating mechanism during that time.[32] Richard Wall, following the same logic that has guided his colleagues at the Cambridge Group for the History of Population and Social Structure, notes that, 'when people marry at a later age there are fewer complex households and more households containing only parents and their unmarried chil-dren'.[33] He then adds that this was, 'the situation not just in England but in much of northwest Europe'.[34] If this logic is correct, there should be a systematic connection between age at marriage and house-hold types, or more precisely between age at marriage, household formation patterns, and the subsequent sequences of types through which households pass. Istanbul men married late, later on the aver-age than Englishmen in the past. Their marriage age fits the Mediterra-nean pattern. Women in Istanbul, however, married a few years younger than their English peers, though later than Mediterranean women in the past, and their marriage age rose a year a decade begin-ning at least as early as the turn of the century. How do these nuptial facts connect with their household formation patterns?

Laslett is convinced that 'neolocalism', setting up a household inde-pendent of one's parents or one's spouse's parents at marriage, is

---

[31] Herlihy and Klapisch-Zuber, *Tuscans*, 218.
[32] Wrigley and Schofield, *The Population History of England*; Richard Smith, 'Fertility, economy, and household formation in England over three centuries', *Population and Development Review*, 7 (1981), 595–622.
[33] 'Introduction' in Wall, *Family Forms*, 16.
[34] *Ibid.*

the 'outstanding point of differentiation among the postulated regional tendencies'.[35] He argues that it is, 'a decidedly structural principle', and that it entails many of the other characteristics of the regions with regard to their household systems.[36] Our problem begins at this point. It is not that we shall claim that Istanbul had a neolocal system. But there were, it appears, strong tendencies in that direction, or at least circumstances that mitigated against multigenerational residence and economic dependency at marriage. This is surprising to find at the very periphery of the European continent and at the edge of the Muslim world. If anything, Istanbul fits into the Mediterranean marriage and household formation system, particularly with regard to age at marriage. There were however, some important differences in domestic group formation, post-marital residence and in the kin composition of households. Our ability to classify the Istanbul system is further complicated when we take into consideration the inconsistencies between household formation and kin composition of households viewed as a cultural system on the one hand – that is as the largely unarticulated generalization of people's deeply rooted preferences – and the ways in which people in the past actually went about setting up their households, on the other.

As Macfarlane points out, a high degree of 'emotional' as well as 'economic nucleation' characterized the relationship between generations in English families in the past.[37] This was, as he tells us, the 'custom' of that society.[38] It was not, however, either the custom or the statistical norm in societies other than a small number of those located at the northwest tip of the Eurasian continental mass according to Murdock and Macfarlane,[39] though recent work has also located the patterns south of that area on the Iberian peninsula,[40] and future studies may show that it is even more widespread than we now know it to be. Complex 'arrangements' between custom and practice are possible. As Macfarlane postulates for example: 'It may be frequently the case that sons settle near their parents, thus setting up a sort of patrilocal system within an apparent system of neolocality.'[41] Reher describes a similar situation in the supposed normatively neolocal

[35] 'Family and household', 531.
[36] *Ibid.*
[37] *Marriage and Love*, 79ff.
[38] *Ibid.*, 91.
[39] *Ibid.* The reference to G. P. Murdock, *Social Structure* (New York, 1949), is from Macfarlane, *Marriage and Love*.
[40] D. S. Reher, 'Old issues and new perspectives: household and family within an urban context in nineteenth century Spain', *Continuity and Change*, 2 (1987), 103–43.
[41] *Marriage and Love*, 91.

Spanish town of Cuenca in the eighteenth and nineteenth centuries, where neolocal residential patterns were embedded in a system of strong ties between family members in different households.[42] The obverse of this pattern is also possible. That is, it may be the case that most sons assume headship of their own households at marriage, setting up a tendency towards a kind of economic neolocalism within a system in which patri- or matrilocality are in fact the preferred forms of post-marital residence, and where the emotional bonds connecting extended family members are quite strong.

The evidence is good that the custom, the ingrained traditional residential preferences of people in Istanbul at marriage, was not neolocal. Occasional suggestions by Ottoman modernists, beginning after the turn of the century, that young couples should set up independent households at marriage and be self-sufficient, reflect, if anything, in their insistence the deeply embedded preferences of parents, and we presume their children, for living together. Some sons and daughters – themselves modernists, perhaps – may indeed have preferred to live apart from their parents. We will, however, never know much about such desires so difficult to express in the gerontocracy of Ottoman Istanbul. While the custom, the cultural preference, was not neolocal, it was not purely patrilocal either, as it most certainly was in rural Anatolia. There is a longstanding tradition of uxorilocal residential preferences in Istanbul, embedded in what seems to be a much more bilateral kinship system than that found in rural areas, particularly rural areas in central and eastern Anatolia. The Aegean area seems to bear a closer resemblance to the Istanbul bilateral tendency than do the central or eastern regions. Though filiation in Istanbul was patrilineal as elsewhere in the Mediterranean region, residence patterns differed from the predominant patrilocalism in the area. Fifteenth-century urban Tuscany seems to have been more patrilocal than Istanbul.[43]

The Istanbul uxorilocal tradition is modelled after the imperial palace tradition where, in the absence of married sons, daughters' husbands, known as *damat*s, traditionally played very significant political roles in palace and state affairs. Many grand viziers were at the same time the sultan's *damat*s. The prestigious status of the *damat* was emulated in the microcosm of the elite households of the city, which were both linked to the palace through intricate patron–client ties and by a kind of institutional mimesis. The high status of the *damat* in Istanbul was

---

[42] 'Old issues', 115–21.
[43] Herlihy and Klapisch-Zuber, *Tuscans*, 282.

not just something limited to the upper crust of society, but pervaded domestic mores in the city in general. In statistical terms, it was just as common to find patrilocal as uxorilocal multiple family households in Istanbul in the late Ottoman period. As we shall see, with men marrying at the age of thirty to women about ten years younger, there would (given the probability of a relatively low life expectancy during the period) have been fewer husbands' parents surviving to that time than wives'. More than half of the multiple family households of which twenty to twenty-nine year olds were the junior married partners, and nearly two-thirds of those in which thirty to thirty-nine year olds were in the same position, were uxorilocal in structure. The majority of resident relatives in Istanbul households were from the wife's side of the family. The position of the Istanbul resident *damat* is inverted in Anatolian Turkish culture, where the term for his rural equivalent, *iç güvey* (literally, internal 'son-in-law'), conveys anything but a desirable status for a young married man. Though the residential 'custom' in Istanbul gave more or less equal weighting to both sides of the family, there was, it seems, an increasingly heavier weight on the patrilocal side as one moves down the social ladder, that is, with social distance from the uxorilocal palace model.

Headship rates for Muslim males in Istanbul in 1907 follow a pattern similar to those characterizing pre-industrial western and central Europe.[44] By the time they reached the thirty to thirty-nine year old age group, over 60 per cent of all men in the city were heading their own households. Rates continue to rise until men reach the ages fifty to fifty-nine and then begin to fall off slightly, indicating an authority system flexible enough to allow some elderly men to be superseded by their sons (see fig. 3.2, p. 65). This is very different from the typically delayed pattern of headship in non-western societies,[45] from certain non-western European societies such as Krasnoe Sobakino in neighbouring Russia in 1849[46] where headship devolved at least ten years later, and even from other Mediterranean urban centres in the past, such as Renaissance Tuscany,[47] where at the age of thirty fewer than 50 per cent of all men headed households, and where 'marriage and the establishment of an independent household do not coincide'.[48]

The relationship between marriage and household formation in

[44] See Wall, 'Introduction', 37, fig. 1.1.
[45] Hajnal, 'Two kinds'.
[46] Wall, 'Introduction', 37–8.
[47] Herlihy and Klapisch-Zuber, *Tuscans*, 302–3.
[48] *Ibid*.

Table 3.7. *Marriage and household headship, Istanbul, 1907*

Age group of household head	Proportion of males in all age groups who are:		
	Evermarried*	Household heads	Evermarried household heads*
15–19	6.2	14.6	2.0
20–9	42.4	34.9	20.9
30–9	87.9	61.0	55.7
40–9	94.3	78.5	75.6
50–9	90.1**	83.7	78.9
60+	87.2**	79.6	75.7

Source: Istanbul population rosters, 1907.
 * Includes all currently married and widowed heads.
 ** These proportions are lower than might be expected due to the classification of some widowers as single at the time of the census.

Istanbul was a close one in comparison to what it must have been in Turkish rural society in the past. The fact, though not the rule, was that a young couple formed a household independent of the control of their parents at marriage. We can only presume what the situation must have been in rural areas on the basis of what we know about the relatively high percentages of multiple family households in past times, since there are no figures available that would give us a clear picture of headship rates in the Ottoman Turkish country-side. When the relationship between marriage and household forma-tion is close, a great percentage of individuals set up new households at marriage rather than including their spouse in their parents' house-hold. They begin their married lives in charge of their own families, rather than under the tutelage of one set of their parents. They are the masters of their house and bear the burden and responsibility for running the household economy. These are some of the things we mean when we say that the relationship between marriage and household formation was close in Istanbul just after the turn of the century.

The threshold for headship in Istanbul in 1907 was clearly located between the twenty and twenty-nine and thirty to thirty-nine-year-old age groups, that is, more or less at the age of thirty, the same age at which men on the average married in the city at that time (see table 3.7). Only 35 per cent of all men in the twenty to twenty-nine age cohort headed their own households. By the time men reached the ages of thirty to thirty-nine, the majority (61 per cent) were heading their own households, and the percentages rose to 78.5 at the ages of forty to forty-nine, remaining at a high plateau until after sixty, when the curve begins to dip slightly (see fig. 3.2, p. 65). If we look at the same phenomenon from its other end, the ages at which men head non-family households, which we take to mean a combination of solitary and no family units, we get the obverse of the pattern we have observed above. Forty-nine per cent of all household heads between the ages of twenty to twenty-four were heading non-family households; only 33 per cent of the twenty-five to twenty-nine-year-old-cohort were in the same position. By the time they reached the thirty to thirty-four age group, only 13 per cent of all men were heading households that were not really families. Again age thirty seems to be a rough threshold point. The time that most men were getting married in Istanbul was also the time they were setting up and heading their own family households. Most city men began their married life in charge of their own household. They did not marry and bring in a bride to their father's household as their rural compatriots were more likely to have done.

The relationship between the proportions married and those heading households is an indicator of the connection between marriage and autonomous household formation. The Istanbul data appear to fall somewhere in between the western European and Mediterranean patterns (see table 3.7). In 1907 88 per cent of men in the thirty to thirty-nine-year-old cohort were married, as compared with only 42 per cent of the twenty to twenty-nine-year-old cohort. The majority, 61 per cent to be precise, were heading their own households. That figure is less than that which typifies western European societies, though greater than the percentage found in parts of the northern Mediterranean world in the past. It appears at first glance that over 30 per cent of the cohort had not set up autonomous households at or soon after marriage, and one might presume that they were living with their parents in a joint family household. These crude figures are deceptive. A breakdown of the kin composition of the households of the married non-heads reveals a different and more complex picture (see table 3.8).

Approximately a half of married non-heads between the ages of thirty to thirty-nine were living as the secondary unit with one or the other set of parents. The rest were living with age-peers, usually with their own siblings or with those of their spouse, in a household the management of which they presumably shared responsibility for with the head in a way they would not have had they been the juniors in a multiple family unit. The situation is similar for the twenty to twenty-nine year olds. If we combine the percentages of such indivi-

Table 3.8. *Kin composition of households containing married male non-heads for selected age groups, Istanbul, 1907*

	Age groups			
	20–9		30–9	
Household type	Number	%	Number	%
No family	5	8.2	4	5.9
Simple family	1	1.7	1	1.5
Extended family				
Extended upwards	2	3.3	2	2.9
Extended downwards	1	1.7	–	–
Extended laterally	2	3.3	1	1.5
Combinations of these	4	6.6	4	5.9
Subtotal	9	14.8	7	10.3
Multiple family				
Secondary units up	–	–	2	2.9
Secondary units down	29	47.5	27	39.7
Secondary units lateral	1	1.7	3	4.4
Frérèches	2	3.3	5	7.3
Combinations of these	3	4.9	5	7.3
Subtotal	35	57.4	42	61.8
Unclassifiable	11	18.0	14	20.6
Total	61	100.1	68	100.1

Source: Istanbul population rosters, 1907.

duals with those for the household heads in these cohorts, we get figures of 31 and 73 per cent for the twenty to twenty-nine and thirty to thirty-nine age cohorts respectively. This curve, representing proportions of what we might call 'non-gerontocratic' family household living, rather closely parallels the total evermarried one, and is an indicator of a residential relationship between generations in Istanbul quite different than that characterizing joint household systems (see fig. 3.4). It is interesting to note that there is a greater uxorilocal tendency among the thirty to thirty-nine-old cohort than among their juniors. Fifty-three per cent of the twenty to twenty-nine-year-old non-heads live uxorilocally, whereas 61 per cent of their seniors do so. That may be because the probability of the husband's father or mother surviving at that age is lower than that of their wives' parents, given the age difference between spouses.

Three-quarters of male household heads in their prime marriageable years, ages thirty to thirty-four, were heading households that were either simple (51 per cent) or extended (22 per cent) in structure. We

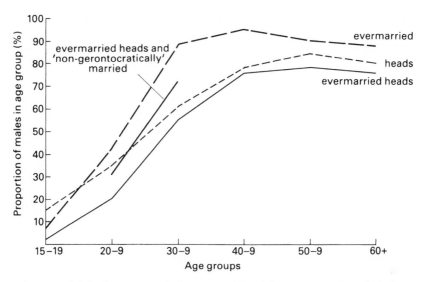

Figure 3.4 Males by age, marital status and headship position, Istanbul, 1907

know that in most cases the extension resulted from the presence of a mother, or less likely, a mother-in-law. Widowed mothers would not as a rule head households if their sons, especially their married sons, were alive to do so. This meant that by the time men reached the age of thirty or thirty-five they were very likely to have been in charge of their own household. Only 45 per cent of the next youngest age group, those between twenty-five and twenty-nine were in such a position. Only 13 per cent of all households in 1907 were multiple, and only 8.6 per cent were in the multiple generation family household that so many have presumed to be the typical form of residence for Ottoman Turks in Istanbul. In sum, only a small percentage of men setting up households at marriage were doing so with their father present in the households in which they were born and grew up. They were largely on their own, either having succeeded to the head-ship of their father's house at his death, or having set up an indepen-dent household, possibly with another relative not too much older than themselves. In either case they were supporting their own house-hold, or they shared the responsibility for doing so with others of their generation. They may, as in nineteenth-century Cuenca, have resided for a short period with their parents after marriage.[49] Perhaps a percentage of those married non-heads that we have found living

[49] Reher, 'Old issues', 113.

with their parents were only doing so for a short time. That would not be surprising given what we know about the strength of intergenerational ties in urban Turkey even today,[50] and about the difficulties of setting up a household in the past. Unfortunately our data do not provide us with clues about such temporary residential arrangements.

At the time most men in Istanbul were getting married, or in any case soon thereafter, they were assuming the headship, that is the material and moral responsibility for the running of their own households. Many of them may have been doing that in the house in which they grew up if their father was not alive, rather than moving out and establishing a completely new domestic unit. Our data do not shed any light on that important distinction. Even if they were replacing their father's household, they were in a very different position of responsibility than they would have been had they been the junior couple in a joint family household. Roughly half of those marrying, but not heading their own households, joined their parents; the other half resided with relatives closer to their own generation. As we have seen, in 1907 only 13 per cent of all households were complex, and only 8.6 per cent multigenerational, so that one hesitates about classifying the turn of the century Istanbul household formation system as a joint one in Hajnal's sense, even though we know that the bonds, both emotional and economic, between generations were, and are, very close at all levels of Turkish society.

In the past the correlation between social stratum and multiple family households was, perhaps, stronger than it is today in Istanbul. In 1907, 21 per cent of elite household heads were in charge of multiple family households, 14 per cent of the civil servant/military strata, 13 per cent of the artisan-shopkeepers, and only 6 per cent of the wage-earners (see table 3.4 p. 61). By and large, the population of ordinary people in Istanbul, such as Kâzım Bey's childhood family, spent at most a small part of their lives in such households. Even after age sixty, the optimum time in life for being a household patriarch, when 42 per cent of elite and 33 per cent of civil-servant household heads were in charge of multiple family units, only 24 per cent of artisans and shopkeepers were in that position. Sixty-five per cent of such artisans and shopkeepers were heading simple or extended family households; only 42 per cent of the elite and 44 per cent of the civil servant/military classes were doing so. Household size also exhibited different age-specific patterns for the various social

---

[50] Duben, 'The significance of family'.

strata. Elite households continued to increase in size even after the primary reproductive period, those of civil servants and the military stabilized, whereas households of the artisan–shopkeeper strata dropped in size, especially after age sixty at a time when elite households continued to expand. Clearly the size of the households of ordinary Istanbul residents appears to have been more directly a function of fertility within their households than was the size of those of very high rank and position, whose households frequently grew with the addition of individuals (especially servants) other than the offspring of the head.

Three ostensibly demographic events in the lives of many Istanbul residents seem to have played a major role in fracturing families and setting men and their wives on their own at marriage in the midst of a cultural environment which quite strongly emphasized just the opposite – intergenerational solidarity. The cultural emphasis on such solidarity and joint residence in Istanbul may have been a reflection of common cultural connections between the metropolis and its hinterlands. But economic and social circumstances differentiated city and countryside and these resulted in differing demographic regimes. One of the demographic events was the late age at which men married, another the age at which their fathers died, and the third, patterns of migration. As Wall has indicated, when people marry late there are fewer complex households.[51] This is, if for no other reason, because the likelihood that the father of the person or persons marrying being dead increases with their own increase in age. Given a mean male marriage age of thirty throughout our period, an age at which we will assume both fathers and sons married, and also given certain presumptions about life expectancy, we have calculated that only 39 per cent of all men would have their fathers alive at the time they were to marry. If we assume that it would take them six years on the average to have a first son after marriage, then only 28.3 per cent of the fathers of married men would have been alive to witness the birth of their first grandchild.[52] In other words, only a minority of all men marrying in our period would have had the benefit of the demographic conditions allowing for the possibility of setting up

---

[51] Wall, 'Introduction', 16.
[52] In this calculation we proceeded under the assumption that the mean birth interval was three years, and that the sex ratio was equal to one. The probability at birth of a man still being alive when his son's son is born is 0.27. The probability of the same man being alive when his son's first child is born is 0.283. We have used Model Life Tables (East – Level 14) and have assumed that both fathers and sons marry at age thirty. See Ansley Coale and Paul Demeny, *Regional Model Life Tables and Stable Populations* (Princeton, NJ, 1966).

a multiple family household should they have wanted to do so, and an even smaller percentage would have had the possibility of being the patriarch of a full three-generation family household.

Migration was also an impediment to the establishment of complex households, especially under the extremely disruptive domestic circumstances under which many Turks departed from the collapsing Ottoman provinces of Europe and western Asia.[53] Permanent migration may lead to the fragmentation of families; often old people choose not to make the traumatic move. This clearly decreases the probability of there being enough family members at the destination point to form complex households. It may be that there was a greater propensity for fathers and sons to be separated from each other among the refugee population, or for migrating fathers to have lower survival rates than Istanbul born fathers. In either case, it is not surprising that, whereas 17 per cent of Istanbul born household heads lived in multiple family households, only 10 per cent of those born elsewhere did so. We know that a large proportion of the Istanbul population was composed of people born elsewhere: some refugees, some simply migrants from the provinces; in either case, potentially fractured families.

Despite widespread misconceptions then as well as now, the modal household in early twentieth-century Istanbul was small as well as simple in structure. Most couples began their married lives charged with their own survival, not jointly with their parents. This does not mean that extended family ties were not strong, for they were and still are very tight in Istanbul, as well as in the rest of Turkey. Households were rather fluid structures, changing over the life-cycle of individuals and as a result of the more random processes of coming and going of relatives. Relatives often lived near each other, and there was a common interpenetration of activities and involvements. In this period of extraordinary change, such household structures and extended family values seem to have been less affected than many other major institutions. They provided an anchor of relative stability in a sea of changing relationships and meanings. Even the meanings attributed to households and families fluctuated in step with the tempo of westernization. The first and perhaps the most disturbing changes in perspective and meaning came in relation to the modes of entry into marriage.

---

[53] Nejat Göyünç, '"Hane" deyimi hakkında' (On the term 'household'). *Tarih Dergisi*, 32 (1979), 331–48; Karpat, *Ottoman Population*, 60–77.

4

Love and marriage: meanings and transactions

In most parts of the world, and for most of history, marriage has been an alliance between families or kinship groups in which the bride and groom were very often passive participants in a larger social drama. Marriages took place more for social and economic reproduction than for individual fulfilment. The emergence of love marriage, in the sense we know it, was a radical intrusion by the individual into the hegemony of family groups in society. This was true in European history as well as elsewhere in the world. In Ottoman society the introduction of the idea that a man and a woman should unite in matrimony of their own volition and only if they were in love caused great intellectual and emotional turmoil. Alongside this turmoil, however, traditional expectations of marriage disguised in new forms persisted even in modernist circles. To a large extent this was because families continued to play an important role in shouldering the social and financial burden of marriage and household formation.

Love

Love, like all other social phenomena, takes different forms and carries somewhat different meanings, depending on the particular cultures, and the times. Densely laden with diffuse meaning, love can in fact come to stand for so much more than just the relationship of a man and a woman. Love is a symbol, and like so many major cultural symbols can carry a wide range of meanings and evoke a great spectrum of emotion for individuals in society. Therefore, in order to understand the role that love played in late Ottoman Istanbul family life, it is first necessary to attempt to understand the weight of meaning and affect that it carried in society in general at that time. We shall, accordingly, first begin with a discussion of love as a cultural phenomenon and then move into an analysis of love in action.

The turbulence felt in the economy, society and culture of late Ottoman Istanbul came to focus particularly intensely on the smallest, most private social institution – the family and the intimate relationships between men and women. This upheaval and the questioning of age-old ways of relating were articulated in various views about the meaning of love, women, marriage and family in that society, views which appear to have played a formative role, paradoxically, both in fomenting the crisis and in providing points of orientation for individuals by connecting them to larger systems of ideas within which the new directions made sense. At the same time there was, quite naturally, also a defence of the traditional values and relationships by the spokesmen of the offended, threatened and often inarticulate majority.

By the second half of the nineteenth century the ideas of the French Revolution, particularly *liberté*, socially the most radical of them, had begun to influence even the intimate personal and domestic arrangements of literate circles in Ottoman society. Love, or *amour*, as it was often referred to by privileged Ottomans, came to stand for so much more than just an intense personal relationship. It came to be associated with a political passion at the same time. The state was equated with the father, and autocratic, backward political arrangements with patriarchalism and restrictive marriages. *Amour* and *liberté*, then, went hand in hand in a wave of intellectual liberalism that swept Istanbul intellectual society in the politically oppressive decades before the turn of the century. Such passions were domesticated, repressed and channelled in socially acceptable ways during the pre-First World War years.

The domestication of love took two forms. In the hands of the Young Turk ideologues, particularly Gökalp, it was harnessed to the political goals of the Young Turk Revolution. *İlân-ı hürriyet*, the proclamation of freedom, as the Young Turk political revolution of 1908 is known, symbolizing the triumph of political liberty and reason over oppression and absolutism, also, paradoxically, marks the ideological subordination of love (*ilân-ı aşk*) by the dominant political class to a new political cause, the modern Turkish nation. At the same time, the passions of love were routinized in the ostensibly apolitical ideology of the western conjugal family, about which eager modern-minded Ottomans were learning from an abundance of popular sources available in Istanbul beginning in the late nineteenth century.

Modern drama and the novel made their appearance in late nineteenth-century Turkish society with the themes of love and free marriage choice.[1] These remained the obsessions of Turkish writers into the 1920s, most of whom saw literature as a major vehicle for setting Turkey on the path to modern civilization.[2] The family was central to this story. Such literature begins in the 1860s with the exaltation of love and liberty, and climaxes in the 1920s with love as the hand-maiden of treason: from idealized romantic love to social disorder within sixty years. How did it happen?

The most advanced minds in Istanbul of the 1860s were thinking about love and marriage, and were critical of traditional nuptial arrangements. It was as if the oppression and backwardness of the family were a microcosm of the larger society.[3] The first Turkish play in the western mode, *Şair Evlenmesi* (The Marriage of a Poet), written in 1860 by the poet Şinasi, a Young Ottoman intellectual who had been a student in Paris in the early 1850s, takes as its theme the critique of arranged marriages. The hero, Müştak Bey, one of the new modern-minded men of the time, is in love. His is a 'love marriage', he boasts to an uncomprehending friend. On the wedding night he discovers that his bride-to-be has been replaced by her elder sister, an arrangement in accord with traditional, familistic *mahalle* values. The play ends happily, however, as Müştak Bey succeeds in substituting his rightful bride for her sister.[4]

During the decade of the 1860s numerous translations of French novels began to appear on the Istanbul scene, consumed by a reader-ship first male, soon increasingly female, all eager to partake of Euro-pean civilization. Many of these individuals from the elite of society would read such works in the original French. They were very open to western values, and the novels must have had a great impact on their lives. The writer Hüseyin Cahit [Yalçın] tells us in his *Edebî Hatıralar* (Literary Reminiscences) that, 'it was the French language and culture above all things which were responsible for my awaken-ing'.[5] Nusret Hanım, the heroine of Ahmed Midhat's *Bahtiyarlık* (Happiness), is one of those modern-minded women with love on her mind. The author, perhaps the most popular and influential of the period, tells the reader that:

[1] Berna Moran, 'Tanzimat'tan Cumhuriyet'e roman' (The novel from the *Tanzimat* to the Republic), in *Tanzimat'tan Cumhuriyet'e Türkiye Ansiklopedisi* (Istanbul, 1985), I, 412.
[2] Moran, *Türk Romanı*, 11.
[3] Namık Kemal, 'Aile' (Family), in A. H. Tanpınar, ed., *Namık Kemal Antolojisi* (A Namık Kemal Anthology) (Istanbul, 1942), 55–6 [originally in *İbret*, 56, 1872].
[4] *Şair Evlenmesi* (The Marriage of a Poet) (Istanbul, 1982 [1860]).
[5] *Edebî Hatıralar* (Literary Reminiscences) (Istanbul, 1935), 26.

She was not just thinking about becoming a bride. She wanted a husband. When a girl thinks of a husband, she wants to know who he is ... She had read so many novels ... Yes, Nusret Hanım was also thinking of marriage, but she was thinking of it in this way.[6]

Ceylân, the heroine of Ahmed Midhat's *Jön Türk* (*Jeune Turc*), 'tried to apply everything she read to our Ottoman life (*ahvâl-i Osmaniye-miz*)'.[7] 'The eyes of a bride-to-be were opened wide after reading so many novels in French, or if she did not know French, reading the "New Literature" (*Edebiyat-ı Cedide*), or at least following [the popular early twentieth-century novelist] Hüseyin Rahmi [Gürpınar]', Refik Halid emphasizes.[8] By the turn of the century, with the appearance of a literate middle class, novels, often released in serial form in the newspapers, became even more widely read, and presumably even more influential.[9]

It is difficult to evaluate the impact of novels and other forms of popular fiction or non-fiction on the diffusion of the love ideal in Ottoman society. Macfarlane tends to downplay such influences in society and argues that 'there have been many highly literary civilizations that have contained all these art forms without producing romantic love'.[10] That is certainly true in the pre-modern period, where Macfarlane looks to features of English social structure that promoted such aspirations as, for example, the lack of the need for parental consent in marriage. One could with little difficulty locate the opposite tendency in most other societies, and certainly in pre-modern Turkey. But when cultural institutions such as love are transplanted late to foreign soil, the influence of ideas as transmitted in literary forms is perhaps much greater. And the process, often rather an unnatural one, begins at the top of society and works its way down. This does not mean that it has no social structural roots. Something has to have changed for the ideas to take hold. In late Ottoman society increasing differentiation, the impact of education, particularly on women, the impact of western institutions in general, all had their effect and eventually led to a conflict between generations which was only exacerbated by the desires of some young people to select their own marriage partners. Our concern with literary forms here is then a dual one: because they apparently had a great impact on the lives of people,

---

[6] *Bahtiyarlık* in Ahmed Midhat, *Letaif-i Rivayat*, 124–5.
[7] From Ahmed Midhat, *Jön Türk* (Istanbul, 1326/1910), as quoted in Okay, *Batı*, 194.
[8] *Üç Nesil Üç Hayat* (Three Generations, Three Lives) (Istanbul, 1943), 38.
[9] M. Belge, 'Türk romanında tip' (Character in the Turkish novel), *Yeni Dergi*, 4 (1968), 33–6.
[10] *Marriage and Love*, 23.

but also because they portray the issues and conflicts which are central to our interests in ways that cannot be duplicated with other sources.

The first French novel to be translated into Turkish was Abbé Féne-lon's *Télémaque*, published in 1862, followed soon after by *Les Misér-ables*. By the end of the decade romantic themes gained in prominence with the serialization of Chateaubriand's *Atala*, and Bernardin de Saint-Pierre's *Paul et Virginie*, followed by many others.[11] The 1870s saw the beginning of Turkish short stories in the European style and of the Turkish novel serialized in popular newspapers. According to Namık Kemal, 'even shopkeepers and servants are reading papers or listening to those who can'.[12] The collections of stories, *Letaif-i Rivayat* (Finest Stories) by Ahmed Midhat, and *Musammeretname* (Night Entertainment) by Emin Nihat, began to appear in 1871, the same year as the first Turkish novel, *Taaşşuk-i Talât ve Fitnat* (The Love of Talât and Fitnat) by Şemseddin Sami, was published. They all, in one way or another, take up the themes of love versus arranged marriages. That is the central focus of *Taaşşuk-i Talât ve Fitnat*, the melodramatic and tragic story of a young man and woman who fall in love, but, as was so often the case in these early Ottoman novels, whose amorous desires are thwarted by their families. The end is suicide after the arranged marriage of the heroine, Fitnat. As in Namık Kemal's classic novel, *İntibah* (Awakening), a story resembling Dumas Fils' *La Dame aux Camélias*, and those of the popular novelist Ahmed Midhat, the objects of men's affections at the time were often women who lived on the edge of society: non-Muslims, slaves, prostitutes or fallen (*aşifte*) women. While love was in the forefront of the novel-ists' concerns, it would have been difficult at that time to have por-trayed 'proper' young Turkish girls in the role of a lover.

By the turn of the century, some men and women of the elite came to regard love as the proper stepping-stone to marriage. Unadulterated *amour* is what we find in Halid Ziya [Uşaklıgil's] *Aşk-ı Memnu* (Forbid-den Love), in the protagonist, Peyker's, rather melodramatic pining for love, the essence of life.[13] Bihter, the heroine, desperately wants love in her marriage. Through the voice of the author, we learn of her feelings for her husband: 'she was his companion . . . but she wanted more than that, not affection, but "love"'.[14] For the old-fashioned mind, 'love or affection (*muhabbet*) comes after the wed-

[11] Evin, *Turkish Novel*, 44–5.
[12] Quoted in Niyazi Berkes, *The Development of Secularism in Turkey* (Montreal, 1964), 277.
[13] *Aşk-ı Memnu* (Forbidden Love) (Istanbul, 1978 [1900]), 154.
[14] *Ibid.*

ding', as young Şefika's mother tells her in Namık Kemal's play *Zavallı Çocuk* (Pitiful Child) published in 1873; Şefika is married off to a wealthy pasha of thirty-eight, and commits suicide because she is unable to unite with Ata, her lover. Bihruz Bey, the prototypical nineteenth-century *alafranga* fop in the well-known novel *Araba Sevdası* (The Carriage Affair), perpetually in search of *l'amour*, is the subject of Recai-zade Mahmut Ekrem's satiral pen in 1896.[15] Three years later the widening gap between the older generation with its unease about love marriages, and the younger, with its impatience at the restrictions of its seniors, comes to the fore in Sami Paşazade Sezai's *Sergüzeşt* (Adventure). Generational conflict, especially over marriage arrangements, becomes a prominent and increasingly painful theme from then on, reaching its peak during the disruptive war years.

Love was a dangerous business. Not just because it subverted the authority of parents, but because, as a result, it also undermined the moral foundations of society. Clearly, it was a threat to authority, but it also jeopardized family honour (*namus*), family boundaries and personal identity, hence social order. In the years of Hamidian censorship it was also often a euphemism, perhaps one might say a displacement, for liberty. It was, as it emerged in the form of *grand amour* from the 1860s onward in the Ottoman upper strata, a foreign intrusion, as Ahmed Midhat correctly observed. Bahtiyar Pasha, a character in one of his stories, is not able to conceal his delight that the marriage arrangements he is making for his daughter, who has fallen in love with a young man of her choice, are a mere formality, a joy that the author with his more traditionalist views does not share. In discussing the plans with the father of the groom-to-be, Bahtiyar Pasha tells him: 'Sir, this *alafranga* thing is really something. *Liberté*! Freedom! . . . That's what it's all about! A man needs a woman; a woman a man. Why nowadays should parents demand that this natural freedom (*hürriyet-i tabiiye*) be restricted?'[16]

Love and liberty; libertinism and, perhaps, anarchy; love or suicide; liberty or death: these were not just personal matters; they were also intensely political. The connection between love and liberty was clearly drawn in Ahmed Midhat's short story 'Teehhül' (Marriage), published in 1871, by the hero Mazlum Bey, who tells us that, 'when there are still no individual liberties (*hürriyet-i şahsiye*) in our country how can a man choose the girl he wants, or a girl the man she

---

[15] Şerif Mardin, 'Super westernization in the Ottoman Empire in the last quarter of the nineteenth century' in P. Benedict, *et al.*, eds., *Turkey: Geographic and Social Perspectives* (Leiden, 1974), 406ff.

[16] From Ahmed Midhat, *Karnaval*, as quoted in Okay, *Batı*, 206.

desires?'[17] Celâl, in the novel *Sergüzeşt*, complains to his uncle of the injustice, the evil, of the painful consequences of marriages arranged against the will of those marrying.[18]

Was this rebellion against parental (and, indirectly, state) authority in the literary world of late nineteenth-century Istanbul a reflection of a nascent individualism in Ottoman society? It is difficult to imagine individualism taking root in the thick communalist soil of Istanbul. Yet, the sociological implications of love as the basis for marriage clearly lead in that direction. Love denies social structures, traditional social constraints and established social patterns. It is the bond uniting two individuals, two people whose priority is their relationship – ideally at any expense, and in the novels of the period, most often at the cost of their lives. Berkes argues that a kind of 'utopian individualism' served as an ideological force among those intellectuals most alienated from Ottoman Islamic society: 'They aspired for the life of the European *individual* in which material comfort, scientific progress, and individual liberty reigned.'[19] The individualists rebelled, he says, against everything that represented tradition, against everything irrational.

Ziya Gökalp has a somewhat different perspective on the same issues. His stance, though set on a sociological base, is in fact a reflection of a deep-rooted Turkish moralism. For he sees individualism as a social corruption. He says that the individualism which developed in Turkey after the *Tanzimat* is 'really egotism (*hodgâmlık*)'.[20] And it arose, he argues, as a response to the moral vacuum created by a weak collective conscience in the transition from an Islamic communalistic (*ümmet*) type of society to a more differentiated modern one in the nineteenth century.[21]

Gökalp, like his mentor Durkheim, devoted much of his life to a search for a satisfactory replacement for the older communalistic social morals of a 'pre-modern' society, and he found it in the social bonds of the modern nation, in a kind of corporatist solidarity.[22] Perhaps more than Durkheim he believed that: 'A society can only rest on shared beliefs and shared ideals, not on common interests (*menfaatlar*).'[23] He was concerned that romantic love untamed by social morality, was leading 'to sexual immorality or even amorality

[17] 'Teehhül' (Marriage), in *Musahebat-i Leyliye* (Istanbul, 1304/1887), 170.
[18] Sami Paşazade Sezai, *Sergüzeşt* (Adventure) (Istanbul, 1978 [1889]), 99.
[19] *Development of Secularism*, 295. Italics in the original.
[20] *Türk Ahlâkı* (Turkish Morality) (Istanbul, 1975).
[21] *Ibid.*
[22] Taha Parla, *The Social and Political Thought of Ziya Gökalp, 1876–1924* (Leiden, 1985).
[23] Gökalp, *Türk Ahlâkı*, 160.

in our country'.[24] Uncontrolled love, he correctly perceived, was a force that might get out of hand, and he felt this as a special threat in an Islamic society, a society where family honour was so dependent on the chastity of women, and where an association of modern life with what was perceived as immoralistic behaviour could be very destructive to the cause: 'women should regulate (tanzim) their attitudes and thinking (meşver) in terms of the society of which they are a part.'[25] Though he gives no evidence for it, he claims that there was a weakening of family ties in his time and an increase in divorce, which he connected to such moral corruption, 'to husbands and wives ignoring their children and giving in to their selfish feelings'.[26] Egotistical individualism was, then, perceived as a threat to social order, both past and future.

Interestingly enough, among other things, Gökalp blamed such 'egotistical individualism' on the French influence in Turkish society and on 'the sick morality that began with the Servet-i Fünun movement in literature'.[27] Like many Ottomans, he attributed great importance to the influence of literature and ideas. The journal Servet-i Fünun was the organ of the 'New Literature' (Edebiyat-ı Cedide) movement, late nineteenth-century followers of the French symbolists. The Servet-i Fünun movement aroused the wrath of most elements of Ottoman society, both the modern nationalists like Gökalp and the traditional-minded modernists like Ahmed Midhat, all of whom shared an antipathy for such cosmopolitanist, 'unTurkish' elements. Berkes wrote, 'It was the ideology of the decadents against whom Ahmed Midhat fought to the end.'[28] He fought to the end because he knew that their beliefs meant the demise of family and mahalle (community), the moral foundation-stones of the Ottoman society he so highly valued. Gökalp reacted in a similar way because the movement represented a threat to the new moralism resting in family and the state, to which he was devoted.

Individualism, as the late nineteenth-century Ottomans first came to know it, whether in love or in politics, was the expression of a rejection of the past, and of the shackles of repressive family, community and authority. However, in the intense nationalistic years beginning with the Young Turk period, it also came to be associated with anti-nationalism, moral corruption and even treason. Despite

[24] Ibid., 173.
[25] Ibid., 172.
[26] Ibid., 165.
[27] Ibid., 173.
[28] Development of Secularism, 295.

the enchantment of Ottoman intellectuals with science and rationality, their individualism had greater affinities with the passionate, iconoclastic rebellion of Nietzsche than with the utilitarian individualism of a Locke or Bentham. As such, it evoked, as we shall see, the dangers and fears associated with anomie or even anarchism. Gökalp used the ideological power of his sociology to tame such a tendency and subordinate the individual to the state in the name of progress and a new national purpose in the years following the Young Turk Revolution.

Did all this intellectualizing about love and liberty in the novels and short stories of the time have anything to do with the way people in Istanbul actually met and married? That is much more difficult to know, since there are few records left of such intimate details of people's personal lives. As noted earlier, when educated Ottomans wrote their autobiographies, or kept journals, they were more often political than personal. And most of these were left by men. Two of the most prominent women of the period who wrote their life stories, the poetess Nigâr in the late nineteenth century, and the novelist and feminist Halide Edip [Adıvar] in the early twentieth, both had arranged marriages, although later they divorced and remarried, largely on their own initiative.

Arranged marriage did not necessarily mean that the young couple did not see each other or even get to know one another before the wedding. As one elderly lady named Nimet explains: 'In general it is true that people had arranged marriages in the past. But not without seeing each other, meeting one another.' The line between arranged marriages and love marriages was often not as clear as the polemic about them would have us believe. The same informant tells us the story of Tahir, a close relative, whose marriage was arranged with Nezihe in 1919. After the arrangements, but before the wedding, they got to know and 'like each other'. Nimet's own story, however, is more interesting. Before he met her, her husband was 'in love' with a young girl whose beauty he had only heard about. When he finally met the girl at a formal occasion set up for that purpose, his dream was shattered in disappointment. Later a friend recommended Nimet, and his mother and aunt visited her with the intention of making the preliminary nuptial arrangements. This time they did not want him to see the bride-to-be, but his elder brother was able to convince their mother that he had a right to see her, arguing that: 'He can't go ahead with this without seeing her; his lifelong companion.' In the end he did meet her and they married soon afterwards. Nimet Hanım's daughter, who was present at the interview, then asked

her: 'Did you like father when you first saw him then?' And she
replied: 'I had lost my father. My mother thought it appropriate. Of
course I did.'[29]

No doubt many, perhaps most marriages in our period, even into
the 1920s and 1930s, were arranged by families. But they seem increasingly to have taken the desire for the relationship of the young couple,
even perhaps a genuine love for each other, into account. This might
range from parental accession to the meeting of the betrothed before
the wedding to parental sanction for a relationship that they did not
entirely initiate. We shall, however, never know the real extent of
the variations on this theme, since there are no systematic records
of such things. It does seem, however, that what were called 'love
marriages' were becoming more frequent, especially after the First
World War. The majority of our middle-class informants who married
in the 1920s and 1930s said that their's were love marriages, and novels
of the period give a similar impression.

We also know, however, from the interviews that although these
were labelled as love marriages, they did not involve the radical departure from family norms that, perhaps, the ideal type required. While
the relationship was often initiated by one or both partners, once
they had decided to get married it was necessary to turn the matter
over to their families. The groom-to-be had to ask for the hand of
his bride-to-be from her father. And parents might object and use
their power and influence to dissuade their children. In any case,
whether parental sanction was symbolic or not, the institution of marriage still ultimately involved the arrangements of two families. It
had not really become solely a matter of individual choice.

Certainly the 'national custom' (*âdet-i milliyemiz*), as Ahmed Midhat
labelled it, was arranged marriage. And it is quite unlikely, even with
all the talk of love in the novels, that in the late nineteenth century
many young men and women would have had the courage to have
love affairs and then get married. For 'proper women', that was out
of the question. For men, love affairs or sexual escapades with non-
Muslim women, with *cariyes* (servant-slaves), or prostitutes and other
'loose' women (*aşifte*), were an accepted part of the dual standard.
Refik Halid, in describing love in Istanbul over three generations,
tells us that during the Aziz period (Sultan Abdülaziz, 1861–76), the
first of his generations, words like 'love' (*sevmek*) or 'making love'
(*sevişmek*) that were so commonly used during the early Republican
years when he wrote, were rarely uttered, certainly not by children,

---

[29] We thank Harun Turgan who conducted this interview.

Plate 4.1 Wedding photograph, 1926, from a well-to-do and quite modern family.

and when they were used it was with the greatest unease and embarrassment.[30] We learn from him that such words became more popularized during the very late years of the century. In the protected society of the Aziz period it was difficult for young men and women to meet,

---

[30] *Üç Nesil*, 33–9.

Plate 4.2 Wedding photograph, 1933; a rather intimate and confident pose, not possible publicly in an earlier period.

and even more so to fall in love. When such scandalous affairs became the basis of marriage, the bride was said to be whorish (*aşifte*) and the groom engaged in debauchery (*çapkınlık*) by the spokesmen of *mahalle* morality.

By the 1870s it became somewhat easier, Refik Halid argues, for young men and women to see each other, flirt and fall in love. This is probably an exaggeration, though no doubt there was a tendency in that direction. For him the destruction by fire and reorganization of the grid of streets in many parts of intramural Istanbul came to symbolize some of the many other changes taking place in Ottoman society. The following, Hamidian, period (1876–1908) was a time when love and love marriages blossomed in Istanbul, he says. This too is no doubt an exaggeration, and it is probably closer to the truth to interpret him to mean that 'love' had begun to enter the acceptable vocabulary of middle and upper strata families during those years of rapid change. Parents, he claims, seemed to have become a bit more lenient with their children during that time. Hester Jenkins, who was in Istanbul during the latter part of this period describes some of her acquaintances, from what she calls 'advanced' families of the time:

Rabieh was permitted to know and learn to care for her husband between the betrothal and the marriage. She and Reshad read together, and became good friends in the six months that preceded their marriage. Saliha's father permitted Hussein Bey to court her while she was still in school.[31]

Despite the veil and chaperoning, it became somewhat easier for young men and women of the literate classes to meet in public places, in parks, picnic spots, theatres, at weddings and celebrations. A furtive glance, a flirtatious turn under the veil, a handkerchief dropped, a flower in one's lapel, a secret love-letter passed from hand to hand, these were some of the public symbols of a still forbidden, though increasingly tolerated, romance. And once again, we learn that 'novels and plays had a powerful impact on lovers during that time'.[32]

Clearly, then, all this romantic activity was not just a matter of an expanded amative physical topography. People's expectations were also changing. But we would doubt that the numbers of those actually falling in love and building their marriages in such romance were very large. Even at that time in France, the place where Turks believed *amour* in this sense originated and which they so idealized, the gap between the ideal and fantasy of *grand amour* and the realities of most people's lives was great. Theodore Zeldin argues: 'The changes that

---

[31] Hester Jenkins, *Behind Turkish Lattices: The Story of a Turkish Woman's Life* (Philadelphia, Pa., 1911), 380.
[32] *Ibid.*

did occur were more subtle than a radical rejection of the values of the past.'[33] This was also the case in Turkey.

The jubilation that accompanied the Young Turk Revolution, the fall of Hamidian despotism and the restoration of parliamentarianism in Ottoman society provided an enormous stimulus for the opening up that had begun in a more restricted way in the late nineteenth century. This opening up was felt in the lifting of restrictions on the press, in a burst of women's journals, some quite feminist in approach, in the establishment of associations for the advancement of women's rights, in advances in female education and in the beginnings of public employment of women. Such a relatively open society, along with increasing female education and literacy, provided a more suitable soil for the diffusion of the 'love revolution' that had begun during the century just ended.

In Hüseyin Rahmi [Gürpınar's] popular novel *Kadın Erkekleşince* (When a Woman Becomes Like a Man) set in the middle-class Istanbul of 1916, a girl too shy to show her love for a young man is presented as 'a girl of the past century'.[34] In the same novel, the mother of a young man of twenty-five from a middle-class family tries unsuccessfully to arrange for the marriage of her son to a rich girl. But he is in love with someone else. 'One marries someone who suits one's heart, not for money',[35] he informs his exasperated mother, who has a very different idea of marriage and tells the reader that: 'In this world most people do not get a wife through love. Most marriages spring from necessity.'[36] Love marriages received greater legitimacy in Ottoman Istanbul with the increase in modern publications after 1908 advocating a freer choice in such things. But Hüseyin Rahmi, who was a modernist, a feminist and an enthusiastic advocate of romantic love, could not but help draw out the social dangers of love in his novels. Like Ahmed Midhat of the previous generation, *amour* for Hüseyin Rahmi raised the spectre of *ihanet*, a word which can be translated as 'unfaithfulness' or as 'treason'. His novels relate one case of *ihanet* after another. We learn from him that love is not a sound basis for marriage because it is so ephemeral.

Romantic love increasingly came to be seen as a threat to family stability by modernist thinkers. This position is carried to its logical extreme in Yakup Kadri [Karaosmanoğlu's]' novel *Kiralık Konak*

[33] *France 1848–1945: Ambition and Love* (Oxford, 1979), 286–7.
[34] Hüseyin Rahmi Gürpınar, *Kadın Erkekleşince* (When a Woman Becomes like a Man) (Istanbul, 1974 [1916]), 13.
[35] *Ibid.*, 22.
[36] *Ibid.*, 26.

(A Mansion for Rent) set in Istanbul of the 1910s. The drama of generational conflict comes to a peak in this novel, which in so many ways captures the social and moral tensions of those painful years of Ottoman decline. Naim Efendi, the grandfather, and the representative of traditional morality cannot accept the 'new style marriage', that is developing around him. His granddaughter, Seniha, a very advanced young woman, in love with Faik Bey, cannot even accept the idea of marriage. Because for Seniha and Faik marriage is not the fruition of love. As she tells us:

> For us marriage is not a matter of the heart. Nor is it a biological (*uzvî*) necessity. He and I both look upon it as a matter of accounting (*hesap*) and of the mind; something to do with money.[37]

In the end they decide not to marry, and Seniha shocks her grandfather, when she learns that he has spoken to Faik's father hoping to make arrangements for her marriage to him, declaring:

> Neither is Faik Bey under his father's control if he wants to marry me, nor am I under yours if I decide to go with him. I am just about twenty. He is approaching thirty; we know each other much better than you know us, and we love one another ... If I wanted him now I would marry him; if I wanted him today he'd take me. But, I'm afraid that's not what we want.[38]

She explains to her uncomprehending grandfather that though they love each other now, if they married they would start quarrelling, they would become a burden for each other, and eventually would come to hate each other. In the end Seniha pays the price for her free thinking. She lives the life of a loose woman, a state of moral corruption that is the alternative to a proper marriage and family. Yakup Kadri had, however, marked her even earlier in the novel, when her love affair with Faik Bey became known, with some of the heaviest words of disapprobation in Turkish society, noting her 'harlot-like inner balance' and 'whorish voice'.[39]

In Yakup Kadri's *Sodom ve Gomore* (Sodom and Gomorrah) (1928), set in allied-occupied Istanbul after the war, we see the ultimate degradation of the modern Turkish woman: treasonous love affairs with the English and French officers stationed in the city. Free sex, free love and their destructive effects on morality and on the family

---

[37] *Kiralık Konak*, 131.
[38] *Ibid.*
[39] Moran, *Türk Romanı*, 131.

were among the central themes of novels of the 1920s. In his novel *Cânân*, Peyamî Safa classifies the women of Istanbul into three types: the vulgar (*avam*), the middling (*orta hallı*), always faithful to their husbands and families, and the contemporary (*asrî*) woman, egocentric, pleasure-seeking, and unfaithful, 'because she finds the family system comical, and she knows that this system is bound to collapse some day. This is the woman of the future'.[40]

Interestingly enough, the magazine *Resimli Ay* presents a very similar classification in 1924, one year before *Cânân* was published. In a clear sign of the increasing residential differentiation of Istanbul by class and life-style, the author calls the contemporary woman the Şişli woman, the middling one the Kadıköy woman, and the vulgar one the Beyazıd woman. But he does not hesitate to add that the Beyazıd woman's daughter has begun to emulate the Şişli woman.[41] In an interesting article in the popular magazine *Sevimli Ay* in 1926, Feridun Necdet, complains about these modern female types, who are selfish, unfaithful, negligent of their domestic duties, the products of a misunderstood modernism. He observes, articulating the fears of social collapse stemming from the moral centre of Turkish society: 'that these are the behavioural attributes of a female minority, but let us not forget that the majority always follows the minority.'[42] This is often the way fads and fashions move. While such women did indeed remain in a minority during those years, the voices of libertinism continued to make the connections between love and liberty that most Turks so feared. In *Cumhuriyet* newspaper, the organ of the Kemalists, an agony-aunt columnist gives parents the following advice:

Love, happiness, peace of mind, all these things follow their natural course through life. Neither mother, father, nor society and the law can protect one from them. If they want love, if they want freedom, give it to them.[43]

Cumhuriyet also 'describes' for its readers the 'girl of 1930', perhaps

---

[40] *Cânân* (Istanbul, 1980 [1925]), 156.
[41] 'Bugünkü Türk kadınları' (Turkish women today), *Resimli Ay*, 2 (Mart 1340/March 1924).
[42] 'Bir erkek karısından neler bekler' (What does a man expect from his wife?), *Sevimli Ay*, 3 (Mayıs 1926/May, 1926).
[43] 'Bana sorarsanız: anne baba reşit olan kıza karışmalı mı?' (If you ask me: should parents tell a mature daughter what to do?), *Cumhuriyet*, 2222 (19 Temmuz 1930/19 July 1930), 2.

a projection of the fears that untrammelled love had engendered in society: 'Love is merely an experiment for her, marriage a temporary friendship, home a hotel she shares with the man she loves.'[44] This was hardly even the caricature of the modern woman only half a century later.

The corruption of the female in the novels of the early twentieth century symbolizes the moral degradation which it was felt had penetrated Turkish society. Perhaps woman was even held responsible for such corruption. In *Kiralık Konak* and *Sodom ve Gomore* it was clearly women who symbolize the negative aspects of a westernization that has even penetrated the Turkish family. Women uncontrolled and uncontrollable by their families and the moral community have always been the nightmare of Turkish society, and those who advocate such libertinism are portrayed as morally corrupt, even traitorous.

The purposes of marriage

There is no doubt that marriage and reproduction were viewed as necessary and inevitable stages in the life-course of individuals in Istanbul in past times. Other than for a few radical modernists in the twentieth century who made a point of rethinking the institution, all Turks who could, got married. No decision was necessary about whether to get married or not. Marital statistics from the two censuses during our period make that very clear. Only 2 per cent of all women did not marry before reaching the end of their childbearing years. Only 8 and 5 per cent of all males in 1885 and 1907 respectively did not marry by their mid-fifties. While proportions remaining single may, as contemporaries argued, have gone up slightly during and after the war years, this is most likely a reflection of the sex-ratio imbalance caused by male losses in the wars and of difficult economic conditions – not of a re-evaluation of the institution of marriage. The alarm that was expressed in the press about what were perceived to be large numbers of men and women choosing not to marry beginning with the immediate post-war years and continuing into the late

---

[44] 'Bana sorarsanız: 1930 kızı annesinden daha mesut mu?' (If you ask me: is the girl of 1930 happier than her mother?), *Cumhuriyet*, 2150 (1 Mayıs 1930/1 May 1930), 2.

1920s,[45] proved to be entirely unwarranted. Proportions remaining single beyond their fifties continued to be extremely low even into the post-First World War Republican years. Clearly no revision of the place of marriage in the life-course of an individual had, or has, taken place to this day.

The earliest writings that we have encountered during the span of our period indicate quite clearly, to quote a typical one from the newspaper *Terakkî'i Muhadderat* of 1869, that 'the purpose of marriage is to raise children'.[46] The newspaper *Sabah* elaborates upon this theme in an article entitled 'Kadınlara mâlûmat: izdivaç' (Information for women: marriage) in 1894. Two purposes of marriage are indicated: 1) child-rearing and social reproduction, and 2) setting up a family and household so as to increase one's well-being.[47] Here, the emphasis is on the division of labour between male and female. The author does not neglect, however, to inform the reader that these social functions of marriage rest, in the first instance, on companionship (*muhabbet*).

That marriage was viewed within a familial rather than conjugal context by traditional Istanbul residents, is quite clear from the terms within which young women articulated their marital expectations. Ahmed Midhat Efendi contrasts traditional and modern expressions of this in his story *Bahtiyarlık*. He writes that most Ottoman girls think, when they conjure up their future marital life, about becoming a *gelin*, which translates as 'bride', but implies a connection to a family rather

---

[45] See, for example, 'İzdivaç dünyanın en emin sigortasıdır' (Marriage is the world's best insurance), *Resimli Ay*, 4 (Mayis 1341/May 1925), 23; 'Bekârlık' (Being single), *Cumhuriyet*, 1751 (24 Mart 1929/24 March 1929), 3; or Dr Nusret Fuad, *İzdivaç: Şerait-i Sıhhiye ve İçtimayesi* (The Hygienic and Social Conditions of Marriage), 3rd edn (Istanbul, 1338–9/1920–21), 21ff. The argument, always with reference to European statistics, was that bachelors had higher rates of morbidity, and died younger than those who got married. See 'Teehhül' (Marriage), *Terakkî'i Muhadderat*, 10 (17 Ağustos 1285/29 August 1869), 1–2; Dr Rusçuklu Hakkı, 'Elvah-ı hayat: 2- İzdivaca dair' (Tablets of life: on marriage), *Sabah*, 4047 (25 Şevval 1318/15 Febuary 1901), 3–4. Like the Europeans, the Turks attempted to deal with the problem through various legal means. In the early 1920s there was a proposal for a mandatory marriage law, a code which, however, never materialized. See Yahya Halid, 'Zorla nikâh' (Mandatory marriage), *Vakit*, 1898 (24 Mart 1924/24 March 1924), 3. This was followed in the late 1920s by a proposal for a bachelors' tax around which there was quite a heated debate, but which, however, was never enacted into law. See also 'Bekârlık vergisi: çok çocukluları da dinleyelim, (Bachelors' tax: let's also listen to those with many children), *Cumhuriyet*, 1749 (22 Mart 1929/22 March 1929), 4; Yunus Nadi [Abalıoğlu] 'Bekârlık vergisi' (Bachelors' tax), *Cumhuriyet*, 1757 (31 Mart 1929/31 March 1929), 1.

[46] 'Teehhül', 1–2.

[47] 'Kadınlara mâlûmat: izdivaç' (Information for women: marriage), *Sabah*, 1889 (13 Cemaziyülevvel 1312/12 November 1894), 3–4.

than a groom. Since the *gelin* did not choose her future husband under the traditional arrangements, her attention was on her role and her potential for happiness within the larger family, though no doubt her secret hopes were for an agreeable relationship with her husband, for support and possibly even for sexual satisfaction. All the members of her husband's family will refer to her as *bizim gelin*, or 'our bride', and there is a rich body of folklore in Turkey about the subordination of *gelin*s to family interests.

For the modern Turkish woman of 1885, in the character of Nusret Hanım in *Bahtiyarlık*, the goal was a more individuated one. It was not that of becoming a *gelin*, but of getting a husband (*kocaya varmağı düşünüyordu*).[48] Most significantly, she has a particular man in mind: 'When a girl thinks of *getting a husband*, she also thinks about who that man will be.'[49]

The procreative purposes of marriage, whether expressed in traditional community terms or in the then current nationalistic terms, were at variance with the actual fertility experiences of women in Istanbul, as was the pronatalism that characterized the last years of Ottoman society and the early ones of Republican Turkish society. As we have noted earlier, Istanbul women gave birth to very modest numbers of children even at the beginning of the period and perhaps earlier. It is possible, as we shall argue, that low fertility may have been a long-standing feature of Istanbul life. Fertility decline in Istanbul in the late nineteenth century begins from an already rather low level. Istanbul women were seemingly inured to the pronatalist campaigns that raged in the press during those years.

In an article published in 1897, at a time when Turkish nationalism was coming to the forefront of political discussion, the reader is told that 'the major duty of the family is to raise up young children, the hope for the future of the people [*millet*, here meaning Turkish people].'[50] This was more clearly articulated in 1913 in the journal *Kadınlar Dünyası* (Women's World) by Aliye Cevad: 'The purpose of the family is the future. The family provides the future of national life. Family means nation (*millet*), nation means family.'[51] In the same year, from the same journal we read that: 'It is the family which

---

[48] Ahmed Midhat, *Bahtiyarlık*, 124–5.

[49] *Ibid.*, 124. The emphasis is our own.

[50] Hüseyin Mazhar, 'Aile' (Family), *Çocuklara Mahsus Gazete*, 41 (9 Kânun-i sâni 1312/2 January 1897), 2–3.

[51] 'Aile – 1' (Family), *Kadınlar Dünyası*, 37 (10 Mayıs 1329/25 May 1913), 2.

causes the nation to increase in numbers, which gives it power and strength . . . Everyone is obliged to get married.'[52]

By the early years of the Republic, readers are told that: 'Marriage, above all things, means becoming a responsible citizen.'[53] And conversely, not marrying had come to mean being irresponsible, egocentric and even immoral. These were certainly the sentiments deterring those who might contemplate not marrying in the traditional Islamic setting in Istanbul and elsewhere, although the concern is not with the nation but with the family and the community. The emphasis in the more mature nationalistic family literature was on children and on the child-rearing function of families, in a qualitative as well as quantitative sense. As Ali Tevfik Bey tells the reader in *Kadın Erkekleşince:'* The real skill is not giving birth, but raising up the child.'[54] This became the theme of *Gürbüz Türk Çocuğu* (Robust Turkish Child), a publication of the Turkish Society for the Protection of Children which began to be issued in the early 1920s. Child health, child-rearing and education were its major causes, which were also given a wide press in the popular literature of the time. It is in such an environment that the magazine *Sevimli Ay* published a booklet in 1927 advocating for the first time, to our knowledge, birth control – largely translated from the work of the well-known American advocate of birth control, Margaret Sanger – as the preferred way to ensure the survival of healthy and quality children for the nation. Istanbul residents clearly seem to have chosen this path even before the population propaganda machine got started.

Though there were many people whose personal and family lives were captivated by the nationalist spirit so pervasive in the early twentieth century, there were also those whose motivations for marrying and raising a family were more prosaic. The conjugally based, small, child-centred family that the nationalist ideologues and the popular writers following in their footsteps were advocating, was, as we shall see, none other than a variation on the western bourgeois family to which many modernist Turks had been aspiring. There was no incompatibility, except in their ideological veneer, between such European bourgeois family aspirations and the ideals of companionate marriage

[52] Seniye Ata, 'Türk kadınlarına: aile – 1' (For Turkish women: family), *Kadınlar Dünyası*, 70 (12 Haziran 1329/25 June 1913), 3–4.
[53] Tevfik Nuri, 'İzdivaç hakkında evlenmesinden evvel çocuklarıma nasihatlerim' (Advice to my children about marriage before matrimony), *Resimli Ay*, 6 (Temmuz 1341/July 1925), 40.
[54] Gürpınar, *Kadın Erkekleşince*, 80.

and child-centredness that the Young Turks and later the Kemalists advocated as 'nationalist'.

In the late nineteenth century modern approaches to love and marriage, whether they be nationalist or Europeanist, were largely limited to the elite, but, by the post-First World War years, both these styles appear to have become quite widespread among the middle and perhaps even lower-middle classes. It is often difficult to distinguish between them. Novelists in particular, beginning in the Young Turk years, tend to set these social innovations farther and farther down the social scale. They would not have discussed love marriages in middle-class families unless there was some truth to the matter, otherwise their stories would not have been credible to their middle-class readership.

Marriage transactions

In late Ottoman Istanbul, marriage was jurally constrained by a mixture of Islamic law and local custom. The basic underpinnings of the institution were provided by orthodox Islamic jurisprudence, but many of the practical details, and as a result much of the variation found in the various parts of the Empire, stemmed from local custom and tradition.

Under Islamic law marriage is not considered a religious function. It is only a contract between two people or, if these are not of age, between two families or guardians. A declaration of intention in the presence of two witnesses is, in principle, enough to constitute a marriage agreement or contract, provided certain minimum legal conditions are satisfied. A marriage is not an act which has to be religiously sanctified or recorded. The presence of a man of religion has never been considered a necessary condition, and the short religious ceremony which sometimes takes place (though never in a mosque) is in no way a seal of legitimation. The voluntary presence of a local imam in the drawing up of the marriage contract – and all the Muslim schools of legal interpretation are unanimous on this – does not confer upon the marriage contract the character of a religious act.[55] The validity of a marriage act is not dependent, therefore, on its being blessed, performed or recorded by any religious authority whatsoever.

A marriage becomes valid and consummation socially sanctioned

---

[55] For more details on the law of marriage in Islam, see Y. Linant de Bellefonds, *Traité de droit Musulman comparé* (Paris, 1965); A. F. Fındıkoğlu, *Essai sur la transformation du code familial en Turquie* (Paris, 1936); M. Akif Aydın, *İslâm-Osmanlı Aile Hukuku* (Islamic-Ottoman Marriage Law) (Istanbul, 1985).

as soon as the contract is agreed upon by both parties and the nuptial celebrations are completed. There is a great amount of variability with respect to the content of the marriage contract. In general, in Istanbul, the content of marriage agreements occasionally noted down by local imams yield rather meagre demographic fare. The names of the spouses and, if any, their legal representatives, the names of the witnesses, the date of the agreement and the amount of the *mehr* (marriage payment) constitute the usual information. There are no signatures, no exact residential addresses, hardly any information on the ages of either of the spouses, their possible occupations or their social or economic status. Since the contract itself did not have to be put on paper, such scanty notes were sometimes jotted down only as a personal record by certain meticulous or enterprising local imams.

No centralized marriage records existed in late Ottoman Istanbul, except perhaps for the cases of litigation for divorce brought to the *sharia* courts, and these are assuredly not a very representative sample. In 1883 significant changes were made in the marriage registration system, the first in a series of measures which would eventually bring Turkish marriage regulations in line with those of Christian Europe. The regulations of 1883 entailed a legal obligation to declare marriages and have them inscribed in the population register within six months of the event.[56] This compulsory registration of marriages was, however, a bureaucratic formality, and had no legal effect on the validity of the union which was still officiated over by an imam. It was only in 1926, during the early years of the Republic, that civil marriage was prescribed and made the sole form of legally binding marriage. In rural areas, in particular, adherence to the law only took place gradually and traditional imam marriages persisted. In the major cities, it seems that compliance was quite widespread, though some no doubt brought in an imam for a religious ceremony in addition, as is still the case in many parts of the country.

In the years between 1883 and 1926, marriage registration among the Muslim population of the Ottoman capital city was in a state of limbo, since the newly introduced legal obligation of declaring marriages to the population authorities had no social or religious sanctions attached to it, and non-registration entailed no change whatsoever in the validity of the union. Though various penalties were attached to non-compliance with the registration system, they do not seem

---

[56] *Sicill-i Nüfus Nizamnamesi* (Regulations for Population Registration) (Istanbul, 1300/1883).

to have been very effective until after the 1907 census, and even then, there must have been many who did not register.

Things improved somewhat after 1905. Until then there had been almost no official marriage registration in Istanbul, the 1883 regulation having been to the best of our knowledge, virtually ineffective. In 1905, more effective fines and other legal sanctions for non-compliers were introduced in conjunction with the upcoming census. Marriage registration greatly improved and, from that date on, meaningful demographic information on Muslim marriages in Istanbul became available. But even then, and at least until 1926, it is not possible to say that marriage registration in Istanbul was complete and exhaustive. Afterwards, central registration did not, of course, improve overnight. It has been reported that even in the early 1970s around 15 per cent of all marriages in Turkey were not recorded within the legal period of notification.[57] We have used the marriage records (*vukuat defteris*) for Istanbul from 1905 to 1940 for our analyses. One indirect indication of the general improvement in centralized marriage registration on a city-wide scale can be gained from the fact that the few remaining notebooks belonging to imams and containing records of nineteenth-century Istanbul marriages all cease before or around 1906. The relative success of the new centralized system of recording marriages with its sanctions must have prompted these imams to terminate their traditional recording activities.

The question remains, nevertheless, as to whether the still ambiguous status of marriage registration in this period contributed to the introduction of biases in the marriage records after 1905. The sample we have drawn contains 4,939 marriage records from 1905 to 1940. Although it is difficult to be certain, it might well be that especially before 1926, and in the absence of any real social and religious coercion for marriage recording, certain groups, such as those from families with above average levels of education and literacy, more modern-minded families, people with less pronounced religious backgrounds, households of long-standing urban tradition and men working in government posts, may have registered their marriages more willingly than others. Unfortunately we have no way of telling whether this is really true. The post-1905 records themselves do not contain sufficient information as to the social and occupational background of the spouses. Furthermore, even if such a bias existed, its possible effects on the measures of nuptiality we have calculated are, for all

---

[57] Türker Alkan, *Kadın Erkek Eşitsizliği Sorunu* (The Question of Inequality between Men and Women) (Ankara, 1981).

practical purposes, unquantifiable. To the extent that men in the above-mentioned categories tended to marry somewhat later than others (and that is something we will probably never be quite sure of), male mean age at marriage might then be sightly overestimated. Our period is one of transition between a more or less strict practice of the basic Islamic legal precepts on personal matters, to one where a civil code (in this case an adaptation of the Swiss *Code Civil*) governs the legality, procedure and recording of all acts related to marriage.

The fact that a marriage contract was considered a purely personal agreement by Islamic law never meant, however, that there had been no central control of any sort on marriages in late Ottoman Istanbul. Since the sixteenth century religious judges (*kadıs*) appointed in the Ottoman Empire had had among their duties that of ruling on the legality of marriage contracts and of acting as legal guardians in the marriage of orphans. The religious court records (*şeriye sicilleri*) of Istanbul contain numerous instances of decisions as to the legality of this or that marriage act. These court rulings were in fact marriage licences of a sort, certifying that there was no basic religious obstacle to the conclusion of a marriage agreement.[58]

Although Islam does not sanctify the marriage arrangement, Islamic law does prescribe a certain number of fundamental preconditions in order for a marriage contract to be valid. In principle, one must obtain a licence (*izinname*) from a *kadı* stating that no barriers exist to the nuptial arrangements. One of the most important preconditions concerns not falling within the realm of those kinship relations considered an impediment to marriage. Such relations are listed in great detail, and include certain relationships of blood and marriage – and even a category of 'fictive' kinship relationship may also constitute a barrier to marriage. On 5 March 1881 (3 Rebiyülahir 1298) a marriage was concluded in Kasab İlyas *mahalle* between Tahsin Efendi and Ayşe Hanım. On 8 December (15 Muharrem 1299) of the same year the marriage was declared null and void. In the meantime it had been discovered that the bride's father 'had been breastfed by a woman who was co-wife to the woman who had fed Tahsin'. Marriage between what are known as 'milk-siblings' in Turkish is forbidden by Islamic law.

Polygyny is allowed according to Islamic law, but with a maximum of four wives. Having four wives is, for a man, therefore an obstacle to another marriage. Furthermore, a man is not allowed to marry

---

[58] For a thorough review of Ottoman marriage law and procedure, see Aydın, *İslam-Osmanlı*, and Cin, *Evlenme*.

two women who are related to each other. There are also certain conditions which pertain to previous marriages. A divorced woman cannot, for example, remarry unless she has had three menstrual periods since her divorce to ensure that she is not pregnant by the previous husband. A man who has repudiated his wife cannot remarry her unless she has, in the meantime, contracted and consummated a valid marriage with someone else. Furthermore, the religious judges in Istanbul were often unwilling to permit the marriage of individuals who had not yet attained puberty, because later annulment of such a marriage had to be granted upon request.

Unfortunately, there is no way to estimate the proportion of marriages in pre-Republican Istanbul which were contracted with the actual approval of a judge. Since there never were, in Istanbul, specialized officers to whom the *kadıs* could delegate their powers with respect to marriage licences, these were inevitably granted on a case-by-case basis. It is clear from the surviving records that only a small number of Istanbul marriages were performed with such a licence.

The local imam who recorded the marriage contract in his register was, in principle, supposed to ask for such a licence, but here again, the system did not work perfectly. In reality, most imams were probably satisfied with the information given them by the marrying parties. That is not surprising in view of the fact that most of the local imams presumably knew at least one of the spouses personally – the one who lived in the neighbourhood of the mosque where he officiated. Judges, nevertheless, refused to consider cases of dispute of the validity of a marriage, if the marriage had been contracted without a *bona fide* licence.

This situation did not, to the best of our knowledge, create insuperable legal, social or religious problems. An interesting legal case created by an imam registering a marriage contract without an *izinname* from the *kadı* dates from 1922 and appeared as a news item in a daily newspaper:

A young girl from Üsküdar [a district of Istanbul] named Münire had declared to an imam named Hafız Mehmet Nuri Efendi that she lived in that area, that her father was dead and that she desired to be married to Ahmed Efendi. The imam performed the marriage and gave them a copy of the registration. The truth came to light some time later. Münire was the daughter of Abdullah Efendi, an army captain who had, for some time, refused his consent to his daughter's marriage, thence her stratagem. After the inquest, the imam was put on trial.[59]

[59] 'Izinnamesiz nikâh kılma davası' (The case of an unlicensed marriage), *Peyam*, 10 (15 Şevval 1340/11 June 1922), 3. See chapter 5 for a discussion of polygyny.

The basic problem in this case was whether the girl was really of the proper age to marry without her parents' consent, and there was no question of the annulment of this marriage. What the local imam said at court seems to be an accurate description of what, no doubt, had been the common practice in Muslim Istanbul for centuries:

I trusted Münire Hanım, registered the marriage, and gave her a signed copy of the act . . . As to the question of performing a marriage without the spouses producing an *izinname, this happens all the time in the city.* I saw no cause for legal liability, and performed the marriage, as usual.[60]

We have been able to examine one of the very few surviving pre-1905 local marriage registers kept by imams of local mosques within Istanbul in some detail. The registers kept by the imams who officiated at a little mosque (Kasab İlyas *Cami*) situated in the small neighbourhood of the same name (Kasab İlyas *mahalle*) contain a total of 654 marriage registrations. They cover a period of forty-two years, from 1864 to 1906 (1281–1324). Of the 654 records only four contain mention in the margin of a licence previously obtained from a *kadı* and produced during registration. A few others, cases of remarriage, indicate that the bride had produced a court ruling concerning the divorce from her previous husband.[61]

About a third of these records, however, contain the mention of a guarantor (*kefil*) of the legality of the marriage being recorded. The imam, knowing the law, had every reason to protect himself, particularly if he did not know the spouses personally or if one of them lived in another part of the city. In most cases the mention of a guaran-

---

[60] *Ibid.* (our emphasis). Although it is difficult to speak of a real conflict, the perception of the registration fee itself may have been an object of competition between local imams and the *kadı*. That this might have been in many cases the real issue is also upheld in a newspaper article which appeared in 1901: 'The adjunct *kadıs* of small districts should legally receive a fee of 12 *kuruş* for an *izinname*. We hear, however, that many of them ask for as much as one *lira*. As for the *muhtars* [neighbourhood or village headmen], they often shamelessly demand to be paid as much as ten *liras* to deliver to the future bride a certificate saying that 'there is no legal or religious obstacle to her marriage', 'Vilâyette izdivaç, nahiye naibleri, köy muhtarları' (Marriage in cities, district judges, village headmen), *Sabah*, 4263 (5 Cemâziyülahir 1319/19 September 1901), 2. *Sicill-i Nüfus Kanunu* (The Population Registration Law) (17 Şevval 1332/8 September 1914) states in article 26, in conformity with Ottoman common law, that 'the marriages of Muslims will be performed only after an *izinname* has been delivered by the religious judge or his substitute'. Another law, enacted by the Sultan on 24 October 1917 (8 Muharrem 1336) inserts a new article (art. 200) in the Penal Code, according to which any imam drawing a marriage contract without the necessary authorization from a judge would be punishable by one to six months' imprisonment. These legal measures do not seem to have had the desired effects.

[61] A court ruling called *tatlik hükmü* for a case of repudiation and *muhalâa hücceti* for a case of divorce by mutual consent.

tor for the act is simply indicated with a statement such as: 'Mr So and So has guaranteed, in writing, that the bride has no legal or religious impediment to marriage whatsoever.' The guarantor was apparently sometimes a person of high social standing, sometimes a figure well known in the *mahalle*, and quite often a parent or even the guardian (father, elder brother, uncle) of the bride. In a few cases an imam from another quarter of the city – often, presumably from the place of residence of the bride – served as guarantor. In a number of cases, especially in the last years of the nineteenth century, the guarantor's statement becomes more precise and the marriage is frequently recorded 'with all responsibility belonging to the guarantor'. It seems that as far as the strict legal procedures of marriage are concerned, the rather rigorous legal and religious prescriptions could easily be avoided and the whole procedure adapted to the customs and conditions of the city.

From a demographic and even purely historical viewpoint, these pre-1905 imam marriage records are, as we have indicated, rather unsatisfactory. All our demographic analyses are for that reason based almost exclusively on the post-1905 centralized records of the then newly established population registry offices of Istanbul. The few surviving pre-1905 records contain almost no information on the spouses themselves; age, date and place of birth are also absent. Marriage order is almost never mentioned except perhaps in the – assuredly unrepresentative – cases where the two spouses, previously married to each other and later divorced, are reunited in marriage. The records are not signed by the spouses themselves, and seldom give any clue as to economic, social, occupational or geographic background or place of residence after marriage. It is also not clear how the marriage terminated. Since divorce is ruled upon by the court, it does not have to be recorded in an imam's register. Previous widowhood or divorce is only sporadically recorded in these registers and only, of course, when there is no guarantor.

The pre-1905 local marriage records do contain the names of the spouses and those of their fathers (with no mention, however, of whether he is alive or dead), as well as the name of their legal representative. The future husband and wife did not have to be present when the marriage act was drawn. In the overwhelming majority of cases a parent or relative acted as legal representative. When the future husband or wife were present, this extraordinary occurrence was mentioned in the registration. Then there are the names of the two (sometimes four) witnesses and that of the guarantor, if any, as well as the date of the marriage act. The only other significant item contained in the record is the amount of the *mehr*, or marriage payment. We shall return to that shortly.

By contrast, the post-1905 marriage records in the centralized *vukuat defteris*, provide data more amenable to demographic analysis. Dates and places of birth for both spouses are indicated, as well as the premarital status (single, widow, etc.) of the wife. A few of the records also contain some background information (occupation or level of education) on the husband. We have, therefore, used these records to analyse the changes in nuptiality and marriage patterns between 1905 and 1940. These records, however, contain no mention of *mehr*.

Mehr is a fundamental feature of the Islamic law of marriage. *Mehr* is a payment which devolves from the groom's family to the bride upon marriage, and in that sense may be referred to as a form of indirect dowry. From a strictly legalistic point of view, the *mehr* is a consequence, not a precondition of marriage. The woman has a right to *mehr* if, for instance, no *mehr* was specified in the marriage contract, or even if she had clearly waived her right to it.[62] The *mehr* is in principle due to and belongs to the wife, not to her family, and she has all rights of disposition over it, though in practice it might be used to cover part of the wedding and household formation expenses. There was traditionally, at least in Istanbul, no lower or upper limit to the amount of the *mehr*. If the amount was not specified in the marriage contract, the wife could apply to a judge who would then determine, *ex officio*, an appropriate sum.

It was common Ottoman practice to pay the *mehr* in two parts. The first part, paid by the husband upon the drawing of the marriage contract, was called the *mehr-i muaccel* (the urgent or premarital *mehr*, often known as the *ağırlık* in Turkish). The payment of the second part (*mehr-i müeccel*, the deferred *mehr*) was to be made at a later date. This postponement, of course, could not be indefinite for, at least in theory, the woman maintained the absolute right to demand its payment. If the husband repudiated his wife, the postponed portion of the *mehr* had to be paid to the wife for the separation to have legal effect and the wife could always sue him for payment. In case of divorce by mutual consent (*muhalâa, hul*), the financial agreements could, in some cases, include a renunciation by the wife of the as-yet

---

[62] For further legal and religious details on the *mehr*, see Aydın, *İslâm-Osmanlı*, 31–4 and 103–7.

unpaid portion of the *mehr*. The *mehr* was also considered as a debt, and a debt which had priority over the husband's other debts. The legal practice in Istanbul was, in case of the husband's death, to pay the *mehr* due to the wife out of the deceased's estate before it was divided up between any of the other legal heirs. As we have already indicated, and unlike the traditional bridewealth (*başlık*) common in rural areas, *mehr* was in principle at the disposal of the wife herself, and not of her family, father, brother or other kin. Furthermore, payment of the *mehr* could not be used by the husband as a basis for demanding that the wife provide a dowry. This was, at least, quite definitely the case among the traditionally highly urbanized Muslim population of Istanbul.[63] There are cases in the *kadı* courts of women demanding that an appropriate amount be allotted to them as *mehr*.[64]

In the pre-1905 records of Kasab İlyas *mahalle*, we found some cases of the *mehr-i muaccel*, the effective downpayment made at the drawing up of the marriage contract, being paid in the presence of the witnesses. These witnesses to the marriage contract also acted thereby as guarantors to the husband's present (and future) solvency.

Divorce according to Islamic law is an easy matter – at least for the husband. To repudiate his wife it was sufficient for him to openly declare in front of two witnesses that he divorced his wife.[65] The matter was, in actual fact, never as simple and straightforward. Words said in anger had to be retracted, hasty decisions revised and couples were often reunited. The immediate social environment of the *mahalle* in Istanbul seems in many cases to have exercised a mitigating pressure. When divorced couples reunited, a new marriage contract had to be drawn – for the sake of formality – and a new, second, *mehr* was of course specified. Being a second *mehr* it was recorded in the new marriage contract. About 5 per cent of the 654 marriage recordings

---

[63] It is quite another matter that the rural *başlık* (bridewealth) was often thought to coincide with the *mehr* in less urbanized parts of Ottoman Anatolia. The institution of *mehr*, as practised in the Ottoman capital, however, should be considered as a form of indirect dowry or marriage settlement between spouses and not as bridewealth.

[64] When the amount of the *mehr* was clearly set down in the marriage contract, it was called *mehr-i müsemma* (the specified *mehr*). It was called *mehr-i misl* (the comparative *mehr*) when unilaterally dictated by the *kadı* in cases where mention of it was omitted in the marriage contract.

[65] Divorce by mutual consent, although always possible, in the central Ottoman lands required a regular court ruling to make the decision legally binding. By contrast, repudiation had only to be declared by the husband and simply registered by the *kadı* – and even that was often avoided.

in Kasab İlyas *mahalle* were of this sort. The recordings mention the amount of the first and of the second *mehr*s. We even came across, in this small Istanbul *mahalle* between 1864 and 1906, one or two cases of third marriages of the very same couple.

The *mehr* could be paid in cash as well as in kind. Although the *mehr-i müeccel*, being a promise to pay in the future, is always recorded as a sum of money, there seems to have been a significant number of cases in Istanbul in which the *mehr-i muaccel* was paid in kind. There certainly were quite a few cases in Kasab İlyas *mahalle*.

In a marriage registered by the imam on 9 August 1880 (3 Ramazan 1297) the husband, Hüseyin bin Ömer, promises to pay 351 *kuruş* as *mehr-i müeccel* to the wife, Fatma bint-i Ali.[66] The *mehr-i muaccel* consisted of 'thirty quarter-size gold coins, a complete set of kitchenware, an assortment of bedclothes and a chest'. In another registration, that of Mehmed bin Ali's marriage to Fatma bint-i Yusuf on 6 June 1881 (8 Receb 1298), it is clearly specified that the *mehr-i muaccel* consists only of 'a bed and an assortment of bedcovers and bedclothes'. When, on 1 June 1883 (25 Receb 1300) Hanife bint-i Abdülhâlik marries Ahmed bin Abdullah for the second time, the registration specifies that the first, already paid *mehr-i muaccel* had consisted of 'a 50 per cent share in the ownership of house on number three'.

There were also cases where both some goods and a sum of money were given. On 9 October 1891 (5 Rebiyülevvel 1309), Ali Bey bin Topal Hüseyin marries Fatma bint-i Muhammed, and his *mehr-i muaccel* consists of 500 *kuruş*, plus 'a settee, a bed, two quilts and a chest'. Many other instances exist. There is no apparent relationship between economic or social status of the husband or of the wife and the fact that payment is in cash or in kind. A whole house could be given away as *mehr*, but also, more simply, as was the case when Hasan bin Bektaş was married to Fatma bint-i Mehmed on 24 March 1893 (6 Ramazan 1310), 'a bed, a chest and a carpet'.

In the great majority of cases we encountered, however, the *mehr* was given in monetary terms. Payments in kind were really in the minority. What was the size of the *mehr*? What were the amounts of money involved? Table 4.1 gives mean figures for various periods in Kasab İlyas *mahalle*. It gives mean values for fifty marriage regist-

---

[66] A clear and definite bias (most probably stemming from a superstition) against the setting of round figures for the *mehr*, seems to have existed in Istanbul. The two *mehr*s are almost never allowed to total up to a round figure. One of them almost always ends with 1 (151, 301, 501, 3001 *kuruş* etc.), while the second is a more round figure (150, 300, 500, 3,000 *kuruş*, etc.).

Table 4. 1. *Mean values (in* kuruş) *of the* mehr *in Istanbul (Kasab İlyas*
mahalle) *for selected periods*

	Mehr-i muaccel	N	Mehr-i müeccel	N
1864–8	1,493	13	658	50
1889–91	1,123	20	776	50
1904–6	1,141	17	717	50

Source: Notebooks of the İmam of Kasab İlyas Mosque, Istanbul.

rations taken from the beginning of the period when records are available, fifty from the middle of the period, and the last fifty registrations from the record kept by the imam of the Kasab İlyas mosque. The first striking feature in these *mehr* recordings is that, although the *mehr-i müeccel* figure is present in all cases, the *mehr-i muaccel* has been set down in only about a third of all marriage registrations. Since marriage registration was, as we have said, considered to be a pure formality, information on the amount of *mehr* actually paid, an especially private and more confidential part of the marriage transaction, was no doubt easily withheld. Since it is only a promissory payment, the *mehr-i müeccel*, was more easily recorded in a purely formal registration procedure. Since it did not 'cost anything' at the time, the *mehr-i müeccel* might have been used as a kind of status symbol for the husband and his kin.

There is no discernible trend in the mean amount of *mehr* paid during those four decades. If we exclude one single case of an exceptionally high *mehr-i muaccel* during the first period, the mean was 1,201 *kuruş*, giving us an even flatter curve. The range of the *mehrs* is, however, quite large, and the variance is high. Between 1864 and 1868, for instance, the *muaccel* ranged between 51 and 6,001 *kuruş*, with 151 as the mode (six cases). For 1904–6, the mode is 201 *kuruş* (seven instances), although the mean figure is somewhat lower than previously, and the figures range between 101 and 5,001 *kuruş*.

What do the actual amounts of *mehr* paid given in table 4.1 signify in terms of purchasing power? Around the turn of the century, or within the decade that immediately preceded it, an army captain's monthly salary was 666 *kuruş*, and that of an inspector in a ministry around 2,500 *kuruş*. The mean monthly wage of a qualified factory worker was 416 *kuruş* in 1889 and 475 *kuruş* around the year 1900. In 1910 a *kadı* in Istanbul earned a monthly salary of 3,500 *kuruş*, his secretary was paid 1,000 *kuruş* and the various clerks attached to his office got a monthly pay of between 400 and 800 *kuruş*.[67] The mean monthly salary of Ottoman Foreign Ministry officials around 1910 was 1,166 *kuruş*. A schoolteacher could expect to earn as much as 1,000 *kuruş*. Just before the First World War, army salaries started around 700 *kuruş* for a lieutenant who had just graduated from the military academy, who then could expect to earn as much as 3,000 *kuruş* on being promoted to the rank of colonel.

This was a period of relatively stable prices or, at the most, very mild inflation. Considering that in about 50 per cent of cases the *mehr-i müeccel*, and in 24 per cent of cases the *mehr-i muaccel* were either equal to or less than 500 *kuruş*, it is difficult to call the *mehr* 'prohibitive'. Our data from a neighbourhood of average size located in the centre of intramural Istanbul, leads us to the conclusion that the *mehr*, as practised then, was not a serious deterrent to marriage. Indeed, there is some evidence to show that the *mehr* itself was a relatively small portion of the expenses usually incurred during marriage.[68]

One last particularity of the marriage contracts of Istanbul concerns

---

[67] See Eldem, *Osmanlı İmparatorluğu*; Findley, 'Economic bases of revolution', 81–106; Abdülaziz Bayındır, *İslâm Muhakeme Hukuku: Osmanlı Devri Uygulaması* (Islamic Court Law: Its Implementation During the Ottoman Period) (Istanbul, 1986), 88–9.

[68] Contemporaries might have perceived it differently, however. As part of a state policy to encourage marriages, an Imperial Rescript (*Ferman*) published in 1874 aims openly at limiting the expenses incurred during marriage. Potential candidates for marriage are divided into four categories and for each of these precise figures for the *mehr-i muaccel* are given. The highest category is assigned to pay 1,000 *kuruş*, the second 500, the third 100 and the fourth between 30 and 100. Appropriately proportioned amounts are also assigned for the *mehr-i müeccel*. This Rescript may reflect a more or less wide social concern. However, there is no doubt that (1) the Sultan's will was in open contradiction with strict Islamic law, which recognizes no upper limit to the amount of the *mehr*, and (2) that the Rescript could never be implemented. As early as the sixteenth century an Imperial Rescript had set an upper limit of 1,000 *akça* (asper) for the *mehr* to be paid by Janissaries who were getting married, but that order too could not be strictly implemented. See Aydın, *İslam-Osmanlı*, 100–101.

In order to obtain another insight into the financial significance and burden imposed by the payment of the *mehr*, one can try to weigh it against the *nafaka* (alimony) payments in certain cases of divorce. Islamic law prescribes a period of time during which a divorced woman cannot remarry. That period is called *iddet*. The dominant view is that it should last for 'three menstrual periods of the woman'. During this time the husband is liable to pay a maintenance allowance called *nafaka-yı iddet*. This allowance, fixed by the *kadı* as part of the divorce ruling, was supposed to enable the wife (and the children, if any) to have a decent standard of living. We have examined a certain number of religious court rulings of divorce emanating from two courts in Istanbul. Tables 1 and 2 give mean values for the *nafaka-yı iddet*.

The mean values of the *mehr* in a Kasab İlyas *mahalle* are, therefore, only three

the 'special conditions' (*şart*) included in the marriage registrations. Such conditions are perfectly valid according to Islamic law. In previous centuries this opportunity was sometimes used by women to improve their relative position within marriage.[69] Most of these special conditions, however, were only specifications of what was in any case considered as normal behaviour on the part of the husband. The wife specified, for example, that she was agreeing to the marriage on condition that she be treated well, that she be allowed to visit her own parents and family, that her children receive a decent education, or that she and her husband live in a house apart from the rest of the family – all rather normal expectations of married life in Istanbul. These 'special conditions' sometimes also included a sanc-

Footnote 68 continued
or four times the monthly amount officially deemed necessary to ensure decent living conditions for a divorced woman.

Table 1. *Nafaka-yı iddet* in Üsküdar. Istanbul 1884–1917/1302–35

Dates	N	Mean monthly *nafaka* (in *kuruş*)
1884–6/1302–3	14	281.1
1885–6/1303	35	325.5
1886–8/1304–5	32	262.6
1889–91/1307/09	60	228.5
1911–13/1329–31	38	334.0
1915–17/1334–5	74	505.6

Source: Archive of the Istanbul Religious Courts, Court of Üsküdar.

Table 2. *Nafaka-yı iddet* in central Istanbul, 1882–1918/1300–36

Dates	N	Mean monthly *nafaka* (in *kuruş*)
1882–3/1300	20	444.0
1883–5/1301–2	16	358.7
1887–8/1305	19	496.9
1887–91/1305–8	18	367.7
1912–14/1331–2	40	195.0
1917–18/1366	71	358.3

Source: Archive of the Istanbul Religious Courts, Court of Istanbul.

[69] See, for instance, R. Jennings, 'Women in early 17th century Ottoman judicial records: the sharia court of Anatolian Kayseri', *Journal of the Economic and Social History of the Orient*, 18 (1975), 53–114. Aydın, however, does not entirely agree with Jennings' conclusions. See Aydın, *İslam-Osmanlı*, 100–1.

tion, namely, that the wife would acquire the right to sue for divorce in case the conditions were not respected.[70]

The marriage registrations from Kasab İlyas *mahalle* only include two such cases of 'special conditions' to marriage. Strangely enough, one of them emanates from the husband. The first case is the marriage on 14 December 1888 (10 Rebiyülahir 1306) of Hüseyin bin Hasan and Gülsüm bint-i Receb. This was a second marriage. The couple had been married and divorced previously. But Hüseyin bin Hasan was a polygynous husband and also had another wife with whom Gülsüm bint-i Receb rightfully expected to be treated on an equal footing. She therefore made Hüseyin sign an official statement, appended to the marriage contract, in which he declared that he would 'as his other wife, support Gülsüm, treat her well, and give her no further occasion for complaint'. From the point of view of strict Islamic law this statement is redundant, since such 'equal treatment' is the basic condition which every polygynous husband should respect.

The second case of a 'special condition' in a marriage contract occurs in the nuptials of Davut Ağa bin Ahmed and Gülsüm bint-i Osman from Kütahya, on 2 July 1889 (4 Zilkade 1306). This time it is the husband who sets the condition. Davut Ağa must have been a man of small means, for he asks his future wife's representatives at the marriage ceremony to sign a statement on behalf of her, guaranteeing that 'if the aforesaid husband is called for military service, the above mentioned wife will have no right to sue for support'. The husband has, in this case, had the wife relinquish a right to which she was perfectly entitled. It is most probable in this particular case that, if the wife had appealed to a religious court, the 'special condition' would have been declared null and void. These two examples of 'special conditions' inserted in marriage contracts, though surely not representa-

---

[70] It is a point of contention among Islamic jurists as to whether a marriage contract including such a condition with a sanction is to be considered as a 'marriage with a special condition' or as a 'conditional divorce'. Another point which needs mentioning – though it is difficult to do more than just that – is homogamy in Istanbul. Homogamy (*kefaet*) – the existence of similar economic, social, religious status for both bride and groom – is in fact one of the basic obligations imposed by the Islamic law of marriage. Many Islamic doctors of law admit that an annulment of the marriage is possible if the husband is not of 'equal standing' with the wife. Classical Islamic doctrine judges homogamy from the following six criteria: religion, freedom, piousness, fortune, occupation and family origin. The 1917 Family Law (*Hukuk-u Aile Karar-namesi*) which, in many areas, only ratified the existing practices and conventions on marriage matters, admits of only two criteria: wealth and honour. For the husband to be of 'equal standing' to the wife, he should be able to pay the *mehr-i muaccel*, support his wife and children, and his occupation should be as 'honourable' as that of his wife's father or family (art. 45). Unfortunately, we are not able to evaluate to what degree this required equivalence in social status was met in practice.

tive of the real social conditions of marriage in the city of Istanbul, are nevertheless a clear indication that local practice could, and perhaps frequently did, deviate from the letter of Islamic marital precepts.

Despite the furore created about love marriages by people in Istanbul, the joining together of a man and woman in matrimony was still largely under the hegemony of families even at the end of our period. Though there was a freer choice in the selection of spouses by the second and third decade of this century and an ideology of love several steps in advance of reality, the domestic and moral anarchy feared by many during those years was in all likelihood little more than a projection of those fears onto the real situation. In addition to the social arrangements for betrothal and marriage, the important role of families in the nuptial process is witnessed by the arrangements for the payment of *mehr* during the late Ottoman years, and by their continuing financial contributions to the setting up, and even maintenance, of the households of offspring during the Republican period.

5

Marriage age and polygyny: myths and realities

The institution of marriage was, as we have seen, the focus of great attention in late Ottoman Istanbul society. In addition to concern with the mode of entry into marriage, there was a considerable interest shown in the age at which people – women in particular – first got married. Not having produced statistical tabulations from the figures they collected on marriage age, Ottomans were in most cases misinformed about the nuptial realities over which they expended so much effort and emotion. The same was true with respect to polygyny. The reality was not at all what most people imagined it to be. Perhaps it would be more accurate to refer to successive and overlapping monogamies than to polygyny as the prominent feature of the system. Let us then take the figures on marriage age and type that the Ottomans have left to posterity and do what they did not choose to do – use them to calculate trends in marriage age and patterns of marriage type.

Age at marriage

Age at marriage in late Ottoman Istanbul was very high, both for women and for men. This is clear from an examination of the adjusted figures shown in table 5.1.

The data on marital status of women in both censuses present us with a problem: the proportions of single women after the ages thirty or thirty-five show inexplicable irregularities and remain too high. We must deal with this before we can proceed with our analyses. The phenomenon is in fact a well-documented one, for it comes out also in later Turkish Republican censuses. The issue of concern is the underregistration or misreporting of widows and divorced women. Quite a number of divorced and widowed women are mis-

Table 5.1. *Proportions single in the censuses of 1885 and 1907*

Age	1885			1907		
	Male	Female		Male	Female	
		Census	Adjusted		Census	Adjusted
−10	99.7	100.0	100.0	99.6	99.1	100.0
10–14	97.1	93.2	93.2	96.1	91.2	91.2
15–19	90.8	57.3	57.3	93.8	60.7	60.7
20–4	58.4	17.6	17.6	69.4	39.5	39.5
25–9	25.3	14.4	14.4	44.5	17.0	17.0
30–4	11.1	13.5	4.1	15.9	10.5	5.9
35–9	11.5	10.2	2.7	8.0	11.0	3.3
40–4	5.7	13.5	2.1	5.8	12.5	2.3
45–9	5.5	10.4	2.0	5.7	9.5	2.0
50–4	8.2	17.5	2.0	5.4	9.3	2.0
Singulate mean age at marriage			19.1			20.5

Source: Istanbul population rosters, 1885 and 1907.

registered as 'single' or as 'marital status unknown'. This distortion, a systematic cultural phenomenon, exists for younger women as well as for those above thirty, but the numbers involved are certainly smaller at younger ages, and up to age thirty the bias is not clearly reflected in the crude figures.

As a result of this situation an adjustment had to be made using the 'standard marriage schedules' devised by Ansley J. Coale.[1] After adjustment it looks not unlikely that more than half the women above thirty and registered as single must in fact have been widows or divorcees. The difference between the crude and adjusted proportions increases with age, probably because proportions widowed and divorced also increase with a woman's age.

Another indicator of misreporting of female marital status is the proportion widowed among the female population aged fifteen to forty-nine. This proportion is about 2.5 per cent in the two late Ottoman censuses. In the Turkish censuses of 1955 and 1960 the percentage is the same, with a much lower level of mortality, a higher mean age at marriage for women and a smaller age difference between spouses. In addition, there are some indications that a similar

---

[1] 'Age patterns of marriage', *Population Studies*, 25 (1971), 193–214.

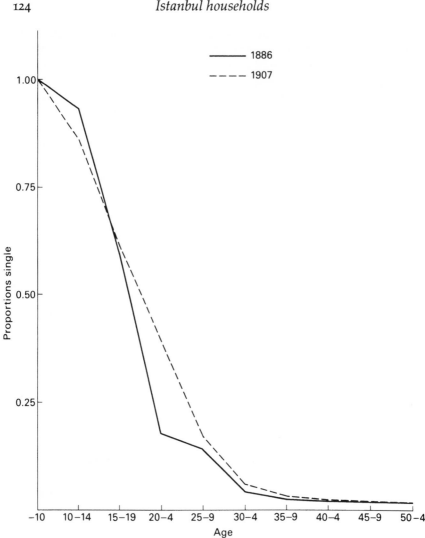

Figure 5.1 Female proportions single (adjusted) in two censuses, Istanbul

phenomenon (of misreporting marital status for divorced and widowed women) also exists to some extent in other Middle Eastern countries, such as Syria and Egypt.[2]

---

[2] Soliman A. Huzayyin, 'Marriage and remarriage in Islam' in J. Dupâquier *et al.*, eds., *Marriage and Remarriage in Populations of the Past* (London, 1981), 95–111.

Figure 5.1, derived from table 5.1, shows the proportions single by age group for the two censuses. The curve showing proportions single for the 1907 census clearly stands out among all the others. Proportions single for women are very high at ages twenty to twenty-four and for men between twenty and thirty. This may be an indication of the fact that a period of delayed or declining nuptiality preceded the 1907 census (assuming that there had been no marked change in the age and sex structure of the Istanbul population during the twenty years prior to that census).

The age at marriage in Istanbul, particularly for women, is especially high by Islamic or Middle Eastern standards (see table 5.2).[3] This is clear when one examines the lower part of the table which gives the age by which 75 per cent of the women are already married (the last quartile). Urban marriage patterns in other major Middle Eastern urban centres such as Cairo and Damascus, for instance, only begin to display a similar age at marriage for females in the 1960s and 1970s, about half a century later than Istanbul.

This rather exceptional situation in Istanbul, as far as female age at marriage is concerned, is not matched by a similarly exceptional proportion of women never marrying. All but about 2 per cent of women get married before reaching the end of child-bearing age. Very few women remain single, but age at marriage is much higher than in other societies where such a high incidence of marriage prevails.[4] About 5 per cent of all men remain single. Marriage in Istanbul was, in sum, both late and universal.

The singularity of the northwest European marriage pattern is well known. It features a high age at first marriage both for men and for women (with a relatively small age difference between spouses), and a high proportion of people of both sexes eventually remaining single. In that system a remarkable stability in female age at marriage – at around twenty-five or twenty-six – is observed throughout the seventeenth and eighteenth centuries and up to the middle of the nineteenth

---

[3] Age at marriage in Istanbul also seems to have been very high compared to Turkish rural areas. The available data show that in rural areas age at marriage was considerably lower, both for men and for women, and that the age differential between spouses was low. See Duben, 'Turkish families', 75–97; Smith, 'The people of Tuscany'.

[4] This high incidence is also to be found in all Turkish Republican censuses after 1935, in which the percentage of women remaining single by age fifty is always around 1 or 1.5 per cent. For a summary of the European pattern, see K. Gaskin, 'Age at first marriage in Europe before 1850: a summary of family reconstitution data', *Journal of Family History*, 3 (1978), 23–36.

Table 5.2. *Singulate mean age at marriage for women in Istanbul and in various Islamic countries.*[a]

Libya 1964	16.8	Syria 1960	19.5
Algeria 1966	18.4	Egypt 1960	19.7
Iran 1966	18.4	Iraq 1957	20.1
ISTANBUL 1885	19.1	Jordan 1971	20.8
Turkey 1960	19.2	Syria 1970	20.5
Iran 1973	19.4	ISTANBUL 1907	20.5
Tunisia 1956	19.5	Kuwait 1975	20.7
Algeria 1954	19.5	Tunisia 1966	21.0
Last quartile			
Syria 1970	23.8		
Tunisia 1956	21.9		
Tunisia 1966	23.1		
ISTANBUL 1907	25.7		

Sources: M. Amani, 'La population de l'Iran', *Population*, 27 (1972), 411–19; R. Dixon, 'Explaining cross cultural variations in age at marriage', *Population Studies*, 25 (1971); M. L. Samman, 'La situation démographique de la Syrie', *Population*, 31 (1976), 1253–89; J. Vallin, 'La nuptialité en Tunisie', *Population*, Special number (1971), 150–4; 'Facteurs socio-économiques de l'âge au mariage de la femme Algérienne', *Population*, 28 (1973), 1172–7.

century. Men marry two to three years later. The proportion of people eventually remaining single seldom falls below 10 per cent for both sexes and is even frequently above 20 per cent.

The late nineteenth-century marriage pattern in Muslim Istanbul (a city much to the east of Hajnal's imaginary line 'from Leningrad to Trieste'), though resembling the northwest European in one respect, is very different in another. Mean age at first marriage is high. For men it is around thirty and shows no perceptible trend in the long run. It is even higher than the mean age for men in western Europe. The mean age at first marriage for women, though not as high as in northwest Europe, rises progressively from twenty to around twenty-three, significantly surpassing what is observed in other 'southern', 'eastern', or 'developing' societies. As far as celibacy is concerned, however, Istanbul stands far apart from Hajnal's northwest European pattern, with very low proportions of unmarried men and women in higher age groups, proportions more akin to those of southern and eastern European societies.

The interval of ten to fifteen years which separated menarche from marriage was, in northwest Europe, also a period when the woman was, perhaps, functioning with her maximum productive capacity. Women's 'professional' life-cycle was under the direct influence of the marriage pattern. This ten to fifteen year period was one when the young woman could contribute financially both to her natal and to her future household and, hence, one when marriage strategies were elaborated within the households. Since work activities of women outside the home were virtually non-existent in Istanbul up until at least the First World War, and family support was almost exclusively a male affair, it is in certain respects surprising to find such relatively high female mean ages at first marriage. High male age at marriage is, for the same reasons, less surprising and, indeed, follows quite naturally from this situation.

If we look at the 4,939 marriage records we have which span the period from 1905 to 1940, we see that the already relatively high female mean age at marriage shows a continuously rising trend throughout the period (figure 5.2), moving from around twenty in the 1900s to over twenty-three in the 1930s. This shows a rise of about a year a decade, a very fast one indeed. The centralized post-1905 Istanbul marriage records contain information on the pre-marital status of the bride (but not of the husband), so that we were able to sift first marriages from subsequent ones for women only.

When we look at the age at marriage of men, we see a salient feature of the so-called 'Mediterranean' marriage pattern: the rather high male mean age at marriage. Almost a third of the men in our sample had married after thirty-five, all marriages taken together. Though men marrying single women do so about 1.5 years below the general mean age, they still marry at about thirty, an age much higher than that which western Europe has experienced during the past two or three centuries.

The series of mean ages at marriage for men (whether it be all men, or only those marrying single women) shows no perceptible trend or tendency, except for a slight rise during the war years. The mean age at marriage for males between 1905 and 1940 is stable at around thirty. This, of course, means that there is a rather significant age difference between spouses, another feature of the 'Mediterranean' marriage pattern. Mean age difference for first marriages is 8.01 and the mode of the series is 7. The variance of this age difference is very high. For an overall mean age difference (for all order marriages) of 7.7, the standard deviation is 8.9. Increasing female mean age at marriage throughout this period has, of course, meant that the age-gap

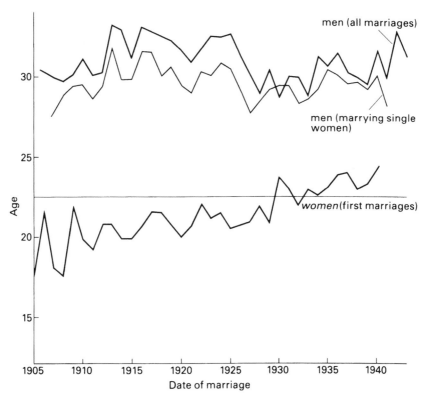

Figure 5.2 Mean age at marriage in Istanbul, 1905–40

Table 5.3. *Marriages and pre-marital status of the bride, Istanbul, 1905–40*

	Single	Widow	Divorced	Evermarried	Unknown	Total
N	2881	160	11	635	1272	4959
%	58.1	3.2	0.2	12.8	25.7	100.0

Source: Istanbul marriage registers, 1905–40.

between spouses narrowed from about ten years in 1905 to not more than seven years in the late 1930s – a demographic prerequisite for a more 'companionate' form of marriage.

Table 5.4. *Age at marriage and marriage order for women,*
Istanbul, 1905–40 (%)

Age	First marriages	Remarriages	Total
10–14	91.1	8.9	100.0
15–19	93.0	7.0	100.0
20–4	86.9	13.1	100.0
25–9	72.1	27.9	100.0
30–4	50.9	49.1	100.0
35–9	38.0	72.0	100.0
40–4	31.7	68.3	100.0
45–9	30.6	69.4	100.0
50+	40.5	59.5	100.0
Total	78.1	21.9	100.0

Source: Istanbul marriage registers, 1905–40.

Remarriage

The late Ottoman marriage records indicate, as we have explained, the pre-marital status of the wife, but not of the husband. Table 5.3 gives a distribution of all marriages in our sample according to the pre-marital status of the bride.

In addition to the usual categories, we have an additional rather vague and very large one, the 'evermarried' (*seyyibe*), which we have carried over from the Ottoman registers. Although certainly not a legally valid denomination it was, as one can see, very widely used. It is symptomatic of two related basic social attitudes at the time towards women of marriageable condition. The first is the marked social preference for never-married women or, in other words, virgins as wives as opposed to widows or divorcees. The second is the clear effort deliberately to disguise or misreport an undesirable marital status, especially that of divorcee. Table 5.4 gives the age distribution of first and of subsequent marriages.

Remarriage seems to have been quite frequent in Istanbul during our period. Indeed, one in every five marriages was a remarriage for the woman (21.9 per cent). The fact that late Ottoman Istanbul women did remarry with such regularity does not fit very well with a 'Mediterranean' type of marriage and the strong emphasis on virginity and posthumous faithfulness which it presupposes. But we know that remarriage was also very frequent in rural areas of central Anatolia. The corresponding percentages for Greece and southern Italy in the second half of the nineteenth century are 7.5 and 12 per cent, respectively. High percentages of remarriage would be understandable in a rural Turkish setting where remarriage was, just as in fifteenth-century Tuscany, an economic necessity. In rural areas in Turkey, households were relatively small and not especially complex. Since the institution of rural service was virtually non-existent in Anatolia, the labour lost by the death of the husband or of the wife might not easily have been replaced. Rates of remarriage and of polygyny might also have been influenced by local disequilibria in the sex ratio, massive male out-migration or mortality in wars.[5] But it is surprising to find the same remarriage pattern in a very highly urbanized environment.

One could argue about possible differential rates of registration between first and subsequent marriages. Higher rates of registration for remarriages are possible, since non-registration of a remarriage also in fact means non-registration of a previous vital event, the death of the husband or a divorce. The rather high proportion of remarriages in the fifteen to twenty-five age group seems to support this view. One cannot avoid the objection that, if there is some sort of a selection in the registration of first marriages, then a double or triple selection process must exist for subsequent marriages.

In fact the overall proportion of one to five for remarriages is not demographically unrealistic. Using an appropriate standard life-table (model South-Level 14) with an age at first marriage of twenty-one for women and thirty for men, it appears that about 12 per cent of women will be widowed before reaching the age of fifty. The proportion of women in any single marriage cohort who would, some time before the end of their childbearing period, become eligible for remarriage could not, with divorce and greater sex differentials in mortality at younger ages coming into the picture, have been very far from 20 per cent. Table 5.5 contains a more detailed tabulation of mean age at marriage and remarriage (the two columns for men indicate the pre-marital status of the wife).

The first thing which attracts our attention in the table is that the mean age at remarriage of widowed, divorced and 'evermarried' women shows a rising trend, especially in the second part of our period. This, we know, occurs against a background of a clear and continuously rising trend in female mean age at first marriage. Later first marriage for women has, therefore, meant, all other things being equal, later remarriage. Furthermore, the mean age at marriage of men marrying widows or divorcees, that is evermarried women, rises

[5] See Duben, 'Turkish families', 75–97.

Table 5.5. *Mean age at marriage and marriage order, Istanbul*

Marriage date	Women		Men	
	First marriages	Remarriages	First marriages	Remarriages
1906–10	19.83	29.00	29.25	36.06
1911–15	20.00	30.81	29.77	36.08
1916–20	20.85	30.76	30.38	37.50
1921–5	21.26	29.03	30.06	37.61
1926–30	21.53	30.38	29.81	37.63
1931–5	22.71	33.31	29.31	37.86
1936–40	23.66	34.16	29.68	41.24
Total	21.82	30.60	29.81	37.63
N	2881	806	2881	806

Source: Istanbul marriage registers, 1905–40.

in the same way from about thirty-six to more than forty-one. This means that throughout our period the age difference between men taking widows and divorcees as their wives remained practically unchanged (at around seven years), whereas for women entering into their first marriage, this age-gap kept narrowing, as we have seen.

The Ottoman Empire was in an almost continuous state of war from 1912 until its final collapse in 1922. Some of the figures in table 5.5 may acquire a different meaning when interpreted with that in mind. Men marrying single women (most probably largely single men themselves) in this period do so at a slightly later age than they did before or following the war years. The connection between this slight rise in male marriage age and the probable lesser availability on the Istanbul marriage market of younger single men during this period must, however, be supported by further and more extensive evidence before any final conclusions about the matter can be reached.

Spousal age and status

The Istanbul marriage pattern was one in which practically all women married by the time they reached thirty-five. One would imagine that as men got older they would be bound to marry widows and divorcees in increasingly greater proportion. Minimal age-matching constraints and the unavailability of single women of a suitable age would, one might expect, push in that direction. And yet table 5.6 shows us that this was not exactly how things turned out.

Table 5.6. *Age of husband and wife's pre-marital status,*
Istanbul, 1905–40

| Age of husband | Wife's pre-marital status | | | |
| | Single | | Evermarried | |
	N	%	N	%
10–14	28	87.5	4	12.5
15–19	260	86.7	40	13.3
20–4	733	89.3	88	10.7
25–9	794	85.4	136	14.6
30–4	465	76.0	147	24.0
35–9	274	72.1	106	27.9
40–9	234	58.1	169	41.9
50–9	67	43.2	88	56.8
60+	26	40.0	39	60.0
Total	2881	78.1	817	21.9

Source: Istanbul marriage registers, 1905–40.

Given the pattern of female marriage which we have isolated, and the level of mortality prevailing, a man marrying at a somewhat later age would, if he showed a marked preference for nevermarried as opposed to remarrying women, have to marry a woman considerably younger than himself. And that is what more than half the men marrying after forty did indeed do. With the age-gap between spouses for husbands marrying widowed or divorced women remaining the same (see table 5.5), and a slowly declining level of mortality throughout our period, the social preference for single women as marriage partners would normally result in increasing age difference between spouses for men marrying late. With time, the later a man married, the greater the age-gap was likely to be if he insisted on marrying a virgin. Many men seem to have done precisely that.

The age preference pattern can be more clearly seen by relating age difference at marriage according to the pre-marital status of the bride to the age at marriage both of the husband and the wife. We have not reproduced the tables here – they are too long and tedious. Looking at them from the point of view first of the husband, the later the marriage the larger the age-gap, but much more so when marrying a virgin. As expected, the mean age difference between himself and his wife for a man marrying at say forty is sixteen years if he is marrying a single woman, but only eight years if he marries a widowed or divorced woman. There is a gap of eight years here. The later the man's marriage, the greater the gap.

Looking now from the wife's point of view, widows and divorced women, when they remarry, marry men much older than those married by single women of the same age on the average. Between the ages of eighteen and forty, and for each single age, remarrying women marry men three to four years older than single women of the same age. Given the level of mortality, in that widows are more readily available at higher ages, there must have been, from the man's point of view a 'trade off' between the age of the bride and the preferred pre-marital status: either a younger widow, or a slightly older virgin.[6]

Returning now to the changes in female mean age at marriage, fig. 5.3 shows us the proportions single at various ages for three groups of female cohorts. It seems, as we have already indicated, that some basic structural changes in female nuptiality, though earlier in origin, took hold within the 1905–9 group of cohorts. Although there is no sudden jump in the mean age at marriage in this group, the age distribution of marriages has shifted considerably. The difference is more striking if we collapse the first two groups of cohorts. In the 1905–9 cohort group more than a third of the women were still unmarried at twenty-five, as compared to 22.5 per cent in the preceding groups. The proportions at age thirty are 16.7 and 11.4 per cent respectively. A much higher proportion of women belonging to this group of cohorts married at a relatively late age than did so in previous female cohorts.

Actual and ideal ages at marriage

There was a great gap between the relatively high and, for females, rising mean age at marriage in the first decade of this century and the perception of it on the part of the public. People had quite clear ideas about the 'proper' age for getting married, both for men and women. There are numerous references to this concern in the Istanbul press of the time, and the ideal age for getting married seems to have been one of the major demographic issues debated.

The references to the matter which appear in the press always stress what we now know is an imaginary discrepancy between the ideal and the reality. The prevailing opinion seems to have been that both

---

[6] We are making these evaluations in the absence of any data on changes in age and sex composition of the population of Istanbul as a whole. We have also had to disregard, in this particular analysis, the influence of the household structure and of its pattern of reproduction on the choice of a marriage partner.

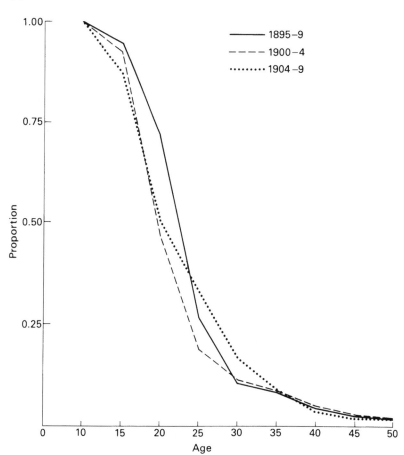

Figure 5.3 Proportions single in various groups of female marriage cohorts, Istanbul

men and women of Istanbul were getting married too early. There was also considerable concern about 'unbalanced' marriages, meaning marriages where there was a great age difference between spouses in one direction or the other. The uniformity and near unanimity of thinking on this topic throughout the period are quite striking.

The ideal age at marriage

One of the earliest references to the problem, dating from 1889 and published in the daily *Sabah*, is a good synopsis of prevailing attitudes.

It is worth quoting at length:

One of the factors influencing the increase and decrease of the population is marriage. Before getting married one should consider whether one is able to support a family. Together with a certain number of other conditions, the man and the wife should be in a position enabling them to raise, provide for, educate and secure a good future for their children. One of the conditions to be fulfilled concerns age. There are, for men as well as for women, proper ages for raising children. Women should not get married before they are eighteen, and men before they are twenty-eight. People unfortunately never conform to these conditions in our country. That an early marriage is a necessary condition for having a large family is an erroneous idea. An increase in population can take place not when a great number of children are born, but when these children are well looked after. Besides, when a girl marries too young, her procreative powers will be impaired by her first birth and she will not be able to have many children.[7]

There is no doubt that opinions on the appropriate age for marriage in Istanbul during the period were directly influenced by current ideas about the traditional gender division of labour at home. Other than for a handful of radical feminists who expressed their views in the periodical *Kadınlar Dünyası* (Women's World) published after the Young Turk Revolution of 1908, the traditional maternal and domestic roles of women and the provider role of men were little questioned.

The ideal marriage age for women was largely a reflection of the roles that they were ideally to have fulfilled after marriage, the traditional ones of managing the household, caring for their husbands and, most important of all, rearing children. In a considerable number of newspaper and magazine articles written about the suitable age for marriage, the major issue, as far as women were concerned, was the minimum age for bearing and rearing children. Marriage and pregnancy at too early an age were thought to be physically damaging to the mother, and both physically and morally damaging to the child. Immature women were felt to make poor wives and mothers. In 1895 the newspaper *Sabah* informs its readers that:

A girl may be fully grown up at thirteen or fourteen, but neither will her body be strong enough for pregnancy and childbearing, nor her mind able to understand and fulfil her responsibilities towards her husband and her children. For a girl, the suitable age for getting married is between eighteen and twenty.[8]

The criteria for the proper age for getting married for men reflected their primary domestic role as household head and economic provider

---

[7] 'Teehhül' (Marriage), *Sabah*, 355 (9 Muharrem 1307/5 September 1889), 2–4.
[8] 'Sin-i teehhül' (Age at marriage), *Sabah*, 1966 (3 Şaban 1312/30 January 1895), 3–4.

for the family. But this was not all. There also prevailed a sense, a social and cultural evaluation, of when men were considered mature enough to undertake marriage. This was something more than purely economic in origin and had to do with an evaluation of the criteria for social maturity in general. Here is a sample of some opinions on the matter:

Men become physiologically able to marry at thirteen or fourteen. But marriage should take place much later, both for hygienic reasons and because the necessary conditions for forming a family have not yet been fulfilled. Men reach mental and educational maturity between twenty-five and thirty.[9]

A young man who gets married before his time cannot adjust himself and behave wisely.[10]

In the cities men's education takes a long time. In addition, they have to perform their military service and establish themselves in a profession or occupation. Living conditions in the cities push young men to marry late.[11]

Males in Istanbul themselves seem to have had a clear idea of when it was best for them to envisage marriage. In 1918 the newspapers *Sabah* and *Vakit* began a special column for marriage advertisements. This rather extraordinary venture is one clear sign of the changing nature – the increased individuation – of the Istanbul marriage market. A young practising lawyer of twenty-seven placed an advertisement saying that he was looking for a spouse between the ages of twenty and thirty who could contribute to the household expenses, since he was still 'in the process of establishing himself (*taht-ı salâh altında*)'.[12] 'I am twenty-five years of age. At last I have begun to think of marriage' is the way one young man began his response to a survey of questions relating to marriage that the magazine *Resimli Perşembe* posed to its readership in 1926.[13] 'First a man must guarantee his future', writes another young man, named Reşid.[14]

Men did not seem to have considered themselves as fully mature, and well established before their late twenties. Another marriage advertisement in the newspaper *Sabah* makes a special point of informing potential spouses that the groom-to-be has matured socially (*hayat-ı*

---

[9] *Ibid.*
[10] 'Kaç yaşında evlenmeli' (What is the proper age for getting married?), *Vakit*, 854 (3 Receb 1336/14 April 1918), 3.
[11] *Ibid.*
[12] 'İlk ızdivaç talibleri' (First marriage advertisements), *Vakit*, 151 (21 Mart 1918/21 March 1918), 1.
[13] 'İzdivaç anketi' (Marriage survey), *Resimli Perşembe*, 58 (1 Temmuz 1926/1 July 1926), 7.
[14] *Ibid.*

içtimaiyeye vâkıf). This individual does not omit to mention his age, which was forty-one. A younger man, aged 'only' twenty-five, looks in 1918 for a spouse who 'is socially mature enough to consider marriage as a moral necessity'.[15] The mean age of those placing the twelve marriage advertisements which we were able to examine in the newspapers of 1918 is 29.3. Even the feminist magazine *Kadınlar Dünyası*, seems to have conformed to these social norms:

> To marry, a man must first have the necessary financial means, secondly he must be at least thirty, thirdly he must be cultured and civilized, fourthly, he must not be addicted to drinking or any other such vice, and lastly he should have had a good education.[16]

It was also commonly believed that premature marriages were conducive to higher divorce rates, as well as to higher infant mortality. For many of the anonymous writers in various newspapers and journals we have examined, as well as for the ordinary residents of Istanbul, be they male or female, getting married at a 'suitable' age was a *sine qua non* for forming a stable, healthy and fecund family. The concerns about marriage age expressed related, as we shall see, to the founding of enduring households, as well as to the more general demographic problems of increasing fertility and decreasing (child) mortality.

What in late nineteenth- and early twentieth-century Istanbul were the recommended or 'ideal' ages for getting married? There seems to have existed a wide consensus on the matter. As we have seen, a reference from the press dating from 1889 gives eighteen and twenty-eight as *minimum* ages at marriage for men and women, respectively.[17] As early as 1869, the magazine *Terakkî-i Muhadderat* publishes an article entitled, 'Marriage', extolling the virtues of the institution and recommending optimal ages for matrimony:

> Remaining single is like preferring savagery to civilization. The Europeans have calculated that between the ages of twenty-five and forty-five, the death rate [sic] is 28 per cent for singles and 18 per cent for married people. The proper age for matrimony is between twenty-four and forty for men and between eighteen and thirty for women.[18]

We have noted that in 1895 the daily *Sabah* put the recommended

---

[15] İzdivaç talibleri (Marriage advertisements), *Sabah*, 10209 (6 Receb 1336/17 April 1918), 2.

[16] Aliye Cevad, 'Aile – 4', (Family) *Kadınlar Dünyası*, 46 (19 Mayıs 1329/1 June 1913), 2–3.

[17] 'Teehhül', *Sabah*, 2–4.

[18] 'Teehhül' (Marriage), *Terakkî-i Muhadderat*, 13 (16 Teşrin-i sâni 1285/28 November 1869), 1–2.

ages of marriage at eighteen to twenty for women and twenty-five to thirty for men.[19] In a series of articles on 'Family life' published in a women's magazine in 1897, the advice given is quite precise:

The minimal ages at marriage recommended by medical authorities are, given our climatic conditions, twenty for women and twenty-five for men ... The most healthy and fruitful marriages are those contracted between the ages of twenty-five and thirty to thirty-five for men and twenty and twenty-six to thirty for women ... The age difference between spouses must also not exceed ten years.[20]

About a year later the same magazine, this time in an anonymous article, stresses again that 'in our temperate climate a girl should not be allowed to marry before she is seventeen or eighteen and a man before he is twenty-one or twenty-two'.[21] In 1901 the expert opinion of Dr Ruşçuklu Hakkı, as published in the daily *Sabah*, seems to sum up many of the recommendations already quoted:

Age at marriage for men should be no less than twenty-four or twenty-five. For a man's health nothing could be worse than too early a marriage ..., early marriage puts in jeopardy both personal and social position ... For women, marriage should not take place before twenty.[22]

The expert medical opinion of the time did not run counter to the recommendations adhered to by the public at large. In 1909 Dr Nusret Fuad published the first edition of *Izdivaç: Şerait-i Sıhhiye ve İçtimaiyesi* (The Hygienic and Social Conditions of Marriage). This book on home economics, puericulture and family life in general was quite a success and went through at least three editions. Dr Fuad writes the following:

The proper ages for getting married have been the object of long debates and discussions. Although it is strongly advised that both men and women do not marry before the ages of twenty-five and twenty respectively, marriage may also take place at around twenty-two or twenty-four for men and sixteen to eighteen for women only if, however, the physiological development of the future spouses is completed and if they are in good general physical condition.[23]

This near unanimity of opinion on the most suitable ages for mar-

---

[19] 'Sin-i Teehhül', *Sabah*, 3–4.

[20] Mehmed Hilmi, 'Hayat-ı aile – 5' (Family life), *Hanımlara Mahsus Gazete*, 117 (19 Haziran 1313/1 July 1897), 2–3.

[21] 'Kaç yaşında izdivaç etmeli' (What is the proper age for marriage?), *Hanımlara Mahsus Gazete*, 138 (13 Teşrin-i sâni 1313/16 November 1897), 4–5.

[22] Dr Ruşçuklu Hakkı, 'Elvah-ı hayat: 1 – izdivaca dair' (Tablets of life – 1: on marriage) *Sabah*, 4038 (16 Şevval 1318/6 February 1901), 3–4; 'Elvah-ı hayat: 2 – izdivaca dair' *Sabah*, 4047, 3–4.

[23] *İzdivaç*, 73.

riage persists well into the twentieth century after the collapse of the Empire, and into Republican Turkey. There is a remarkable stability in the recommended ages at marriage for men and women. In 1920 we read in the daily *Vakit* that:

The purpose of marriage is the perennity of the human race. People should marry therefore at the age most suitable for raising healthy children. The proper age for marrying is twenty-five for men and twenty for women ... Late marriages are just as harmful as ones too early. Besides, the ages of the spouses must be well-balanced. The husband should be from three to ten years older than the wife.[24]

Another expert medical opinion published in 1925 in a women's magazine says nearly the same: 'The mother should be between twenty and twenty-five and the father between twenty-five and thirty'.[25] Medical, hygienic, economic and demographic arguments all concur in defining more or less the same ideal ages at marriage throughout a period lasting for more than half a century. As late as 1927 one could read the following recommendations in a women's illustrated weekly:

The best age for marrying is twenty-four for women and twenty-eight for men. Scientists who have studied the problem in many civilized countries say these are the most suitable ages for marriage. They also add that marriages before the age of twenty almost always end in divorce. The probability of divorcing also seems to be high for marriages after the age of thirty.[26]

The discrepancy

Just as striking as the general agreement on the suitable ages for marriage is the almost as general dissatisfaction with what, in the absence of reliable statistical data, were perceived to be the actual ages at marriage then prevailing in Istanbul. We now know that the female mean age at marriage, which was around twenty at the turn of the century, gradually rose to twenty-three in the late 1930s, while throughout the period the male mean age at marriage showed no upward or downward trend and remained quite stable at around twenty-nine to thirty. The advice and recommendations which appeared in the popular press and in books and magazines during the late nineteenth and early twentieth centuries corresponded almost

---

[24] Galib Ata, 'Kaç yaşında evlenmeli' (At what age should one marry?), *Vakit*, 854 (2 Receb 1338/22 March 1920), 3.

[25] Dr Rifat, 'Yeni doğan çocuklara mahsus hıfzıssıha' (Caring for nursing infants), *Türk Kadın Yolu*, 4 (6 Ağustos 1341/6 August 1925), 5–6.

[26] 'İzdivaç için en iyi çağ hangisidir' (What is the best age for getting married?), *Resimli Perşembe*, 134 (14 Cemaziyülahir 1346/9 December 1927), 2.

exactly to the demographic realities of the time. Most of those who wrote on this topic, however, were somehow convinced that the practice – and the unspoken rule – in Istanbul was teenage marriage. Many of the articles and books we have quoted were written in criticism of teenage marriages and there is little doubt that, though most of them are anonymous, they were penned by the 'modernists' of the time.

The authors of two articles which appeared in 1889 and 1895 in the daily *Sabah* were careful to distinguish the 'ideal' from their own perception of the contemporary reality. We repeat part of the first of these:

There are, for men as well as for women, proper ages for raising children. Women should not get married before they are eighteen and men before they are twenty-eight. People unfortunately never conform to these conditions in our country.[27]

These rules [concerning age at marriage] are never respected and parents try their best to marry off their sons as soon as they are sixteen or seventeen. We frequently observe the unfortunate results of marriages contracted when both spouses are so young.[28]

We should point out here that the singulate mean age at marriage as it appears in our sample from the 1885 Istanbul census was 19.1 years for women. In 1897 *Hanımlara Mahsus Gazete* is just as clear: 'In our country many families have been ruined by an early marriage. Marriages too early are both morally and materially disastrous.'[29]

Kadınlar Dünyası naturally joins the chorus of attacks on premature marriages:

All the mothers in this country are delighted to marry off their children as soon as possible, girls between the ages of thirteen and eighteen and boys between eighteen and twenty. Early marriage is always a real physiological catastrophe.[30]

Demographic data from Europe were also sometimes marshalled as part of the scientific argument aimed at dissuading people from marrying too early. Young men marrying before the age of twenty were said to age faster, besides incurring rates of mortality 'six times higher

[27] 'Teehhül', *Sabah*, 2–4.
[28] 'Sin-i teehhül', *Sabah*, 4.
[29] Mehmed Hilmi, 'Sin-i İzdivaç' (Age at marriage), *Hanımlara Mahsus Gazete*, 99 (30 Kânun-i sâni 1312/11 February 1897), 2–3.
[30] Aliye Cevad, 'Aile – 2' (Family), *Kadınlar Dünyası*, 40 (13 Mayıs 1329/26 May 1913), 3–4.

than those of their counterparts who were single'.[31] Clearly, those whose object it was to give expert advice were also convinced that age at marriage was too low in Istanbul; otherwise, they would not have been troubled to make these recommendations with such insistence.

What is interesting is that while we now know that marriage practice at the time quite closely reflected the recommendations put forth for marriage age, people generally underestimated the age at which their contemporaries actually got married. Ignorance of actual marriage age at the time led people to arrive at rather pessimistic conclusions. They also most likely fell prey to the very common tendency that people have to take extreme – and therefore particularly striking – cases of very young marriage they have heard of and generalize from them to the population at large. This is still very often done today when discussing what marriage was like in the past in Istanbul. Most people have little sense of statistical accuracy.

This persistent discrepancy between real and perceived ages at marriage can be understood as part and parcel of a current of public opinion about population, health and fertility which was taking shape at the time. As we shall see, in the last quarter of the nineteenth century and the first quarter of the twentieth, the prevailing opinion in Istanbul was that the population (or at least the Muslim population) of the Empire was in sharp decline. It is now well documented that this was not the case. However, throughout this period, the press clearly reflected the serious concerns of both those in governmental circles and of the more enlightened sections of the Istanbul community on what was perceived to be a serious danger. War losses, massive population movements and the progressive disintegration of the Empire also focused public attention on a number of purely demographic issues which became more and more vivid.

A significant number of the recommendations on the proper ages for getting married which we have read make a special point of emphasizing the idea that marriage is a social and demographic, as well as a purely personal, event. They also insist on the idea that the overall demographic consequences of early marriages are at least as important as the personal ones, or those relating to the family. We recall that the article we read from *Sabah* of 1889 indicates that: 'One of the factors influencing the increase and decrease of the population is marriage.'[32]

---

[31] Elvah-ı hayat: 1 - izdivaca dair', *Sabah*, 3–4.
[32] 'Teehhül', *Sabah*, 2.

Again in 1901, to give one more example, Dr Ruşçuklu Hakkı starts
his admonition on the suitable ages for getting married by stating
that:

The question of marriage, before being a strictly personal one, should be
considered from a demographic and hygienic point of view. It would be
necessary to review the conditions of marriage in various parts of the world,
their relative endurability and productivity as well as the mutual influences
between morals, custom and marriage.[33]

The various recommendations and admonitions on the proper ages
for getting married should, therefore, be placed in their proper context. They were, in fact, part of an informal population policy which
tried to provide for child health and survival. An official population
policy was only to come in the late 1920s, after the founding of the
Republic. The fear of population decline was quite a common theme
in the press of Istanbul in the first decades of the twentieth century.[34]
In the absence of any significant publicly available statistical data on
population, the dissatisfaction with the demographic conditions of
the time – as construed by the press – was accompanied almost naturally by anxious and rather pessimistic evaluations of basic
demographic phenomena such as nuptiality, fertility and mortality.

The social and economic bases of late marriage

What were the forces that led men to marry so late in Istanbul and
that led women to marry at an increasingly advanced age? As we
shall see, they were economic, as well as social or cultural. In this
section we shall rest our primary focus upon the conditions affecting
the entry of males into marriage and the formation of households.
The conditions that provided the setting for the rise in female marriage
age will be taken up at some length in chapter 7, when we discuss
women's changing position in society. Female age at marriage will,
therefore, only be dealt with briefly at this point.

Much was written about the great expense of getting married and
of setting up a household during our period of focus. There is no
doubt that this was a constant concern of the Ottomans. What is
much more difficult to assay is the extent to which these concerns
actually influenced the decisions of individuals and of families about
the timing of marriage, and the ways in which these were affected

---

[33] 'Elvah-ı hayat: 1 - izdivaca dair', *Sabah*, 3.
[34] For a discussion of similar issues in Europe and the United States, see Michael
S. Teitelbaum and Jay M. Winter, *The Fear of Population Decline* (New York, 1985).

by the cost of living and other economic factors during the period. Few families have left records of such decisions; things of this nature are rarely recorded. And so we are left with the awkward task of extrapolating from the general statements made at different times about the economic hardships of marrying to the bases of the actual nuptial decisions that people have made.

Said Bey, the upper-echelon bureaucrat whose household we encountered in chapter 3, married off his eldest daughter, Semiramis, in 1908. In his meticulous fashion, he kept a detailed record of the nuptial expenses in his daily account book, an account that few others of his own highly literate class, let alone the masses of ordinary parents in Istanbul, would have kept. In its detail it is, however, a concrete example of the more general statements we encounter in the popular literature and even in the legal debates of our period of concern.

Dumont and Georgeon have calculated that the expenses of the wedding and of setting up house for the newlyweds represented the equivalent of nine months of Said Bey's salary and six months of the household expenditure for 1908. These were, without doubt, a great, yet apparently unavoidable, burden for him and his family. Only 9 per cent of the total outlay of 78,000 piastres (*kuruş*) was for the actual wedding expenses. Twenty-one per cent was spent on the wedding gown and the dresses and suits of the other family members. The trousseau accounted for 10 per cent of the money, whereas Said Bey spent 60 per cent, the equivalent of nearly five and a half months of his salary, on fixing up and furnishing the quarters of the newly-weds. The furniture alone cost him 25,000 piastres. All of this expense was for quarters in his own house, since his daughter and her husband were embarking on the uxorilocal residential arrangements that were looked upon with favour in Istanbul at that time. One can imagine what it might have cost to set up an independent household for the young couple.[35]

We do not have such detailed accounts of wedding expenses or of those for setting up house for other Istanbul families, but there is ample evidence that the entire project was an expensive one, a burden weighted relative to the social and economic position of the families involved. As one elderly lady explained to us, it varied, 'according to the place, the person and the family'. Charles White tells us that the *mehr-i muaccel* alone ranged between 5 thousand and 20,000 piastres even in the mid-nineteenth century.[36] This high figure

[35] Dumont and Georgeon, 'Un bourgeois', 166–7.
[36] White, *Three Years*, 202–3.

surely only represents the *mehr* of elite elements of society. White also relates the story of two European-educated brothers-in-law, quite obviously up-and-coming members of elite Istanbul society, married to the daughters of an important doctor who, unable to afford setting up two independent households, decided to share the burden of setting up house and live under the same (it should be noted, 'uxorilocal') roof.[37] Their domestic arrangements seem to have been quite awkward: though under one roof, they did not actually live as one family, since the Islamic dictates of modesty did not permit either man to see the other's wife, though the two women were sisters.

Marriage payments were viewed as an unnecessary burden by Ottoman modernists as early as the mid-nineteenth century. In 1844, the year White's book was written, an imperial decree made premarital payments (*mehr-i muaccel*) entirely voluntary.[38] It is doubtful that the decree had much effect since the payment of *mehr* follows the dictates of the Islamic religion, and few would have thought of opposing such things at that time. Again in 1862 attempts were made to control *mehr* payments, although with little effect due to religious opposition.[39] Marriage payments were an issue of controversy between modernists and the religious-minded in Turkey from at least the mid-nineteenth century to the early years of the Republic.

Despite this controversy, it does not seem that the major burden of marriage was the payment of *mehr*, although it was clearly of some significance, as we have seen in chapter 4. Nor was it the trousseau *per se*. While the wedding no doubt was a major expense, the real problem seems to have been the cost of setting up and managing a household. Despite this, Lucy Garnett claims that some Turks preferred to marry their sons to women who were brought up as slaves, when they could not afford the nuptial expenses they would have to incur if they were to choose a girl of their own social standing.[40] A sophisticated slave was, for some, preferable to marrying down. Slave is perhaps not the best rendering of the Turkish word, *cariye* (concubine, maiden, housemaid), which no doubt is what Garnett had in mind. *Cariyes* were girls, often of Circassian origin, sold off to the homes of the Istanbul elite as servants, with the understanding that they would be emancipated (*azat*) by their masters and properly married off when they were of age. They were very often raised with

[37] *Ibid.*, 215.
[38] Benedict, 'Hukuk reformu', 14.
[39] *Ibid.*, 15.
[40] Garnett, *Home Life*, 215–16.

the manners of proper Istanbul ladies, and, despite their lowly origins and status as a kind of servant, were thought of as attractive potential mates.

The real burden was, as we have seen from the case of Said Bey, setting up house. Part of this expense was shouldered by the parents of the groom in the form of the *ağırlık*, the Turkish word for the Arabic *mehr-i muaccel* which we have called a form of indirect dowry since it devolves, at least in principle, from groom's father to the bride. Though in principle the *ağırlık* belonged to the bride, in practice she might not get to use it directly. The *ağırlık* was sometimes used to defray the cost of the wedding expenses or towards furnishing the house. The second part of the *mehr*, the *mehr-i müeccel*, the sum of money the groom agrees to pay to his wife in the event that he divorces or predeceases her, is, as we have seen, not paid at the time of the wedding, though it is nevertheless a genuine commitment. Being so immediate, the *ağırlık* was, it appears, taken more seriously and was conceived of as a major outlay, the subject of serious bargaining between families. *Şıpsevdi*, Hüseyin Rahmi [Gürpınar's] famous novel set in pre-First World War Istanbul, provides us with a marvellous description of the intricacies of the bargaining process.[41]

It was the custom for the bride's family to provide her with a *cihaz*, which is the equivalent of a trousseau plus a dowry. In its most general sense the word *cihaz* refers to objects or equipment, and, when used in association with marriage, to the furnishings of the house. As we have seen, however, in the case of Said Bey's daughter, the costs of the wedding and setting up the young couple in their quarters could also be borne by the bride's family. Uxorilocal marriages in Istanbul often involved the marriage of a man of lesser status and wealth to a woman of higher position. Such unions were a form of mobility for promising young men.[42] Perhaps that is why Said Bey assumed a disproportionate share of the expenses.

Age at marriage of males in Beirut in the mid-1930s was very close to what it was in Istanbul, with a median of twenty-nine and a mean of thirty.[43] Prothro and Diab attribute this rather late age at marriage to 'the economic barriers to marriage, which keep decisions on these

---

[41] *Şıpsevdi*. (Istanbul, 1971 [1911]), 256–9.
[42] Eldem, *Osmanlı İmparatorluğu*, 210, 220–1. Carter V. Findley, 'Patrimonial household organization and factional activity in the Ottoman ruling class' in O. Okyar and H. İnalcık, eds., *Social and Economic History of Turkey (1071–1920)* (Ankara, 1980).
[43] Prothro and Diab, *Changing Family Patterns*, 30.

matters in the hands of elders'.[44] By economic barriers they mean the *mehr-i muaccel*, also the custom among Lebanese Muslims.

As early as the late nineteenth century, the Ottomans were concerned that heavy wedding and household formation expenses might be a deterrent to marriage, or lead to late marriage and, hence, population decline. *Hanımlara Mahsus Gazete* (Ladies' Gazette) took up the issue of the burdens of getting married in 1896 in a series of articles entitled, 'İzdivaç' (Marriage).[45] The articles are basically vignettes, or prototypical cases, portraying the financial difficulties besetting people from different walks of life embarking upon marriage. One of the most common portraits is of the young man who does not have the resources to support an independent household, yet can neither join his father's household nor that of his father-in-law because of their own precarious financial situations. And so the young man has to postpone his marriage. The author suggests that men contemplating marriage should be in a position to support their own wife and family and not depend upon either set of parents. The father of a daughter of marriageable age is, the author tells us, burdened with the thoughts of how to finance his daughter's *cihaz*. He could, we learn, use the *ağırlık* his daughter would get in order to pay for the *cihaz*; but then, the author asks, what sort of *ağırlık* could an impecunious father expect to attract for his daughter's hand? She too, we learn, must put off her marriage. It was not unusual for families to go into debt to finance the union of their children. These articles, as the author makes clear, reflect the difficulties of the less well-off. We have already seen what marriage means for the well-off in the case of Said Bey's daughter.

The war years after 1914 only exacerbated this situation. Ahmet Emin [Yalman's] 1920 front-page article in *Vakit* entitled, 'İzdivaç ve maişet' (Marriage and subsistence), was one of many which articulated the same concerns, by this time, however, at a higher pitch, since declining economic conditions combined with massive male losses at the front had created a situation which was felt to be a great threat to the Ottoman population.[46] Our informants emphasize the same theme: the expenses of setting up a household. And it seems that the expectation was that men be in a position to do so at marriage, and that they should be able to support their own family. As one

---

[44] *Ibid.*, 33.
[45] 70, 72, 73, 75 (Safer–Rebiyülevvel 1314/July–August 1896).
[46] 'İzdivaç ve maişet', 1.

informant phrased it: 'It was not easy for men to get married ...
setting up a household ... You know they rarely could move in with
the wife's parents ... They'd have to set up their own home.' It
is interesting that it was the uxorilocal arrangement that was the alternative to neolocalism in that elderly woman's mind.

As we have shown, men and women married quite late during
our period. We have argued that the costs of marriage and household
formation were an important factor in the timing of their marriages.
The decision about the right time to get married or to marry off one's
child was not, however, just an economic one. We have seen that
people had a sense about the proper age for doing so, and about
the social and economic attributes that would qualify an individual
for marriage. The popular author Ahmed Midhat lists the ideal quali-
ties of a late Ottoman male marriage candidate in his novel *Felâtun
Bey ile Râkım Efendi* : 'thirty years old, sensible, finished his schooling,
worldly-wise, and a captain in the army'.[47] In the novel, the wife-to-be
of this gentleman is a young woman of eighteen. The book was published in 1875, and its nuptial facts are close to the mean age at first
marriage for females and males which we have derived from the census held ten years later, in 1885.

There was little questioning of the traditional maternal and domestic
role of women throughout our period except by a handful of radical
feminists. The preferred marriage age for women was, as we have
seen, a function of the role that women were ideally to have fulfilled
after marriage – rearing children, caring for their husbands and running the household. In a number of magazine and newspaper articles
written about the proper age for marriage, the major issue for women
was the proper age for childbearing and child-rearing. There is a con-
stancy about these issues throughout the period.

If the criteria for women's marriage age were determined by the
perceived exigencies of childbearing and child-rearing, for men they
were based on their primary roles as household head and economic
provider. These values cut across the social strata. There was, as we
have seen, also a sense, a cultural evaluation of when men were considered mature enough to undertake marriage, of when they had completed the stage of life preparatory to that social watershed. We
observed that this cultural sense has to do with an evaluation of the
criteria for male social maturity, for when a man is believed to be

---

[47] *Felâtun Bey ile Râkım Efendi*, 136.

ready to undertake marriage. Late Ottoman or early Republican Istanbul men did not conceive of themselves as mature enough to support a family until they reached their late twenties. It was, as we shall see in chapter 7, expected that men marrying in Istanbul would be in a position to support their wives and families. We know that most did set up independent households at or soon after marriage, and did not have the benefit of their father's support even had they wanted or expected it.

Polygyny

A considerable literature on polygyny in Istanbul is available, written both by westerners and Turks. One must be cautious, however, when interpreting such work.[48] Most of the western observers of Ottoman society and of Istanbul were fascinated by stories about 'the harem and its mysteries' and looked upon polygyny as an exciting local curiosity. The situation of the Turkish writers was just the opposite. It is clear that in the atmosphere of westernizing social and legal reforms that characterized nineteenth-century Istanbul, views against the institution of polygyny were more readily expressed than those of the silent and most likely uncritical majority. The written sources and opinions on polygyny will, therefore, have to be referred to with caution. Most of the numerous impressionistic accounts of European travellers would, we feel, more suitably fit within a history of the Orientalist tradition in the West than as descriptions of reality in Turkey.

The data to be analysed here were also taken from the 5 per cent sample drawn from the main rosters of the 1885 and 1907 censuses for the five central districts of Istanbul. These data are, to the best of our knowledge, the first direct first-hand data of any statistical significance on polygyny within the Ottoman Empire.

Let us first look at proportions. Only 2.29 per cent of all married men in Istanbul were married polygynously. The percentage is 2.51

---

[48] Much sentimental, picturesque and romantic prose has been written in the Orientalist tradition about polygyny in Islam or the Middle East, particularly in past times, though few serious statistically based studies exist. The surveys conducted in the 1970s in certain Arab cities (Cairo, Damascus) are small and not very homogenous. They are, furthermore, for methodological reasons not comparable with our Istanbul data. See Huzayyin, 'Marriage and remarriage in Islam'.

per cent in the 1885 census and 2.16 in the one held in 1907.[49] This also means that around 5 per cent of married women were at any one time involved in a polygynous union. Even with that combined figure, the proportion of polygynous husbands is unexpectedly low compared to the 10 or 12 per cent rate for the Mormons in the nineteenth century, or to many African communities.[50] Even within the bounds of the Islamic world, these rates are comparatively low. Taking only a few Arab countries situated fairly close to Turkey (and all of which were part of the Ottoman Empire), we see that the percentage of polygynously married men was 3.4 per cent in Egypt in 1947, 7.5 per cent in Iraq in 1957 and 4.3 per cent in Syria in 1960.[51] These are the earliest 'official' statistical data available for these countries, and one would be tempted to assume that the percentages were higher at the beginning of this century.

How polygynous were these Istanbul marriages? Although marriage with up to four wives is permitted by Islamic law, the predominant form in Istanbul was very clearly bigamy. The intensity of polygyny was, therefore, just like its overall incidence, lower than expected. The average number of wives per polygynous husband in Istanbul was 2.08. Out of 108 polygynous husbands in our sample population, only nine had three wives, and none had four. The very low proportion of polygynous unions did not, however, tend to disappear with time, as we shall see.

There is quite a lot of evidence to show that the phenomenon, although a fundamentally accepted part of the basic marriage pattern, was meeting with increasing disapproval and even opposition in rapidly westernizing Istanbul throughout the second half of the nineteenth century. This trend was given legal sanction in the Family

---

[49] The census registers contain a special column, to be filled in for adult married males only, indicating the number of his wives ('*müteehhil olup olmadığı ve müteehhil ise zevcesinin müteaddit bulunup bulunmadığı*'). Though this information was required according to article 2 of the 1902 Census Regulations (*Sicill-i Nüfus Nizamnamesi*, 5 Rebiyülevvel 1320), the column was always left blank in the registers. The information on polygyny, therefore, had to be obtained indirectly, from a global evaluation of household structure case by case, from explicit or implicit relationships to the head of household, father's and mother's names of present children, etc. See Cem Behar, 'The 1300 and 1322 *tahrirs* as sources of Ottoman historical demography', *Boğaziçi University Research Papers* (Istanbul, 1985). The nature of these data brought about another limitation. Given the impossibility of record linkage in the Ottoman censuses, co-wives living in different households had to be recorded as monogamous. Only the *effectively cohabiting* polygynous couples could be reckoned as such. We do not think, however, that this has significantly affected the results of our analyses.

[50] See James E. Smith and Philip R. Kunz, 'Polygyny and fertility in 19th century America', *Population Studies*, 30 (1976), 465–80.

[51] Joseph Chamie, 'Polygyny among Arabs', *Population Studies*, 40 (1986), 55–66.

Law (*Hukuk-u Aile Kararnamesi*) of 1917 which in its article 38, specifies that a woman has, for all practical purposes, the right to forbid her husband from taking a second wife. A clause in the marriage contract stipulating that she will, in that event, automatically be granted a divorce, is admitted by the law as perfectly valid.

That article was an important step taken towards the legal limitation of polygynous unions, as well as a great novelty within traditional Ottoman Islamic law. The legislators attempted, probably under strong pressure from public opinion, to create obstacles to polygynous unions without departing completely from the basic framework of *sharia* law. Z. F. Fındıkoğlu thinks that this legal obstacle was specially designed to produce the same effect as an outright prohibition.[52] Such an effect would clearly have rested on the universal use of this provision by all women, and that would assume perfect equality between the sexes as far as legal information, assistance and power of law enforcement are concerned.

The pressure of public opinion against polygyny must have been quite strong.[53] This law, however, remained in effect for a very short period of time. In 1924–5 the first drafts of the Republican Civil Code were even more stringent. Special permission from a judge was needed in order to marry polygynously. Furthermore, the applicant had to prove that he 'needed' a second wife and also that he would be fair to both. Polygyny was made illegal in the final version of the Civil Code of 1926.

An interesting and unusual public opinion poll was carried out by the daily newspaper *Vakit* in 1925. In February 1925 the paper had printed a series of questions addressed to its readers and pertaining precisely to the articles on polygyny in the new version of the *Hukuk-u Aile Kararnamesi* then being debated at the Grand National Assembly in Ankara.[54] The questions asked were briefly as follows:

(1) Should polygyny be forbidden?
(2) Should polygyny be allowed for cases where the wife does not bear any children?

---

[52] *Essai sur la transformation du Code Familial*, 43.

[53] Similar restrictions on polygyny presently exist in Iraq, Syria and Morocco (see Chamie, 'Polygyny'). Ronald Jennings brings to our attention similar conditions (*şart*), either within the marriage contract or expressed as an oath taken by the husband in the presence of witnesses, existing in the sixteenth-century records of the *sharia* court of Cyprus. Ronald Jennings 'Divorce in the Ottoman *sharia* court of Cyprus, 1580–1640', paper presented at the Workshop on Turkish Family and Household Organization (City University of New York, New York, 23–5 April 1986).

[54] 'Yeni anketimiz: Taaddüt-ü zevcata taraftar mısınız' (Our new survey: are you in favour of polygyny?), *Vakit*, 2195 (25 Şubat 1340/25 February 1925), 4.

(3) Should polygyny be considered as a means to increase the population?

(4) Should Istanbul and the provinces be subjected to different legal systems concerning polygyny?

The inquiry seems to have been quite popular with the paper's readers. At least twenty letters were published in subsequent issues.[55] The answers to the last two questions were almost unanimously negative. These devoted readers of *Vakit*, most probably upper- and middle-class people, were able to separate their personal views on the matter of polygyny from either post-war Ottoman population problems or from the basic principle of the universality of the law. As for the first question, a clear majority of the answers (more than two-thirds of the letters published) were openly against the institution of polygyny as such. One or two letters coming from female readers stressed the issue of equality of the sexes. Letters coming from male readers underlined the idea that a normal and healthy family life and a civilized social life should exclusively be based upon a monogamous marriage system.

The answers to the second question, however, were not entirely consistent with the strong opinions and principles stated in the answers to question number one. The proportions of positive and negative answers were reversed here. Fewer than a third of the answers admitted of no exception to the principle of prohibiting polygyny. More than two-thirds of the respondents approved of the idea that the husband should take a second wife when, after due medical examination, the first wife proved to be sterile. Consent of the first wife was deemed necessary by the majority. The most frequent type of answer to the first two questions seems to reflect not too unfaithfully the basic attitude in Ottoman-Turkish public opinion of Istanbul towards polygyny in the last quarter of the nineteenth and the first quarter of the twentieth century: disapproval in principle, with, however, an approval for exceptional cases where polygyny became legitimated.

We also have some reason to believe that the relatively low incidence of polygyny was far from being a new, nineteenth-century development. Judicial records from the sixteenth century contain almost no

---

[55] See *Vakit*, numbers 2195 to 2213. This newspaper had not undertaken any such inquiry when the *Hukuk-u Aile Kararnamesi* was first published in 1917. At that time it had simply published long extracts from the law itself, had made a few comments and, most interestingly, had stressed that 'the problem of polygyny' has been 'solved' by this new law. See *Vakit*, 9 and 12 (30 Teşrin-i evvel 1917/30 October 1917 and 2 Teşrin-i sâni 1917/2 November 1917).

Table 5.7. *Marriage type and mean age at marriage,*
Istanbul, 1885 and 1907

	Men	Women	Age difference
Monogamous	31.95	22.71	9.25
Polygynous	36.21	23.32	12.89

Source: Istanbul population rosters, 1885 and 1907.

mention of polygyny, while divorces (from monogamous marriages) are amply represented.[56] Many European travellers also took note of the relative absence of polygyny. The situation in another great Ottoman city, Bursa, is also an illustration of the case in point. Fewer than 5 per cent of the men who died in seventeenth-century Bursa, and whose estates were recorded by the *kadı*, were found to be polygynously married.[57]

During the last quarter of the nineteenth and the first quarter of the twentieth centuries, we have seen that about five out of every 100 women either entered into a marriage as a second wife, or into one which would later turn into a polygynous union. There is no indication of a significant decline or change in this incidence. Polygyny was made illegal in 1926 and vanished from the records after 1930. It is well known, however, that it survived in eastern and southeastern Anatolia.

The mean age at marriage of 'polygynous women' is not much higher than that of monogamous ones but the same is not true for men (see table 5.7). Polygynous men marry on the average 4.25 years later than their monogamous counterparts. In addition, there is a greater dispersion in age difference for polygynous marriages. Assuming that no man married more than two wives and that the polygynous men went into their first (temporarily monogamous) marriage at the same age as the evermonogamous men, we calculate a new and corrected table (table 5.8). The point of this correction is that half the marriages of the men in the polygynous group of table 5.7 were in fact monogamous. These men were marrying their first wife. The same is true of half the 'polygynous' wives who, in fact, married monogamously as wife number one. Table 5.8, therefore, concerns

---

[56] See İlber Ortaylı, 'Anadolu'da 16. yüzyılda evlilik ilişkileri üzerine bazı gözlemler' (Some observations on marriage relations in Anatolia during the sixteenth century), *The Journal of Ottoman Studies*, 1 (1980).

[57] See Gerber, 'Social and economic position of women in an Ottoman City: Bursa 1600–1700'.

Table 5.8. *Marriage type and mean age at marriage*
(corrected), Istanbul, 1885 and 1907

	Men	Women	Age difference
Monogamous	31.95	22.71	9.25
Polygynous	40.46	23.93	16.53

Source: Istanbul population rosters, 1885 and 1907.

only those marriages involving wife number two, the truly polygynous ones.

The difference between the two tables is considerable: we have now isolated truly polygynous unions from either monogamous or temporarily monogamous ones. We are, as a result, able to see that women going into a polygynous marriage as wife number two do so slightly later than monogamous ones. Polygynous men marry their second wife on the average 8.5 years after the first, by which time these men are around forty. The age difference is, therefore, much larger with the second wife.

Given the relatively high level of mortality at the time, it seems therefore more than probable that polygynously married men or women in reality spent a relatively small part of their adult married lives in an effectively polygynous state. We have tried to calculate some average demographic features of the life of a 'standard polygynous union' of Istanbul in the last quarter of the nineteenth and the first quarter of the twentieth century. To simplify matters we selected an average polygynous man marrying for the first time at thirty-one and taking a second wife at forty. We have used standard life-tables (model South-Level 14) and have assumed, to simplify calculations (see table 5.8) that wife number one married at twenty-two and wife number two at twenty-four.[58]

Taking a look at the polygynous man himself, we see that by the time his second wife completed her childbearing period, he would be sixty-six and wife number one would be fifty-seven. The combined probability of this event is 0.41. Only 41 per cent of our polygynous men would have led a full polygynous life until both wives reached fifty. The real percentage is probably lower because of divorce. At

[58] 'South' life tables were chosen because of their structural similarity to mortality conditions in modern Turkey: very high infant and child mortality up to age five, 'normal' adult mortality and, after age sixty-five, relatively high levels again. F. C. Shorter has shown that 'split-level East' tables are a better fit to Turkish mortality in general. With regard to adult mortality, however (our only concern in these calculations), there is no great difference. See Shorter and Macura, *Trends in Fertility.*

thirty-one, men had a life expectancy of around thirty-seven years. However, by the time they reached age sixty-eight, more than a third of them would have suffered a bereavement, with the death of at least one of the wives. The remaining two-thirds would have lived around 75 per cent of their married life in effective polygyny (since they were monogamous in the first nine years of their married life).

Consider wife number two, who willingly married a polygynous man. If she lived to be fifty (the probability of which is 0.86), there is a fifty-fifty chance that her husband or her elder co-wife would have been dead by then. Therefore, more than half of these, so to speak, 'hard-line' polygynous women would be out of polygyny by the time they stopped bearing children. The 'innocent' first wife, who married a man who would later turn polygynous, had a probability of 57 per cent of reaching age fifty in a state of polygyny (still with no divorce rates in the picture). Life expectancy at twenty-two (the age at first marriage) was about forty-six years for women, and 60 per cent of them reached age sixty-eight. Only a fifth of those who did so were still in a state of polygyny. And even these would have lived only 80 per cent of their total married lives in effective polygyny.

It is possible to pursue this exercise and calculate tables of survival in a state of bigamy (there would be five possible exits from such a decremental table). The main point we would like to stress here is that the real incidence of polygyny, in terms of effective man/years or woman/years lived in a polygynous union, is certainly lower than our basic 2.3 per cent rate of polygyny in Istanbul. From a purely demographic point of view, a polygynous marriage brings with it greater risks of disruption than a monogamous one. Monogamous marriages last, on the average, longer than polygynous ones (or at least certainly longer than bigamous ones). A greater proportion of polygynous marriages are truncated before the end of the wives' child-bearing years.[59]

This sort of demographic calculation has the advantage of throwing a slightly different light on polygyny by viewing it as a process. Polygyny was only one possible alternative (and a very improbable one, at that) within a broader process of marriage, household formation and reproduction. The model suggests that the real impact of polygynous unions within the life-cycle experience of individuals in Istanbul might have been quite different from what a few dry, cross-sectional indices or percentages could ever suggest. Seen from that perspective,

---

[59] See Larry Logue, 'Tabernacles for waiting spirits: monogamous and polygynous fertility in a Mormon town', *Journal of Family History*, 10 (1985), 60–74.

Table 5.9. *Polygyny and marriage termination, Istanbul, 1885 and 1907*

Timing of termination	Mode of termination	Monogamous		Polygynous	
		N	%	N	%
Wife > 50		741	51.9	27	41.9
	Death of husband	391	27.4	24	36.9
Wife < 50	Death of wife	163	11.4	7	10.8
	Divorce	113	9.3	7	10.8
	Total	1428	100.0	65	100.0

Source: Istanbul population rosters, 1885 and 1907.

Table 5.10. *Marriage type and previous marriages of wife, Istanbul, 1885 and 1907*

	N of previous marriages of the wife			
	0	1	2	Total
Monogamous	2411	53	2	2466
	(97.7)	(2.2)	(0.1)	(100.0)
Polygynous	90	1	–	91
	(98.9)	(1.1)	–	(100.0)

Source: Istanbul population rosters, 1885 and 1907.

one might even be tempted, in the case of Istanbul, to speak, instead of polygyny, of successive though overlapping monogamies. A more or less similar pattern of polygyny was also observed in some of the Black Sea provinces of the Ottoman Empire in the middle of the nineteenth century.[60]

A significantly greater proportion of polygynous marriages last less than the whole childbearing period of the wives. This is confirmed by the reasons given in the registers for marriage termination in cases where the wife was not yet fifty. A significantly greater percentage of disrupted polygynous marriages are so because of the husband's death. The polygynous marriages in table 5.9 include all rank wives. If wives of rank two could have been separated from those of rank one, the difference would perhaps have been even greater.

[60] Justin McCarthy, 'Age, family and migration in nineteenth century Black Sea provinces of the Ottoman Empire', *International Journal of Middle East Studies*, 10 (1979), 309–23.

It seems, as Table 5.10 suggests, that polygynous men marry single women in at least as high a proportion as do monogamous men. This table reflects the marked social preference for never-married women as marriage partners that we already have noted. The point is that polygynous husbands are able to satisfy their preference in their second as well as in their first, temporarily monogamous, marriage.

If we classify the women involved in polygynous unions by their place of birth, a significant difference appears between those born in Istanbul and those born in the provinces of the Empire. A much smaller percentage of women in the former category (2.5 per cent rather than more than 4 per cent) were ever married polygynously. Women of urban origin, born in other prominent urban centres such as Bursa, Izmir or Salonica, also seem to have been involved in polygyny as infrequently as those born in the capital. The same relationship, however, does not hold true for men, for whom there is no significant difference in involvement in polygynous unions according to place of birth.

Statistical data on the social determinants or correlates of polygyny are very difficult to obtain. Subject to further investigation with possibly larger, or more purpose-specific samples, two categories of men seem slightly more involved in polygynous unions than others: 1) men with strong religious backgrounds or having a religious occupation and 2) high-ranking government officials.

About three out of every ten imams and *hafızs* (one who has memorized the Koran) in our sample had been polygynously married. The proportion is about 10 per cent for high-ranking government officials. About half of all polygynous men in our sample whose occupation was known are either part of the religious hierarchy or are top bureaucrats. The rest are evenly distributed among shopkeepers, artisans, tradesmen and professional people, with no marked tendencies, given the paucity of the numbers involved. Of men bearing a religious title (as set down by the census officials), such as *şeyh, hacı, molla, şerif, seyyid,* etc., 12.5 per cent were polygynously married.

One's district of residence within the city also seems to have provided a small clue as to polygynous tendencies. The basic rate of polygyny (2.3 per cent for Istanbul as a whole) is only 1.4 per cent in the districts of Fatih and Eminönü, that is in intramural Istanbul. This figure is more than twice as large (3.4 per cent) for the district of Beşiktaş, an area with a high concentration of palaces and luxurious *sahilhanes* (waterfront mansions) belonging to high-ranking military officers or bureaucrats.

An American journalist who travelled within the Ottoman Empire just before 1908 observed that:

Polygamy is much less common in Turkey than is generally supposed; the Koran permits a man to have four wives . . . But polygamy is an expensive institution . . . only when the first wife is childless is it customary for the Turk . . . and only when his primary desire for offspring is strong will a Turk add this extra expense and risk his own domestic peace.[61]

Fanny Davis is also of the opinion that the incidence of polygyny was high only among the upper ranks of society.[62] Polygyny was, she concludes, considered a very expensive undertaking, and even when the first wife was childless, or in the absence of a male heir, only the richest and the most powerful could freely indulge in it. Davis bases her judgement, however, not on any direct observations or quantitative data, but on a more or less exhaustive review of the writings of 'the more astute western observers' and on a certain number of personal interviews.

Are religion and wealth then the main determinants of the incidence of polygyny in the Ottoman capital? The question, as it stands, has no answer for lack of sufficient data. Perhaps the consistently greater inclination towards polygyny of the high bureaucrats and military is related to a sort of imitation-effect, a mimesis of the Ottoman sovereign's nuptial habits and prerogatives.[63]

Certain aspects of Istanbul polygyny, such as its influence on fertility or household size and composition, or its role and function within the household formation and reproduction system, are almost impossible to evaluate. In addition, it is difficult to obtain information on concubines (*cariyes*) from whom one could, according to Islamic law have legitimate offspring.[64] But here again, there is reason to suppose that *cariyes*, in this sense, were kept only within very restricted circles. The mimetic effect related to the palace may even have been more strongly felt here.

It is a common misconception that Istanbul Turks married very young, both men and women, though especially women, who were thought

---

[61] W.S. Monroe, *Turkey and the Turks* (London, 1908), 65–6.
[62] *The Ottoman Lady: A Social History from 1718 to 1918* (New York, 1986), 87.
[63] The surveys made in the Arab cities referred to above (n.2) seem to indicate that in those cultural areas education and socio-cultural status are inversely related to multiple marriages. See also Prothro and Diab, *Changing Family Patterns*, 182–6.
[64] The household records in the censuses of 1885 and 1907 contain a certain number of individuals labelled as *cariyes* (concubines, female servants). It is not clear from the records whether this generic term designates an actual concubine or simply a female servant, though the latter is the more probable alternative in most cases.

to have been one among several wives in a polygynous union. Nothing could be farther from the truth, as we have seen. The exigencies of setting up and supporting a household and cultural conceptions governing the definition of maturity were factors that led to a particularly late age at marriage for men, very much in line with a pattern common throughout the Mediterranean world in the past. Late age at marriage for men meant a late start in setting up a household, and had a direct effect on relations between the generations, between spouses and between parents and children. Though the late age at marriage for men does not have a direct effect on fertility, it does have an indirect one, and combined with a relatively late age at marriage for women, is part of a marriage system that works against large numbers of offspring.

Polygyny was very infrequent, as we have seen, and where it existed was often one stage in a series of marital experiences. The outcry against polygyny during the late nineteenth and early twentieth centuries in Istanbul was part of a larger ideological battle for egalitarian gender relations and a modern western way of life; it probably had little effect on what were rather low polygyny rates even at the beginning of the period. But polygyny had great symbolic value both for Ottomans and for many foreign observers of the Ottomans.

6

Fertility and birth control: Istanbul's particularities

In an analysis of the origins and social features of the Malthusian marriage system in England, Macfarlane selects Lady Mary Wortley Montagu's quite well-known observations on early eighteenth-century Turkey as the basis for his foil.[1] Non-Malthusian, familistic, and prototypically 'eastern', Turkey in past times stood for all that England was not: a society where women produced lots of children because their status and position in the family (the only status they had) was directly connected to their fertility. Statements such as Lady Mary's are often employed by writers like Macfarlane, not only as a measure of the non-western system, but also as a kind of base-line for future trends. Since, in this important case, the East is Turkey, the observations are of more than passing comparative importance to us. Let us look at what Lady Mary has to say in her role as ethnographer of the Turkish demographic past; there are two important passages:

in this country [Turkey] 'tis more despicable to be marry'd and not fruitfull, than 'tis with us to be fruitfull befor Marriage.[2] Without any exaggeration, all the women of my Acquaintance that have been marry'd 10 year have 12 or 13 children, and the Old ones boast of having had 5 and Twenty or 30 a peice and are respected according to the Number they have produc'd.[3]

Lady Mary was in many respects a fair and careful observer of urban Turkish life in the early 1700s. The first passage on Turkish cultural values concerning fertility seems to be an accurate representation of what we know to be the state of affairs in traditional Turkey, and is even so in many parts of the society today. But what she has to

---

[1] *Marriage and Love*, 60–1.
[2] Robert Halsband, ed., *The Complete Letters of Lady Mary Wortley Montagu* (Oxford, 1965), I, 372.
[3] *Ibid.*

say about the quantitative aspects of fertility is hardly credible – dis-
countable on the basis of internal evidence alone.

We do not know anything about fertility in Turkey before the late
nineteenth century that would meet rigorous demographic standards,
and given the nature of the available sources it is highly unlikely
that we ever will. So we must rely upon observers' accounts, both
local and foreign, about these matters. It is, therefore, important to
place observations such as those of Lady Mary in their proper perspective. We now know that the total fertility rate in Istanbul in the late
nineteenth century was below four, and there is evidence that it may
have been low even earlier. We do not know whether there was a
downward fertility slope extending from the past, or whether the
more dramatic decline of the early twentieth century was preceded
by a rather low plateau in the years (centuries?) prior to it. But it
does not seem at all possible that Istanbul fertility could have
approached the heights of Lady Mary's standard, even if we are to
interpret it as a kind of traveller's hyperbole.

Why would city people have wanted such large numbers of children? Istanbul, with a population of between 600,000 and 750,000 at
the beginning of the eighteenth century was perhaps the largest city
in Europe and the Near East.[4] In such a highly urbanized setting
it would not make sense for most people to raise so many offspring
(even assuming that only half of them survived, as she tells us).[5]
That their fertility ideology, as Lady Mary relates it, may have been
in conflict with the purported reality of their lives does not surprise
us. Perhaps that ideology reflected the interests and realities of the
elite (who could afford many children) and of rural society (where
the labour of children is imperative), and only corresponded roughly
to the family size aspirations of most city people. While, 'they reason
that the End of Creation of Woman is to encrease and Multiply',[6]
it is not clear why that has to mean an unlimited number of offspring.
Ordinary city people just had to ensure the survival of their families
and of themselves in their old age, and they would not need many
children to do that. Furthermore, they had available to them both
the religious sanction and the means and methods for limiting births
in the past, had they desired to do so. Urban Istanbul was no doubt

---

[4] Robert Mantran, 17. *Yüzyılın İkinci Yarısında İstanbul* (originally published in French
as *Istanbul dans la seconde moitié du XVIIᵉ siècle; essai d'histoire institutionnelle, économique
et sociale*, Paris, 1962) (Istanbul, 1986), I, 50.
[5] Halsband, *Montagu*, 372.
[6] *Ibid*, 363.

socially and demographically very different from rural Turkey; we know that such was the case in the 1930s, and we would expect the contrast to have been even greater in earlier times. Either Istanbul was far removed from the so-called eastern model, or the model needs a finer specification.

Fertility patterns, 1880–1940

It was in Istanbul that Turkish fertility first began to decline. The Ottoman capital was far ahead of the provinces in so many ways that it is not surprising that it was also a trendsetter in fertility patterns. The demographic data we have collected clearly support this conclusion. Indicators of some of the so-called 'proximate determinants' of fertility limitation – such as widowhood, breastfeeding and spousal absence – have, at least in quantitative terms, eluded our research net. There is little doubt that male absences and losses during the war years, and the resulting high rates of widowhood had a significant impact on fertility, but we have no way of measuring this effect, since there are no reliable data available on these phenomena. The evidence for other determinants, such as marriage age and deliberate birth limitation have, fortunately, survived. Many clear signs of volitional decline in fertility are there for us to see in addition to the quantitative evidence. Religious and traditional folklore clearly supported what was no doubt a widely diffused popular knowledge of birth-control methods. We shall examine these in some detail. That birth control was really practised – something our quantitative data tell us in an indirect fashion – is given greater credence by the traces it has left in the press and in other written sources of the time and, not least of all, by the oral testimony of some of those who have lived through the latter part of our period.

The Ottoman censuses of 1885 and 1907 give us cross-sectional age-specific fertility and total fertility rates of 3.5 and 3.88 respectively (see table 6.1). (See appendix to this chapter, on p. 189, for a discussion of the methodology used.) For the end of the period, the only data available to use as a basis for comparison with our Ottoman figures are Shorter and Macura's estimates for the 1940s (see table 6.2).[7] Shorter and Macura's indexes are combined rates for Istanbul and Izmir, the two major cities of the late Ottoman and early Republican decades. Though the population of Izmir was only about a third of

---

[7] *Trends in Fertility.* This table is extracted from the much larger table on page 51 of Shorter and Macura's book. These figures are the best available data for the period.

Table 6.1. *Age-specific fertility rates and total fertility rate in Istanbul*

Age groups	Age-specific fertility rates 1885	1907
10–14	0.014	0.010
15–19	0.125	0.096
20–4	0.135	0.180
25–9	0.207	0.178
30–4	0.149	0.182
35–9	0.059	0.098
40–4	0.010	0.024
45–9		0.008
Total fertility rate	3.50	3.88

Source: Istanbul population rosters, 1885 and 1907.

Table 6.2. *Turkish marriage and fertility indexes for 1945 by major divisions*

	CBR[a]	TFR[b]	C(m)[c]	TMF[d]	SMAM[e]
Istanbul–Izmir	18.7	2.41	0.558	4.32	22.4
Other cities	30.1	4.36	0.691	6.31	20.6
Rural areas	49.4	6.99	0.765	9.14	19.5

Source: Shorter and Macura, *Trends in Fertility*, 51.
[a] Crude birth-rate
[b] Total fertility rate
[c] Proportions married
[d] Total marital fertility
[e] Singulate mean age at marriage

Table 6.3. *Marriage and fertility indexes in Istanbul for 1907*

	CBR	TFR	C(m)	TMF	SMAM
Istanbul	29.4	3.88	0.707	5.49	20.5

Source: Istanbul population rosters, 1907.

that of the capital, there is no reason to suspect that nuptiality and fertility were very different in these two cosmopolitan centres. The corresponding indexes derived from the 1907 census data in Istanbul, which we shall use as a basis for comparison, are given in table 6.3.[8] C(m) is a synthetic index of proportions married for females – more precisely, the schedule of proportions married by age. When all women between the ages of fifteen and forty-nine are married (neglecting those very few who have done so before fifteen), the index is one; when none are married, it is zero. Assuming that there are no illegitimate births, this index provides a direct link between the total fertility rate and total marital fertility.[9]

Within the four decades from 1907 to 1945, the crude birth-rate in Istanbul had declined by slightly more than a third (36.2 per cent), total fertility by 37.9 per cent and marital fertility by more than a fifth (21.3 per cent). In addition, the singulate mean age at marriage[10] increased by almost two years, reflecting the continuous rise in female mean age at marriage from approximately twenty around the turn of the century to over twenty-three in the late 1930s which we discussed in chapter 5.[11]

If we break down the total fertility rate into its two components, proportions married and marital fertility, it is possible to show how this rather considerable decline in total fertility came about (see table 6.4). It seems that the fall in total fertility in Istanbul was due to changes in nuptiality as well as to a fall in marital fertility. In contrast to what happened later in Turkey, nuptiality and marital fertility contributed almost equally to the fall. After the 1950s the fall in marital fertility accounts for a much higher percentage of the decline in the Turkish total fertility rate. From the early 1950s to the 1970s only 19 per cent of the decline of the total fertility rate could be accounted for by the

---

[8] The crude birth-rate in this table is that given for the stable population we have been using for our estimations and corrections (model East-Level 10, r = average yearly growth-rate 0.05). See Coale and Demeny, *Regional Model Life Tables*. For the singulate mean age at marriage, see Behar, 'Nuptiality and marriage patterns'.

[9] See John Bongaarts, 'A framework for analyzing the proximate determinants of fertility', *Population and Development Review*, 4 (1978), 105–32. Illegitimate fertility is very difficult to document, or for that matter, to define in nineteenth-century Istanbul, and direct first-hand data are not available. However, one gets the distinct impression from the late Ottoman census data that bastardy and illegitimacy were quite negligible among the Muslim population of the city.

[10] See John Hajnal, 'Age at marriage and proportions marrying', *Population Studies*, 7 (1953), 111–32.

[11] Behar, 'Nuptiality and marriage'.

Table 6.4. *Components of fertility decline in Istanbul, 1907–45*

	TFR	C(m)	TMF
1907	3.88	0.707	5.49
1945	2.41	0.588	4.32
Average yearly rate of decline (%)	1.24	0.61	0.63
Relative contribution to the decline of total fertility (%)	100	49	51

Source: Istanbul population rosters, 1907; Shorter and Macura, *Trends in fertility,* 51.

changes in nuptiality[12]. The key role often attributed to nuptiality as a demographic regulator in so-called 'transitional' periods receives additional confirmation in the case of Istanbul. The frequency and timing of marriage and remarriage have indeed often played a crucial and regulatory role in relation to fertility in many diverse communities in the past.[13]

In order to properly understand this factor, it is necessary to view such a significant impact of changes in marital status and nuptiality patterns on fertility within the framework of the social, cultural and economic evolution of the Ottoman capital during the last decades of the nineteenth and the first decades of the twentieth century. As we shall see in chapter 7, quite radical changes took place in the attitudes and mentalities, and in cultural values bearing upon family, marriage, women and children. There is clear evidence that cultural, social and educational opportunities available to women improved to a significant extent.

The first four decades of the century witnessed a continuous and fast rise in mean age at marriage for women (whereas for men mean age remained quite stable) in Istanbul. This rise of unprecedented speed in female age at marriage has not yet been equalled either in Istanbul or in any other part of the country. The shortening of the average period of exposure to childbearing, which a later age at marriage brings, accounts for half the decline in fertility in Istanbul. It

---

[12] Shorter and Macura, *Trends in Fertility,* 38.
[13] See, for instance, Dupâquier *et al.*, *Marriage and Remarriage*. It remains an open question as to how to incorporate changes in nuptiality into explanations of a demographic transition which have traditionally been concerned almost exclusively with changes in fertility and mortality.

appears that the social and cultural aspects of marriage, family and household formation and reproduction were very different in Istanbul than they were, or are, in other parts of the Empire or the Republic. The inhabitants of Istanbul may be likened in this respect to those European social groups which Massimo Livi-Bacci very aptly called 'forerunners'.[14] In the 1920s and 1930s the women of Istanbul were marrying at an age which females in the rest of the country would barely reach half a century later.[15] As we shall see, Istanbul also stands in the same type of relationship to the rest of the country, as far as fertility is concerned.

In 1907 the city of Istanbul, with a total fertility rate of 3.88, fell well below the 'normal' range of total fertility rates of pre-industrial European populations. The lowest total fertility rates in Europe before the onset of industrialization seem to have been those of Norway, Sweden and Denmark in the 1770s and 1780s (4.1 to 4.2).[16] Furthermore, it appears that the less than moderately high fertility in Istanbul was very likely not a completely new phenomenon (see table 6.1, p. 162), and most probably could be extended farther back in time. There is, in addition to the age-specific fertility rates and the total fertility rate computed from the 1885 census, other cultural and social evidence to support this view. The singulate mean age at marriage for women was also lower in 1885 than in 1907.

Our contention is that the so-called 'transition' process in Istanbul – at least as far as the level of fertility is concerned – may in fact already have been under way even before the end of the nineteenth century, or that fertility may have been resting on a rather low plateau in Istanbul for an as-yet undefinable period of time in the past. Although cross-sectional indexes of fertility are not available – and our estimates from the 1885 census are far from being fully trustworthy – there is a certain amount of indirect demographic evidence which definitely points in that direction. When trying to document the decline in fertility in Istanbul in the first four decades of this century we have, at each step, encountered evidence leading to the idea of an earlier start in the fall of the indexes used. It is very clear from our data that the city of Istanbul was a pioneer in fertility decline, a process which became particularly marked in the early twentieth century. We must emphasize the fact that the total fertility rate of

---

[14] 'Social group forerunners' in Coale and Watkins, *The Decline of Fertility*, 182–200.
[15] Shorter and Macura, *Trends in Fertility*, 39.
[16] Ansley J. Coale and Roy Treadway, 'A summary of the changing distribution of overall fertility, marital fertility and the proportion married in the provinces of Europe' in Coale and Watkins, *The Decline of Fertility*, 31–80.

Istanbul in the first years of this century has not yet been reached in Turkey as a whole.[17]

Age-specific fertility rates and directly related indexes are not available for Istanbul during our period. The presence or absence of parity-related family limitation within marriage must, therefore, be inferred from other more indirect indicators. Our sample of married couples from the *esas defteris* (basic rosters) of the 1907 census enables us to calculate some of these.

We can derive a useful though indirect indication of parity-wise limitation of marital fertility from the age of women at the birth of their last child. Ansley Coale indicates that, in the absence of any parity-related family limitation, the mean value of this age would be approximately forty, and considers any mean age at the birth of the last child below thirty-six to be a good indicator of a significant degree of parity-oriented family limitation.[18] Major declines in this mean age would also be good indicators of the existence of birth-order related family limitation within marriage. The detailed birth histories of couples recorded during and after the 1907 census and presented in table 6.5 allow us to calculate this index with a great degree of confidence and accuracy.[19] The data are also reproduced in fig. 6.1, and fig. 6.2. The figures concerning the last group of birth cohorts were calculated from a rather small number of cases. Pre-1850 cohorts have been excluded for this reason.

Not only is the mean age of Istanbul women at the birth of their last child always – even for the female cohorts born in the 1850s – below what is considered as a lower limit for 'natural' fertility schedules, but this mean age shows a continuous and significant downward trend. We start with a mean age at the birth of the last child of around thirty-four for the first two groups of cohorts, and end up with a figure below thirty half a century later, with the cohorts born in the first years of the twentieth century. There has been an overall decline at the rate of almost a year per decade. Collapsing the data in ten-year cohort groups would eliminate some of the see-saw movements in the graphs.

Women born in Istanbul have a mean age of completion of childbearing which is almost uniformly below those residents born outside

---

[17] For the whole of Turkey, the total fertility rate was 4.05 in 1983. See *1983 Turkish Population and Health Survey* (Ankara, 1987), 63.

[18] 'The decline of fertility in Europe since the eighteenth century as a chapter in human demographic history' in Coale and Watkins, *The Decline of Fertility*, 11.

[19] Assuming, as we have, that birth underregistration is independent of a woman's birth cohort, her age at the birth of her child and birth order.

Table 6.5. *Age of women at the birth of their last child,*
Istanbul (completed marriages only)[a]

| Birth cohorts | Birthplace | | Total |
	Istanbul	Non-Istanbul	
1851–55	33.3	34.4	34.1
1856–60	31.5	34.8	34.3
1861–5	31.5	31.7	31.4
1866–70	30.1	35.3	34.3
1871–5	32.3	32.6	32.9
1876–80	32.4	32.3	31.8
1881–5	32.6	32.9	33.7
1886–90	30.8	29.5	30.0
1891–5	31.7	32.9	33.2
1896–1900	30.8	32.0	32.4
1901–5	29.7	28.5	29.6
1906–10	27.0	29.4	29.0
1911–15	28.0	27.7	28.3

Source: Istanbul population rosters, 1885 and 1907 (including
post-census recordings).
[a]The figure in the 'Total' column does not always fall in
between the other two. We frequently encountered women
whose places of birth was not known.

the city. The mean age for the earliest groups of cohorts of Istanbul-
born women suggests that fertility control within marriage must have
been going on in the city for some time before the end of the nineteenth
century. The only instance where the mean age of women at the
birth of their last child is significantly lower for women born out of
Istanbul concerns the period between 1912 and 1922 when Turkey was
almost continuously at war. Potential births within this 1886–90 group
of cohorts, at their most fertile ages, in all likelihood had to be postponed, never to resume again. Provincial women must have been
affected more than those born in the capital.

The last quarter of the nineteenth and first years of the twentieth
century thus witnessed an extraordinary diminution in the number
of effective childbearing years of Istanbul women. Their mean age
at first marriage had risen from around twenty at the turn of the
century to twenty-three towards the end of the 1930s. Not only did
these women marry increasingly later, but they also stopped bearing
children much earlier. The childbearing years of Istanbul women were
being cut simultaneously at both extremities: by later marriage at one
end and by a higher concentration of births within the first years

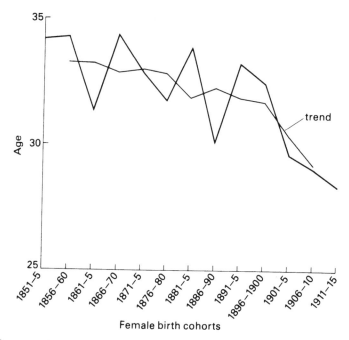

Figure 6.1 Mean age at birth of last child, Istanbul (completed marriages)

of marriage at the other. This funnel effect resulted in an extraordinary shortening of the number of effective childbearing years, which declined from about twelve to thirteen years on the average for those women marrying around the 1900s, to less than seven or eight years for those born soon after the turn of the century.

Of the thirty-three women we interviewed whose children were counted, nineteen had achieved either one or two live births and ten had had three, giving us a figure of 2.36 live births per woman as an average. Their mean age at the birth of their last child was quite low, at around twenty-seven. This means that, given what we know of the mean age at marriage at the turn of the century and soon thereafter, terminal family size was reached only eight years after marriage on the average. Of the twenty-nine women whose age at the birth of their last child was known with certainty, twenty-one had stopped bearing children within ten years after marriage and, of these, nine had reached final family size within five years after marriage. The mean length of the effective childbearing period was 8.3 years for those born before 1905 and 7.6 years for those born in 1905 and after. These already low figures might indeed even be a slight overestima-

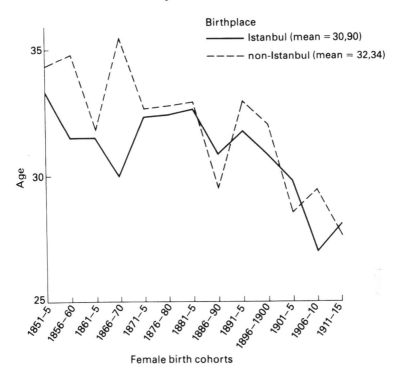

Figure 6.2 Mean age at birth of last child, Istanbul (completed marriages)

tion, since our sample of elderly Istanbul women was biased against married women with no children.

The other indicator of the prevalence of parity-related fertility limitation within marriage is provided by the Coale and Trussell index *m*, which measures the deviation of the age structure of fertility from the standard schedule of a population with 'natural' fertility.[20] We have calculated *m* within a number of marriage cohorts in table 6.6. These figures are also reproduced in figure 6.3. The complete absence of paritywise family limitation would have resulted in a value of *m* equal to zero (plus or minus 0.1). A value of *m* of approximately 0.2 would then indicate a very moderate level of fertility control within marriage. Here too, not only does our *m* index start off at a level

[20] Ansley J. Coale and James Trussell, 'Model fertility schedules', *Population Index*, 40 (1974), 185–258; 'Technical note: finding the two parameters that specify a model schedule of marital fertility', *Population Index* (1978), 203–13. The *m*s for Istanbul have all been calculated by the indirect method described by Coale and Trussell in their second article cited above.

Table 6.6. *The Coale and Trussell*
index m *for various female*
marriage cohorts in Istanbul

Marriage cohorts	m
1861–70	0.248
1871–5	0.400
1876–80	0.250
1886–90	0.447
1896–1900	0.400
1906–10	0.448
1911–15	0.611
1916–20	0.669
1921–5	0.645

Source: Istanbul population rosters,
1885 and 1907 (including post-census
recordings).

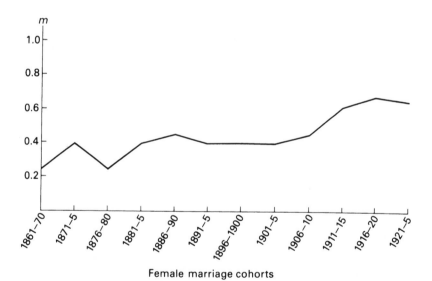

Figure 6.3　*m* within various marriage cohorts, Istanbul

which already suggests the existence of a certain degree of control
over fertility, however modest, but it also indicates a continuous rise
throughout half a century of successive marriage cohorts. As one
might expect, *m* moves up to a higher level of control among the

Table 6.7. *Percentage of completed family size attained after N years of marriage in Istanbul*

Marriage cohorts	N	
	5	10
1886–90	27.0	44.8
1891–5	31.1	49.7
1896–1900	28.3	43.3
1901–05	36.7	60.2
1906–10	33.5	55.7
1911–15	33.5	65.7
1916–20	31.7	59.3
1921–5	34.4	60.4

Source: Istanbul population rosters, 1885 and 1907 (including post-census recordings).

groups of marriage cohorts immediately confronted with the war years.

When parity-oriented family limitation within marriage prevails, marital fertility will show a steeper decline as age increases, because many couples will have achieved the ideal, desired or accepted number of children. If there is no significant change in the degree of fertility control, and assuming no significant change in age at marriage, the distribution of births between marriage and the end of the childbearing period should remain more or less stable in successive marriage cohorts. If, however, there is increasing use of parity-related fertility control, the proportion of births occurring within the first N years of marriage to completed family size will also tend to increase. Births will have a tendency to occur sooner after marriage and the distribution of births will, all other things being equal, be skewed towards the beginning of the relevant period of time, that is towards the time of marriage. An increasingly smaller percentage of total births will then occur in the latter part of married life. Findings of this sort would lead to the conclusion that an increasing degree of control over fertility within marriage had been taking place. And that is, indeed, precisely what we observe in Istanbul. As indicated in table 6.7, the 1886–90 group of marriage cohorts achieved 27 per cent of their completed family size within five years of marriage, and about 45 per cent within ten years. For the 1921–5 group of marriage cohorts these percentages were 34.4 and 60.4 respectively.

As fig. 6.4 also indicates, births are concentrated in the first years of marriage in an increasingly greater proportion. This is another indi-

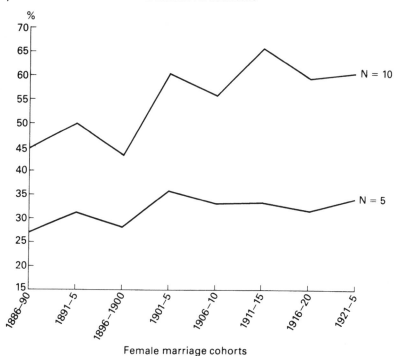

Figure 6.4 Percentage of completed family size attained after N years of marriage, Istanbul

cation of the increasing prevalence – or possibly the more efficient use – of parity-related means of birth control within marriage. It is clear, however, that concentration within the first ten years of marriage increases much faster than that within only the first five years. This may be an indication that family limitation practices were motivated not only by the desire to avoid further pregnancies once the desired family size had been achieved, but also in order to postpone the first birth or births.

One last indication of the extent of birth-control practices within marriage is revealed by the parity progression rates within various female marriage cohorts. In the absence of radical changes in nuptiality or mortality, the probability of having an Nth birth among families already having N-1 living children will depend directly on the existence of parity-related family limitation. Each parity progression rate expresses, within a group of marriage cohorts with N children, the probability of having at least one more child. Table 6.8 and fig. 6.5 indicate that there was first a fall in the probabilities above rank two

Table 6.8. *Parity progression rates, Istanbul (completed marriages)*

Marriage cohorts	a0	a1	a2	a3	a4	a5
1860–80	0.906	0.760	0.678	0.586	0.585	0.412
1880–1900	0.866	0.775	0.684	0.504	0.509	0.448
1900–25	0.834	0.686	0.598	0.500	0.531	0.471

Source: Istanbul population rosters, 1885 and 1907 (including post-census recordings).

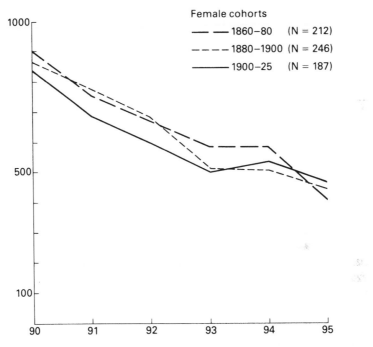

Figure 6.5 Parity progression rates, Istanbul (completed families only)

in the 1880–1900 group of marriage cohorts, and then a quite general-ized decline in the last group of cohorts.

The relatively low fertility rates in Istanbul appear to have been widely diffused throughout the social fabric of the city. They were not just limited to the elite or to the most modern, westernized strata of society. The total number of children ever born to wives of civil servants (the most modern of the occupational groups, both in terms of mentality and of their connection with a modern bureaucratic wage economy) was approximately 4.4 in 1907. For the artisans and shop-keepers, who we know to be socially the most conservative elements of Turkish urban society, and who were still largely embedded in a more familistic subsector of the urban economy, the number was only slightly higher at 4.6. While artisans and shopkeepers, like their more modern-minded fellow Istanbul residents, were also controlling their fertility, they were doing so in a slightly less marked way. The wives of civil servants concluded their childbearing years at the age of twenty-eight, whereas the wives of artisan-shopkeepers waited approximately three more years until thirty-one.

In general, the variation in fertility rates between social strata in a certain type of location in Turkey is much less than that between the same strata in different types of locations. This appears also to have been the case in the recent past, though it seems that as one moves back in time the differences between strata become somewhat more pronounced. Studies in Taipei suggest that this may also have been a feature of Chinese society.[21] In 1968 the fertility of artisan-shopkeepers, the one group perhaps most in need of a family labour force in the urban context, was 2.4 in the metropolises of Istanbul, Ankara and Izmir, 3.4 in other cities, 4.0 in towns and 3.9 in villages. The breaking-point is between the metropolis and the city,[22] not between occupational classes, whose fertility by and large shows a great consistency by location. The fertility of the major metropolitan occupational groups in 1968 was more or less the same except for a slightly lower rate among the professionals and a higher one among the workers. In cities there was also a great consistency at a higher fertility level, with, for example, city professionals – who in the metro-polis have a very low fertility rate – exhibiting a higher rate than metropolitan artisan-shopkeepers.

Sixty years earlier the artisan-shopkeepers of Istanbul had a slightly greater number of children than the bureaucratic white-collar strata in the city, though presumably much lower than that of their peers in small towns or rural areas. There is no demographic evidence of a strikingly prominent group of 'forerunners' in the decline of fertility in Istanbul in the sense that Livi-Bacci, Stone or Banks,[23] each in

---

[21] Sophie Sa, 'Marriage among the Taiwanese of pre-1945 Taipei' in S. B. Hanley and A. P. Wolf, eds., *Family and Population in East Asian History* (Stanford, Calif., 1985).

[22] Serim Timur, 'Socioeconomic determinants of differential fertility in Turkey' in J. Allman, ed., *Women's Status and Fertility in the Muslim World* (New York, 1978).

[23] Livi-Bacci, 'Social group forerunners'; Stone, *Family, Sex and Marriage*; Banks, *Prosperity and Parenthood*.

very different circumstances and times, have described for European societies, though bureaucratic and elite classes during the late Ottoman period seem to have been, to some extent, in the forefront of the movement.

Although impossible to document and analyse in greater detail, the almost uninterrupted period of war and devastation from 1912 to 1919, and the immediate demographic consequence of those years – spousal absence, postponed marriages and births – appear to have provided the bases for a significant dip within an otherwise generally declining trend in nuptiality and fertility. This is documented in the various tables and graphs we have presented, and displayed in a critical fall in the parity progression rates, a jump in m and a sudden fall in the age at birth of their last child for the female cohorts most affected during those years.

The direct demographic effects of the war were, however, much more muted than in the other belligerent countries, perhaps because of the great strength of the pioneering demographic trends already under way in Istanbul. In countries like France or England, for instance, the effects of wars on fertility and nuptiality were quite significant. Demographers, such as Hajnal or Henry, have shown that for female cohorts affected by the wars in those countries, the demographic indices concerning the timing and incidence of marriage and childbearing were deeply and irreversibly affected.[24] Despite several major military mobilizations, direct losses, military occupation of the city and a state of war which lasted longer than anywhere else (from 1912, the onstart of the first Balkan Wars, to 1919 when the army was demobilized), nothing of the sort seems to have happened in Istanbul.

It appears, then, that fertility had entered a period of rapid decline in Istanbul during the first four decades of this century. A drop in total fertility of more than a third was also accompanied by a substantial rise – of about three years – in female mean age at marriage. The city of Istanbul was no doubt a 'forerunner' within Turkey's 'fertility transition' process. As we have noted, the levels of total fertility and the crude birth-rate in Istanbul at the beginning of our century have not yet been reached for present-day Turkey taken as a whole. Some of the data lead us to believe that the relatively low level of fertility in Istanbul was not a completely new phenomenon

---

[24] John Hajnal, 'Births, marriages and reproductivity in England and Wales, 1938–1947', *Papers of the Royal Commission on Population Section A* (London, 1950), 307–22; Louis Henry 'Perturbations de la nuptialité résultant de la guerre 1914–1918', *Population*, 2 (1966), 273–333.

in the 1900s. Many of our indices suggest that, at least for Istanbul-born women (as compared to latecomers to the capital city), this low fertility pattern was already well established in the last quarter of the nine-teenth century. Whether fertility in Istanbul-born women was on the decline before the turn of the century, and for how long, or whether it had maintained a long-standing stability at a rather low plateau up to the late 1800s, are questions which, at least for the time being, cannot be answered.

Family planning

Muslims were, from the very early years, able to think about contra-ception quite differently than Christians and Jews. Musallam, in his study of Islam and contraception, argues that this difference in per-spective on these crucial issues rests on the complete absence in the Koran of any reference to contraception.[25] Since there is nothing like the Christian concept of the church in Islam, the Islamic attitude largely rests on the opinions of jurists and of the various schools of legal interpretation. The starting-point of the Islamic doctrine on contraception is the example of the Prophet Muhammad himself as given in the *hadith* (the reports of his words and deeds). There are a large number of *hadith* bearing on the issue of contraception, more specifically on *azil* (*coitus interruptus*).[26] Let us look at an example of one of these: 'The Jews say that coitus interruptus is minor infanti-cide, and the Prophet answered, "the Jews lie, for if God wanted to create something, no one can avert it".' The conclusion to which one comes from a reading of the relevant *hadith* is that the Prophet knew about the practice and did not forbid it – that in fact he permitted it – and that, in any case, it is not possible to tamper with God's infinite power.

Muslim jurists were almost entirely concerned with one contracep-tive method: *coitus interruptus*. Well into the twentieth century, the history of contraceptive methods in Islam was largely the history of withdrawal. When, in 1960, the Turkish government decided to begin implementing its newly developed family-planning policy, the opi-

---

[25] This section relies heavily on the important works by Norman Himes and Basim Musallam. Cf. Norman E. Himes, *Medical History of Contraception* (New York, 1936); Musallam, *Sex and Society in Islam*. See, also, Mahmoud Seklani, 'La fécondité dans les pays Arabes: données numériques, attitudes et comportements', *Population*, 15 (1960), 831–56.

[26] Musallam quotes those occurring most often within Islamic jurisprudence.

nion of the Directorate of Religious Affairs (*Diyanet İşleri Başkanlığı*) on the religious legitimacy of various means of contraception was sought. In its response, it is quite significant that the theologians of the Directorate chose to mention only withdrawal:

azil, which can be considered as a method of contraception, has been accepted as licit by the majority of religious authorities and doctors of the law, including many companions of the Prophet. To practice it the consent of the wife is necessary, except in a situation of war or if there is a danger that the child cannot be brought up in favorable circumstances.[27]

The careful wording of the highest Turkish authority on religious matters is an accurate reflection of the Islamic attitude towards contraception in general.

Muslim jurists by and large viewed contraception as an acceptable practice, one which was, however, not to be recommended unless there was a pressing need to avoid pregnancy, although it was not really prohibited even when there was no such need for it. Economic reasons occupied the forefront in the medieval understanding of 'need'. The desire to protect family property and its devolution, and the wish to protect the health and the well-being of children, are the most frequently quoted motives for practising contraception. One school of Islamic jurisprudence, the *Hanbalis*, went so far as to prescribe contraception as mandatory in some particularly unfavourable economic, social and political circumstances.

The most thorough analysis of the religious permissibility of contraception was made by the great theologian and jurist al-Ghazali (1058–1111), whose opinions later became the standard for most of the subsequent jurists and commentators. For al-Ghazali it was only the motive that could be objectionable, never the act of trying to prevent pregnancy in itself. The permission to practise withdrawal is not, for him, dependent on these motives:

Ghazali supported contraceptive practice with one's wife or concubine to protect her from the dangers of childbirth, or simply to preserve her beauty. He especially favoured the economic motives for birth control . . . to safeguard one's property . . . A more general motive that he also supported was the wish to limit the family to a manageable size . . . Ghazali strongly disapproved of people who practised contraception through the fear of having daughters . . . [or of] women who practised it because they disliked pregnancy, or because they had a fetish for absolute cleanliness, or simply because they did not

---

[27] Opinion of the Directorate of Religious Affairs, 19 December 1960, as published in *Research on the Practice of Family Planning in Turkey* (Ankara, 1961).

want to bother with childbirth and nursing ... It was the intent that was
objectionable, not the actual prevention of pregnancy.[28]

There was no simple and straightforward Islamic religious position
on abortion, and the opinions of the jurists were far from being as
consistent as those concerning contraception. Such opinions were in
most cases based on the religious view of foetal development. All
Muslim jurists held that the foetus was 'ensouled' and would only
become a real human being after the fourth month of pregnancy,
or, more precisely, in 120 days. All the jurists unconditionally prohibited abortion from then on. After 'ensoulment', abortion was strictly
prohibited because it was equivalent to murder. The only exception
reluctantly admitted was when childbirth might constitute a vital
danger for the mother. As for the early 'unformed and unensouled'
embryo, some schools of Islamic law tolerated abortion in the case
of real necessity, while others condemned it absolutely and considered
it as a human tampering with the divine process of uninterrupted
creation and destruction.[29] Musallam believes that 'on the whole,
abortion was religiously tolerated'.[30] Indeed, as he also points out,
there was no dominant view on the matter and he quotes as supporting
evidence the fact that medieval, Islamic medical, popular and erotic
literature treated contraceptive and abortifacient means and recipes
as if they were two aspects of the same process – birth control.

The sanction of contraception by religious opinion enabled medical
and other writers to discuss all manners of birth control quite freely.
Medieval Islamic physicians, for example, gave extraordinary attention to birth-control techniques. Such eminent physicians as Ibn Sina
(Avicenna) and al-Razi (Rhazes) cited literally hundreds of methods
for preventing pregnancy. In his now classic work on the history of
contraception, Norman Himes identifies sixty-one different 'Islamic'
contraceptive techniques which he classified as: those to be taken
orally, magical means, suppositories and tampons, techniques used
by the male and miscellaneous techniques.[31] Adopting the same
classification, but covering a wider range of medical texts, Musallam
identifies no fewer than 112 different techniques.[32] Most of these were
'reasonable or functional', and only five of them relied exclusively
upon magic. Many of the medieval Islamic contraceptive techniques
bear a close resemblance to those within the corpus of the 'folk'

---

[28] Musallam, *Sex and Society in Islam*, 22–3.
[29] Himes, *Medical History of Contraception*, 136; Musallam, *Sex and Society in Islam*, 57–8.
[30] *Sex and Society in Islam*, 57–8.
[31] *Medical History of Contraception*, 158.
[32] *Sex and Society in Islam*, 88, 104.

contraceptives of Istanbul. In addition to the contraceptive techniques recommended directly by the highest Islamic medical authorities, Musallam also covers a type of intermediate popular-scientific Islamic literature which he calls 'erotica' and which is, in a sense, a more faithful reflection of actual popular knowledge and of the practice of contraception. Here, too, Musallam counts no fewer than seventy-seven different techniques and recipes, only six of which can be clearly considered as purely 'magical'.

The use of magical and folk means to control fertility has drawn the amused attention of both social historians and demographers. The existence and the extensive use of such means are often regarded as proof of the lack of real contraceptive knowledge and of the inevitable failure of all attempts to limit fertility in the absence of the necessary technology.

Accounts of Istanbul's sexual folklore contain a great number of magical recipes, potions, amulets, religious incantations and prayers destined to curtail a woman's ability to bear children. Among the recipes there is, for instance, a concoction of grated broom mixed with honey to be taken by the woman just before intercourse and a potion made by boiling earthworms in water to be imbibed by the husband.[33] There are also detailed accounts and descriptions of written charms to be put in triangular amulets and worn by the woman in order to prevent her from becoming pregnant. Some of these amulets were used to completely curtail pregnancy from then on, and others to avoid becoming pregnant at a particular time.[34] The first type was to be worn permanently by the woman and the second only to be slipped under her pillow after sexual intercourse. Some of the sources indicate that these folk means were used only by women who had already borne a certain number of children, but this view is contradicted by the very nature of the various charms and amulets used in Istanbul.

For the traditional historian or demographer, the magical or folk contraceptive is nothing but an ineffective contraceptive. Recent historical and anthropological research, however, has begun to shed quite a different light on these supposedly irrational, inefficient and non-scientific practices.[35] Anthropologists suggest that the use of such means, far from signifying sheer ignorance or simple-mindedness,

---

[33] Mehmet Halit Bayrı, İstanbul Folkloru (Istanbul Folklore) (Istanbul, 1972), 212.
[34] İsmet Zeki Eyüboğlu, Anadolu Büyüleri (Anatolian Magic) (Istanbul, 1978), 132–3, 140–1.
[35] Angus McLaren, Reproductive Rituals: The Perception of Fertility in England from the Sixteenth to the Nineteenth Century (London, 1984).

implies a complex view of conception and fertility in which both the physical and the spiritual are involved.[36] It is significant from our point of view that the men and women of Istanbul in the past quite commonly attempted to control their fertility, and that they often did so by use of a conceptual framework clearly deeply rooted in an indigenous folk etiology of conception, one alien to many features of contemporary scientific thought. Quite obviously, then, earlier generations in Istanbul did attempt to space or limit births, and they were far from being totally indifferent 'to the real dangers repeated pregnancies could pose to the health and happiness of the household'.[37]

We have good reason to believe that well before the end of the nineteenth century in Istanbul, the control of conception was, therefore both *thinkable* and *possible*. The traditional and folk contraceptives are part of a psycho-physiological view of conception in which men and women are considered as having at least some control over fertility. Furthermore, it would be erroneous to surmise the general inefficiency of these methods. It is very likely that these 'charms' may, in many instances, have been used along with other fertility controlling strategies, such as extended breastfeeding, sexual taboos and withdrawal, the knowledge or the practice of which is more difficult to document for the pre-First World War period. That this is not very far from the mark is also supported by the fact that these charms, amulets and potions are quoted in most written sources alongside many forms of more familiar 'positive contraception'.

People in Istanbul definitely knew about the 'barrier' method by which a mechanical or chemical device is used to prevent the meeting of egg and sperm. Many sorts of pessaries were known. Their effectiveness would, of course, be related to their ability to immobilize or kill spermatozoa. The most frequently quoted pessary is that made of salts of lemon, containing citric acid. The use of ammonium chloride (called *nişadır*), of aloes (called *sarısabır*, also used as a purgative), of asphodel root (called *çiriş*, also used for making glue), of tannin and of soap are also frequently mentioned, as well as pessaries made of various combinations of all of these elements. Although some of these may be qualified as attempts at sympathetic magic (a purgative being used in order to purge the womb of male semen), there is no doubt that the acidic substances or astringents used (lemon, tannin or soap) are highly efficient as spermicides. The mixture of magic

---

[36] *Ibid.*, 5.
[37] *Ibid.*, 147–8.

and of traditional popular medicine which this list of 'charms' reveals should serve as a precaution against any hasty judgement concerning their inefficiency.

Birth control, deliberate and fortuitous

Abortion

Significant glimmerings can be collected from various sections of the Ottoman press which indicate a growing awareness of the widespread use of means of family limitation. The great majority of the articles published concern abortion. In 1889, an article entitled, 'Memâlik-i Osmaniye'de tezayüd ve tenâkıs-ı nüfus' (Population increase and decrease in Ottoman lands), was published by the daily *Sabah* (one of the newspapers with the widest circulation at the time). The anonymous author of the article upholds the mistaken though widespread view that the population of the Ottoman Empire had considerably declined since 'olden times', and stresses that this decline had been particularly dramatic for the Muslim population, as compared to other religious communities.[38] Alongside very high infant mortality, venereal diseases and 'disproportionate and thoughtless marriages', the author does not hesitate to mention abortion as one of the main reasons for what he perceives as the especially rapid decline of the Ottoman Muslim population.

Another long article appears the same year in *Sabah*. It is simply entitled, 'İskat-ı cenin' (Abortion), and contains the following:

Abortion is perhaps not the most important reason for population decline, but it is surely the most terrible. Abortion is not an error or an offence. It is a terrible crime. We know that there are people who try to silence their conscience by pretending that 'the product of abortion is not really a child, it is only a clot of blood'. But they are wrong. A child is a creature of God from the very moment it is conceived. Article 193 of our Criminal Law concerns abortive practices. If a pregnant woman, with or without her consent, uses or is made to use drugs or any other means in order to abort, the perpetrator of this crime is punishable by six months to two years imprisonment. If the criminal is a doctor, a surgeon or an apothecary, he would be sentenced to hard labour. . . . In summary, it is absolutely necessary to prohibit abortion.[39]

---

[38] 'Memâlik-i Osmaniye'de tezayüd ve tenâkıs-ı nüfus' (Population increase and decrease in Ottoman lands) *Sabah*, 346 (1 Muharrem 1307/28 August 1889), 2–3.

[39] 'İskat-ı cenin' (Abortion), *Sabah*, 349 (3 Muharrem 1307/30 August 1889), 2.

This piece was published in August 1889. The Criminal Law to which it refers was passed – with article 193 prohibiting abortion – in 1858 and was very strongly inspired by the Napoleonic Penal Code of 1810. It appears, therefore, that illegal abortions were still, more than thirty years after so strict a prohibition, sufficiently numerous to draw the attention of the Ottoman press, usually so prudish and so sensitive to various moral and sexual taboos. The wording of this long article in *Sabah* also suggests that the public at large must have been quite ignorant of the prohibition.

We have good reason to consider this as an indication of the way abortion was perceived in general by the Muslim population of the Empire. Foreign observers' reports seem to confirm the popular attitude of relative indifference towards abortion. We read in a British Consular Report of 1878, that, 'The Mussulman population of the Osmanli race in Constantinople ... resort[s] to means for procuring abortion to an alarming extent'.[40] The report insists on the role of abortion in the perception of a relative decline of the Ottoman Muslim population. Similar reports were also written concerning the western Anatolian towns of Bursa and Izmir. The British Consul in Izmir as early as 1861 wrote about, 'the horrid system so generally practised amongst the Mussalmans of causing abortion which they do not consider as criminal.'[41]

Once more in 1889, in order both to edify and to warn its readers, the newspaper *Sabah* publishes an account of the proceedings of a court case concerning abortion in France. The mayor of the city of Toulon had had an affair with the wife of a French officer posted to the colonies and, after having made her pregnant, tried to obtain an abortion. *Sabah* reports that the case had aroused great interest in France and had been played up in the press there. These echoes in the French press, probably largely due to the personality of the accused, are transformed by *Sabah* into an edifying example for non-compliers to the law on abortion in Istanbul.[42] Unfortunately, we have not encountered any information on the means used to perform abortion in Istanbul, nor are there estimates of the number of such abortions performed. In a section on abortion in Dr Nusret Fuad's

---

[40] *Parliamentary Accounts and Papers*, 74 (1878), as quoted by Issawi, *Economic History*, 23.

[41] Foreign Office 198/14, as quoted by Issawi, *Economic History*, 23.

[42] 'İskat-ı cenin muhakemesi' (A court case concerning abortion), *Sabah*, 500 (6 Cemaziyülahir 1307/28 January 1890), 3.

zdivaç: Şerait-i Sıhhiye ve İçtimaiyesi, after severe condemnation on moral and hygienic grounds, the author writes: 'We constantly hear of cases of abortion causing the death of many women. Such illegal abortions are performed with the help of numerous instruments, all as unimaginable as they are unhygienic.'[43]

The private memoirs of an Ottoman Jewish gynaecologist practising in Istanbul after the turn of the century contain many cases of medical complications following attempts at self-induced abortion.[44] The frequency and the fierceness of the attacks on abortion clearly indicate that, whatever their real number or their demographic weight or impact may have been, abortion was widely perceived to be a means to limit the numbers of births.

'It is impossible not to be opposed to the abortive practices of our women', writes the author of an article in a women's magazine in 1904.[45] 'Such practices have greatly increased recently,' he continues. The author also mentions 'the terrible events in Arnavutköy [a village in the suburbs of Istanbul] following certain abortive practices'. The reference here is to a police-department case involving the death of a woman following an attempt at self-induced abortion. Apart from global condemnations of abortion as such on social, moral and hygienic grounds, specific concrete references in the Ottoman press to what was most likely quite a widespread practice only seem to emerge when an instance has sustained the attention of the police or the courts.

The widespread use of abortion was also viewed as a serious problem in the highest governmental circles. Sultan Abdülhamid himself seems to have been aware of the extent of abortive practices in Istanbul and to have taken steps towards a stricter prohibition. As early as 1889 the Sultan became alarmed at 'the unhealthy practices of abortion which have been increasing recently in our dominions and have been causing a decrease in the Muslim population',[46] and had asked the government to present him with 'a proposal for necessary measures to be taken'.[47] We know that on 5 January 1891 the government handed him a memorandum containing the proposed legal measures. On 16

---

[43] *İzdivaç,* 84.
[44] We thank İrvin Cemil Schick for permitting us to use the notes and memoirs in his family's possession.
[45] 'Çocuk düşürenlere ibret' (An exemplary case for abortionists), *Hanımlara Mahsus Gazete,* 27 (5 Receb 1322/15 September 1904), 422–3.
[46] Istanbul, 'Başbakanlık Arşivi' (Archives of the Prime Ministry), İrade-Dahiliye, 97491. Many thanks to Dr Selim Deringil who discovered the relevant archival materials.
[47] *Ibid.*

January 1891 Abdülhamid returned the memorandum to the government for amendment and improvement. A few months later, on 16 September 1891, the Sultan issued an official imperial rescript (*irade*) strongly urging the government 'to consider the matter urgently and present the results to the Imperial Threshold'.[48] Abdülhamid had, in all likelihood, been impressed and influenced by the articles on abortion which had been appearing in various newspapers and journals around that time. Unfortunately, we have no information about the new proposals subsequently brought to Sultan Abdülhamid's attention by his government. In the end, however, we do know that no new legal measures were taken with regard to this matter.

Abortion continued to be perceived as a serious problem during the 1920s. When an Economic Congress convened in Izmir in 1923, just months before the founding of the Republic, one of the participants called for the, 'outright removal of the calamity of abortion'.[49]

Nearly half the Istanbul women we interviewed admitted to having had at least one abortion. Some of them had more abortions than live births. All of these abortions (the legal ban on abortion in Turkey was lifted only in 1983) were performed by doctors in relatively good hygienic conditions. Since most of our informants were from the middle- and upper-middle classes that is not surprising. We do not know very much about the conditions for the lower classes, though no doubt many women from such backgrounds underwent abortions in less than desirable conditions. All the women, nevertheless, without fail, considered abortion only as a solution of last resort, never to be used lightly or without careful deliberation. This was not due to a moral stance against abortion, but to practical concerns. All of those interviewed had either witnessed or had heard of various cases of insalubrious attempts at self-abortion practised by women in Istanbul. At least two women implicitly confessed to having taken drugs (quinine?) to induce an abortion – and, indeed, of having succeeded. 'I also used to lift heavy things, make violent bodily movements, dance, and the like', all for the same purpose, Nezahat Hanım confesses. Another informant from a very poor family background, the mother of three children with hardly any other knowledge of family-planning methods, told us that 'we lifted and carried heavy things and the child "fell"'.

---

[48] *Ibid.*
[49] *Türkiye İktisat Kongresi – İzmir 1923: Haberler, Belgeler, Yorumlar* (The Turkish Economics Congress – Izmir, 1923: News, Documents, Interpretations) (Ankara, 1968), 273–333.

Breastfeeding

Breastfeeding is not, strictly speaking, a birth-control technique. Though it may act as a determinant of fertility by virtue of its effect on postpartum amenorrhea, and hence birth intervals, it is not often conceived of by the women who practise it as a way of limiting births. This seems to have been the case in Istanbul during our period. In other words, alongside the deliberate efforts that many people were making to limit their family size in late Ottoman and early Republican Istanbul, we must account for the impact of fertility-related activities, such as breastfeeding, which were unconnected in the minds of most women with their probable end result. Unfortunately, since breast-feeding data for the population at large do not exist, we cannot measure their impact on fertility.

One finds quite a number of references to breastfeeding in the Otto-man press. It appears that it was quite common practice to breastfeed children for a considerable period of time. As early as 1869, we read in a popular journal warnings to its female readers not to wean their children, 'before they have sixteen fully grown teeth',[50] an event which does not usually take place before they are eighteen months old. In fact even more precise guidelines were given: 'The suitable time for weaning children is between their eighteenth and twenty-second month.'[51] All publications for women agree on these points and seem to reflect what was no doubt the predominant practice at the time.

Most of these articles, however, are basically concerned with the proper feeding and the health of children and not directly with the possible effects of prolonged breastfeeding on future pregnancies or on overall fertility. There is no written evidence which indicates that breastfeeding was perceived as an efficient obstacle to pregnancy. However, a popular dictum, one which still has currency in Istanbul, gives the following sensible advice: 'süt korur' (milk protects). The long-standing practical experience of the people of Istanbul must have taught them that some breastfeeding is better than no breastfeeding at all. This popular belief is not in any way connected to a post-partum sexual taboo. There was in fact no such post-partum sexual taboo in Istanbul except perhaps for the first forty days after childbirth, a kind of period of confinement (*loğusa*) when the new mother was

[50] 'Süt emen çocuklar' (Breastfeeding babies), *Terakkî-i Muhadderat*, 3 (28 Haziran 1285/10 July 1869), 7.
[51] 'Çocuk büyütmek: memeden kesme' (Child care: weaning) *Hanımlara Mahsus Gazete*, 2 (27 Zilhice 1320/27 March 1903), 30–2.

accorded special care. In the first book that we know of on contraception ever to be published in Istanbul, the question of the effects of breastfeeding on fertility is very carefully worded:

Question: Is pregnancy possible during breastfeeding?

Answer: It is said that a new pregnancy is impossible during breastfeeding and especially during the first three or four months. But I have known many women who have become pregnant while breastfeeding a two-month-old child. It is not right, therefore, to trust breastfeeding as an obstacle to pregnancy.[52]

Though they did not think of it as a means of birth control, all our informants breastfed their children if they had the milk, and for an average of about one year. They took breastfeeding as quite a natural maternal activity, and, indeed, were usually rather surprised when asked if there were women who were opposed to the practice. The majority of these women were from the middle- or upper-middle classes, the wives of upper-echelon bureaucrats or businessmen, and the types of women among whom, if it existed, one would expect to find opposition to breastfeeding. But they felt no antipathy to it, nor did they use wet-nurses. Perhaps some of the women of that generation, or their seniors, the first generation of modern-minded Europeanized women, who came into maturity around the turn of the century, were opposed to breastfeeding, as were some of their European bourgeois peers, on the grounds that it was uncivilized. We have encountered a few references to this in the interviews, though it does not seem to have been widespread. The press throughout our period was unanimous in encouraging women to breastfeed.

Other methods

The written sources in late Ottoman Istanbul contain precious little on other means of fertility control. Nothing is to be found, for instance on sexual abstinence or on withdrawal, a method well known to Istanbul couples. As we indicated earlier, the first fully fledged modern publication on contraception appeared only in 1927. It is a rather free translation with a long introduction by Dr Fuad, Secretary General of the Society for the Protection of Children, of Margaret Sanger's famous *Family Limitation*. This small booklet of about fifty-five pages starts with the well-known social, hygienic and eugenic arguments in favour of a limited number of healthy, well-cared-for children

---

[52] Dr Fuad, *Gebe Kalmamak İçin Ne Yapmalı?* (What Should One Do to Avoid Pregnancy?) (Istanbul, 1927), 50.

instead of a large number of children, which could be a burden both to families, to the state and to society at large. The author and translator then follows through with rather detailed descriptions of and recommendations for the use of such family-planning methods as the condom, the vaginal diaphragm and various types of vaginal douches, as well as many kinds of pessaries. The section of the book dealing with pessaries begins by noting that, 'pessaries are the most frequently used means of protection from pregnancy'.[53]

The emphatic insistence of Dr Fuad on vaginal pessaries (*fitil*) assumes a knowledge – if not the use – of these devices on a wide scale in Istanbul. Dr Fuad attempts in this section of the book to urge women using 'folk' pessaries to replace them with more 'scientific', and, presumably, more efficient ones. The making and the use of the new pessaries are described in great detail. Among the ingredients of the various recipes recommended are citric acid, boric acid, quinine, salicylic acid and cocoa oil – some of which we have seen in the traditional potions.

The press and other publications do not seem to have played a significant role in the dissemination of information on family planning. None of our informants ever mention having *read* anything about family-planning methods. It is interesting to note that the only precise source of information ever mentioned by any of these informants, 'my mother-in-law had taught me', is a reflection of the most traditional mode of transmission of such information.

As we have noted, none of our written sources ever mention the existence of the practice of withdrawal. However, it appears that it was generally known and widely practised in late nineteenth- and early twentieth-century Istanbul. We learn this from many of the interviews which we conducted with elderly middle-class Istanbul women. The interviews have provided numerous insights into the knowledge and the practice of birth-control methods in the latter part of our period. Most of our informants were born around the turn of the century or immediately thereafter, were married in the late 1910s or early 1920s, and had all stopped bearing children by 1940, the greatest portion of their childbearing period having been in the late 1910s and 1920s.

These women all demonstrate a considerable knowledge of all the family-planning methods available at that time and are, in the majority of cases, willing if not enthusiastic respondents to questions concerning their personal experiences. Almost all state that they knew of

[53] *Ibid.*, 46–7.

no friends or relatives in Istanbul who had had more than two or three children. All agree in saying that the couples they knew almost always found the means to limit the size of their family.

Ayşe Hanım, who was born in 1900 and married in 1921, gave birth to only two children because, using the Turkish euphemism for withdrawal, her husband 'was very careful ... always'. Another informant, born in 1908 and married at the age of twenty-two, also gave birth to only two children. She emphasizes the conjugal nature of the decision, telling us that she, 'agreed with [her] husband ... and he used to take the necessary precautions'. Zeynep Hanım, born in 1907, married at twenty-one and the mother of two children, repeats the same: 'My husband used to be very careful ... we took great care not to have another child.' Sara Hanım, born in 1907, married at twenty-six, and the mother of one child, is very clear about why she was limiting her fertility. She told us that: 'We were careful ... we knew that too many children bring trouble and responsibilities ... besides, all my friends had either one or two children.'

The use of withdrawal does not seem to be associated with any socio-cultural or economic variable such as wealth, educational level or occupation of the husband. Our informants all seem to have considered withdrawal as the easiest, least costly and most practical contraceptive method. Some doubts were expressed, however, as to its long-run overall efficiency. Almost all the informants who regularly practised withdrawal also told us about one or more abortions. Melâhat Hanım, married in 1929, and the mother of one child, also tells us that, 'My husband was always very careful ...' But that does not seem to have solved their problem, because she later admits that: 'I had three abortions ... [the pregnancies] were all accidents.'

The douche was also well known and seems to have been used quite frequently. Binnaz Hanım, a woman of seventy-five and the mother of four children, tells us that: 'I used to get up and wash ... my mother-in-law had taught me that ... I would wash with cold water ... it used to protect me.' 'Cleanliness', as they phrased it – that is, washing after sexual intercourse – was thought of as a means of protection from pregnancy, and is frequently alluded to in the interviews. The condom is also mentioned once or twice in the interviews, but it does not seem to have been very popular or to have been extensively used. The husband of one woman born in 1905 used the condom after the birth of her second and last child in 1930. She was quite open about its use, but did not hesitate to add that, 'it was hardly necessary, since my husband was away on business so much of the time'. Presumably, condoms sold during those years were often not of the best quality. One of the women complained that they would easily 'break' during use. None of the informants, however, mentioned more 'modern' methods of contraception, such as the diaphragm or the rhythm method, which were beginning to be introduced in the late 1920s in Istanbul.

When we first became aware of the low level of fertility that prevailed in Istanbul as compared to Anatolia during the 1930s, we knew that we were viewing the tip of a social iceberg. It is often the case that the level of fertility is a sign of other social and cultural phenomena of great import. The fertility decline in Istanbul, which we intercept in the 1880s, began at quite a low level. Since it is very likely that families in the city did not have the same need for large numbers of children as their rural compatriots, relatively low fertility – and small families – may have been a long-term feature of urban life. A great variety of age-old birth-control methods were known to people in the city, and received the sanction of Islam, so no practical or moral barriers to having a small family existed. These very same methods were called into play in the period of fertility decline which we have documented, at least up until the 1920s, when more modern ones were introduced.

The continuously rising female age at marriage was, we now know, one of the major factors in the decline of fertility during our period. No doubt levels of mortality also entered into the picture and affected the numbers of children produced, and it is likely – though there is no direct evidence to prove it – that declining mortality during the decades of improved urban living conditions during the late nineteenth century may have been a factor in the drop in fertility levels. Another likely factor in encouraging families to have fewer children was, as we shall see, changing views about the value and meanings of family and children amongst the rapidly westernizing segments of the population.

Appendix: procedure for estimating total fertility rate in 1885 and 1907

The data from the censuses of 1885 and 1907 allow us to classify infants less than one year old by the age of their mother. Infants and young children were probably very heavily under-counted in late Ottoman censuses, as they would be in later Republican Turkish censuses. The underregistration of infants and young children can be observed also in the age pyramids of our samples from the two censuses. The data in table 6.9 have, therefore, to be corrected before they can be used

Table 6.9. *Children aged less than one year by age of mother – sample from*
the Istanbul censuses of 1885 and 1907

| | 1885 | | 1907 | |
Age	Women (total)	Children (<1)	Women (total)	Children (<1)
10–14	172	2	312	3
15–19	199	16	249	21
20–4	179	21	222	35
25–9	173	31	194	30
30–4	163	21	207	33
35–9	137	7	177	15
40–4	113	1	145	3
45–9	102		147	1

Source: Istanbul population rosters, 1885 and 1907.

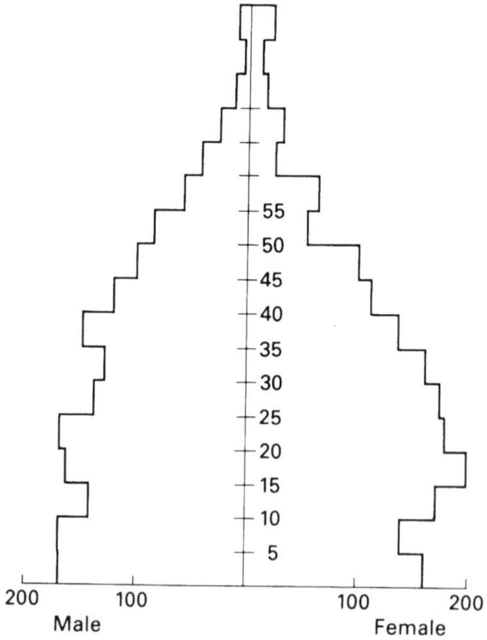

Figure 6.6 1885 Istanbul age pyramid

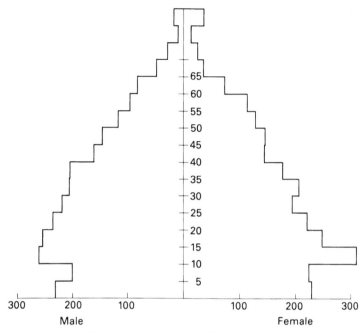

Figure 6.7 1907 Istanbul age pyramid

in fertility estimation. The undercounting seems to have concerned the first three age groups in the 1885 census and only the first two in 1907 (see figs. 6.6 and 6.7). It is well known that the procedures and the coverage of the second census were much more accurate and complete than those of the first.

Given the size of our two census samples and their distance from each other, it seemed preferable to use a method for age-smoothing excluding the use of single year age groups and involving the data of only one census at a time. The use of adequate model life-tables and attached stable populations seemed appropriate.[54] The draw-backs of such a method will be discussed briefly later. The correction factor for the number of young infants in the two censuses has been calculated by comparing the age pyramids of our sample populations to those of appropriate stable populations. The ratio P(O-n)/P in the chosen stable populations divided by the same ratios in our real popu-

---

[54] *Manual IV – Methods of Estimating Basic Demographic Measures from Incomplete Data*, United Nations, Department of Economic and Social Affairs, publication no. 42 (New York, 1967).

lation give us the required coefficients; n is taken as equal to fifteen in the first census and as equal to ten in the second.[55]

The choice of an adequate life-table hinges upon the existence of a more or less precise indication on the level of mortality and the knowledge of an average yearly growth-rate. The two late Ottoman censuses contain particulars for each individual listed as to whether his father and mother (if not actually present in the same household at the time of the census) were still alive or not.[56] This information enabled us to calculate paternal and maternal orphanhood rates by age for both censuses. Conversion of proportions of children (and adults) with surviving fathers and/or mothers into life-table survivorship probabilities obtains reasonable estimates of adult mortality. The methods devised by William Brass have been used for this purpose.[57]

Present Turkish mortality has a particularly skewed age structure which does not fit very well into any of the known sets of model life-tables. The East model life-tables would be the best fit for adult mortality, but infant and child mortality in modern Turkey are exceptionally high. As Shorter and Macura have shown, split-level East tables (i.e. with a higher level for mortality below age five) would be the most appropriate.[58] In the absence of any indication to the contrary, we have had to assume that the age structure of mortality in Istanbul about a century ago was similar to that of present-day Turkey.

Adopting as a basis for our estimation the level of mortality obtained through the Brass method, estimates of adult mortality alone would lead to a sizeable underestimation of overall mortality. Paternal and maternal orphanhood rates, once converted into life-table survivorship probabilities, lead us to a level 11 life-table for 1907, and a level 7 life-table for 1885. Moving one notch down, we have chosen to use levels 10 and 6 respectively.

There remains the problem of the rate of growth of the Istanbul population. A number of official and unofficial estimates exist but few are really trustworthy.[59] The only census result for Istanbul is that of 1885 and it gives a total population of 873,565. The other most

[55] We had to assume, in the absence of better data, that the rate of underregistration is of the same magnitude for all age groups below n.
[56] Behar, 'The 1300 and 1322 *tahrirs*'.
[57] *Estimating Fertility*.
[58] *Trends in Fertility*. See, also, *Vital Statistics from the Turkish Demographic Survey* (Ankara, 1970); and Cem Behar, 'Les tables de mortalité de la Turquie' in *Colloque National du CNRS sur l'Analyse Démographique et ses Applications*, (Paris, 1976).
[59] See, for example, Toprak, 'La population d'Istanbul', 63-70; and, Shaw, 'The Ottoman census system', 325-38.

reliable figure we have, 977,262, is from the Metropolitan Bureau of Statistics for 1914. These two figures give us an average yearly growth-rate of approximately 0.4 per cent. We have adopted, therefore, an R of 5.00 for both the 1885 and the 1907 estimates.

While this may be a reasonable rate to use for 1907, it appears to be totally unfounded for the period around the earlier census. The central lands of the Ottoman Empire, and especially the capital city, Istanbul, had witnessed the influx of large numbers of refugees during this period.[60] After the disastrous 1877–8 war with Russia and the resulting loss of territory both in the Balkans, eastern Anatolia and the Caucasus, a large number of Muslim inhabitants from these areas sought refuge in Istanbul and Anatolia. A similar phenomenon took place during the 1912–13 Balkan Wars, and Istanbul was once again flooded with great numbers of refugees (*muhacirs*). It is quite hazardous, therefore, to use a method of correction and estimation assuming a more or less stable population for 1885, as compared to 1907. As a result, fertility estimates for 1885 are much less precise than those derived from the later census.

Using this method, it appears that the rate of underregistration for infants and young children was around 15 per cent in both censuses. (To be more precise, the rate was 15.6 per cent in 1885 and 14.8 per cent in 1907.) We have assumed that this rate is independent of age at motherhood and have calculated the age-specific fertility rates and the total fertility rate accordingly. However, the rather unusual pattern of age-specific fertility rates in 1907, especially for the ages twenty to thirty-five may well be due to differences in the rate of registration according to the age of the mother, as well as to the contingencies of our sample. This is true for the last age group in the 1885 census as well. The mean age at motherhood, as it appears from these data, is 26.9 in 1885 and 27.9 in 1907.

---

[60] For some estimates of the figures involved in these population movements, see Karpat, 'Population movements in the Ottoman state', 385–428.

7

Westernization and new family directions: cultural reconstruction

Family deconstruction

What a strange time we live in. A crisis in every family ... Are we to be re-educated by the children whose cradles only yesterday we rocked?[1]

Family life was a major point of attention of late Ottoman intellectuals and writers. These individuals articulated, highlighted and dramatized, often in an exaggerated fashion to drive home the point more emphatically, what many people felt but could not easily express. They were also able to leave such thoughts and feelings in a form accessible to posterity, which was something beyond the inclinations or abilities of most. Some of the writers upheld Turkish-Islamic family values and morality in the face of the increasing onslaught of western ways in the home. Others rejected what they perceived to be a rather romanticized traditionalist view of the family and criticized the Turkish family for its stubborn conservatism, oppressiveness and dissension. All agreed that the family was a major focal point for the tensions between East and West felt in Ottoman society at the time. Perhaps, as we have earlier argued, during the Hamidian years (1876–1908), when political oppression and censorship did not permit an analysis of the body politic, the family became a kind of displacement for the frustrations and anger felt by many about society at large. Finn argues that in the late nineteenth century novelists chose to view the 'seeds of decay [in Ottoman society] within the framework of the Ottoman family'.[2] The family was increasingly utilized as a metaphor for society, with its problems taken up in a rather hyperbolic style that may have compensated for its micro-sociological dimen-

[1] Gürpınar, *Kadın Erkekleşince*, 50.
[2] *Early Turkish Novel*, 169.

sions. This idiom continued even after the liberation from Hamidian autocracy. It was from then on, indeed, that it was seen to be in 'crisis'.

The major thinkers of the period - Islamicist, westernist, or Turkish nationalist - were convinced that there was a crisis in family life. The major novelists and playwrights made it their theme, especially beginning with the war years, and this only heightened people's consciousness of a problem. These intellectuals felt that something very important - and, at least in its short-term implications, usually negative - was happening at the very core of Turkish society. The sociologist Z. F. Fındıkoğlu was very explicit in describing 'the family crisis' (*ailevî buhran*) when he wrote a social history of the period in the late 1930s.[3] He made special reference to Ziya Gökalp, who more than any one else gave intellectual articulation to these events at the time they were happening. While Gökalp was very concerned about what he perceived to be the disintegration of family ties, increasingly egotistical behaviour within the family, the rise of divorce and a change in the nature of the relationship between parents and children, in many ways he viewed these as inevitable stepping stones in the evolution of the family from its ancient tribal forms to the modern conjugal 'nest' (*yuva*) type, as he called it.[4] Gökalp was well versed in nineteenth-century French evolutionist family sociology and he viewed his own society within that framework. He drew parallels between the democratization of the state - the case in point being the Young Turk Revolution - and the democratization of the family,[5] both of which he approved of. But he and many others were very concerned about the moral crisis which accompanied such changes. Of course, most people did not view what was happening from the analytic distance which Gökalp was able to maintain, and there was much alarm expressed in the press about the unravelling of family life, indeed of the essential social fabric.

Namık Kemal, poet, novelist and radical intellectual Young Ottoman, was one of the first to begin this idiom with what we might now call a 'deconstruction' of the Turkish family. In a scathing article called 'Aile' (Family) published in *İbret* in 1872, he dissects the Ottoman Turkish family, calling attention to its backwardness, internal dissen-

---

[3] 'Tanzimatta içtimaî hayat' (Social life during the *Tanzimat*) in *Tanzimat* (Istanbul, 1940), 655.

[4] 'Aile ahlâkı - 1' (Family morality), *Yeni Mecmua*, 10 (13 Eylül 1917/13 September 1917), 181.

[5] 'Aile ahlâkı - 3', 321-4; 'Aile ahlâkı - 4, *Yeni Mecmua*, 18 (8 Teşrin-i sâni 1917/8 November 1917), 341-3.

sion and violence and its oppression of females and youth. He ends by drawing the following analogy: 'The homes in a society are like the rooms in a house. Can one find comfort in a house constantly plagued by hatred and infighting? Could it prosper? Would happiness be possible?'[6]

This theme is taken up again and again in newspaper and magazine articles published throughout the period, calling attention to inadequacies in the Turkish family, to polygyny, arranged marriages, oppressive male–female relationships, to the domestic division of labour and to the management of the household. The scene is invariably set with a critique of Turkish family life and then continues with a comparison of families in European, American and even Japanese society. The moral of the story is, as we have seen, that failure in the family will inevitably mean failure on the part of the nation. This is the way Gökalp phrased it in 1919:

We Turks do not know anything about family life. A man should place the highest priority on his family after his people. He should work hardest for his home after his nation.[7]

But not everyone saw the Ottoman family in a negative light or looked up to European domestic institutions. Though it is difficult to enumerate, there was a significant body of opinion in Istanbul, in all likelihood the great majority, which saw the Turkish family as superior. While this was clearly the opinion of the Islamicists, it was even that of moderates such as Ahmed Midhat Efendi, who was very critical of the European family with what, in his eyes, were its loose sexual morality and weak social relations. It is often said that Ahmed Midhat reflects the world-view of the average Istanbul resident. A trip he took to Europe in the late 1890s gave him the opportunity to observe the European family first hand, and this reinforced the negative view he had of that institution, formed earlier from his readings. He praised the Ottoman family for its warm, attentive relationships and for its spirit of mutual support.[8] Many of those who praised the Ottoman family did not, quite naturally, see a crisis in the Ottoman family except as it was influenced by European manners and morals, though they may have been critical, as was Ahmed Midhat Efendi, of such things as the neglect of women's education. Even the feminist magazine *Kadınlar Dünyası* could, in 1913, conclude that, 'Other than

---

[6] 'Aile'.

[7] *Limni ve Malta Mektupları* (Letters from Limni and Malta) (Ankara, 1965), 47.

[8] Okay, *Batı*, 222.

with a few exceptions our family life is very satisfactory'.[9] But, then, in another article later in the year, a different author complains that, 'In the first instance, we have no family life'.[10] So there were, quite expectedly, differences of opinion even among the modernists.

Most of the writing about the problems of the Turkish family refer to the families of the Ottoman bureaucratic or commercial classes, the classes most directly influenced by westernization. Most of the writers themselves came from such backgrounds, and they in all likelihood reflected a situation experienced in certain homes belonging to those classes. It is unlikely that the lower classes were prey in any large numbers to the permissiveness and moral flux that some of those at the top of society were experiencing. A relatively small number of cases was, however, sufficient to excite the passions and the pens of the writers of the period who did not ordinarily think in statistical terms. And there was definitely a sense of crisis in the air, a perception which so often has little to do with the frequencies of events and which was, moreover, reinforced by the economic and political crises of the time. One rather sociologically astute observer wrote the following in the magazine *Sevimli Ay* in 1926:

These days women have become alienated from many of their responsibilities. They neither want to look after their children, nor do anything else! These women are the daughters of men who raised them in dance halls ... Well, you may say that these are the behaviour patterns of a minority of women, but let us not forget that the majority follows in the footsteps of the minority.[11]

Perhaps that was the basis of a fear seemingly out of proportion to the event. The author of the article then goes on to explain that, 'a misunderstood modernity has made women lazy', and that, 'perhaps this situation results from their rather sudden emergence from seclusion into a free style of life'.

The revolt against traditional gender definitions and roles and the reaction of the senior generation began in the late years of the nineteenth century. In the turn of the century novel, *Mutallâka* (The Divorcee) by Hüseyin Rahmi [Gürpınar], an exasperated mother expresses her frustration to her daughter-in-law:

In our time girls had their spinning wheels and looms, now they have libraries, inkwells and pens. We used to weave. You read novels ... And what was that all about the other night? Taking issue with your husband.[12]

[9] 'Bizde hayat-ı aile' (Our family life), *Kadınlar Dünyası*, 27 (30 Nisan 1329/13 May 1913), 2.
[10] 'Çocuklarımız' (Our children), *Kadınlar Dünyası*, 29 (2 Mayıs 1329/15 May 1913), 1.
[11] Feridun Necdet, 'Bir erkek karısından neler bekler?'
[12] *Mutallâka* (The Divorcee) (Istanbul, 1971 [1898]), 12–13.

The dreaded gender role reversals were immortalized in his play *Kadın Erkekleşince* (When a Woman Becomes Like a Man).

The revolt reached its peak during the war years. Though no doubt very few in number, some women could think of rejecting traditional domestic roles. This was not, in many cases, a feminist response. One female author writes: 'There are many women who think doing housework is disgraceful. They enjoy making themselves up and just sitting around or flitting about town. The influence of novels is great in this respect.'[13]

The locus of the changes was clearly Istanbul. Women and the authority of men over them were the focal points of the crisis. In a 1926 magazine article entitled, 'What sort of women do men look for when they decide to set up a new life for themselves?', we clearly see the connection between the dissolution of male authority in the family and the corruption of women. The exaggerated style of the author addresses the emotional issue, though no doubt misleading us about the behavioural facts. The reference to 'the new way of life' was a Gökalpian phrase used by nationalist modernists:

The new way of life made its strongest appearance in Istanbul. The old families run in a patriarchal way are falling off one by one. Young girls are dropping into the streets, the bars, the dance halls ... and ruining their futures in the process.[14]

Most elements of society united against this perceived loosening of sexual morality and a redefinition of gender roles. The 'woman issue' struck deep chords in sexually restrictive Ottoman society. While novels of the pre-Young Turk period focused on the negative aspects of the Ottoman marriage and family systems, and on the debasement of the family and sexual morality stemming from over-westernization, the problems were not yet viewed in crisis dimensions.[15] The family and family relations, not women or sexuality *per se*, were the major points of focus. The absence of the father in many of the early novels is, as Finn observes,[16] quite striking, presenting a vacuum of authority which underpins the moral flux within which the characters, and no doubt some families of the period, found them-

---

[13] Aziz Haydar, 'İçtimaî dertlerimizden: izdivaç, kadınlık' (Some of our social troubles: marriage, femininity), *Kadınlar Dünyası*, 82 (24 Haziran 1329/7 July 1913), 1–2.
[14] 'Erkekler yeni bir hayat kuracakları zaman hangi kızları ararlar?' (What sort of women do men look for when they decide to set up a new life for themselves?), *Resimli Perşembe*, 2, 71 (Eylül 1926/September, 1926), 2.
[15] See for example, Uşaklıgil, *Aşk-ı Memnu*.
[16] *Early Turkish Novel*, 138.

selves. At the beginning of the 1910s the situation starts to be viewed in crisis proportions as Ottoman society frees itself from nearly three decades of repressive authoritarian rule under Abdülhamid II. It is during this period, and especially during the war years and the 1920s, that reference is made to a 'family crisis'. The theme of the absent father is now replaced by that of the clash of generations and the immorality of women following western ways. The members of the younger generation are depicted as the bearers of western morality and manners, with the seniors rather helpless to turn back the clock. Most descriptions of the crisis focus on fathers who no longer have the authority to control the sexual morality of their women, or on the fear that modern women will not want to perform their traditional gender duties. There is a growing and increasingly unnerving sense that women are getting out of hand.

The critique of arranged marriages had now taken its inevitable course in the threat of young women to the authority of the senior generation. This is a reflection of fear, rather than the sociological reality, but who could know in those tumultuous decades of the early twentieth century where indeed events would lead, and whether or not fears might turn into reality? The themes of the decline of authority and the growth of sexual immorality continue to provide a central focus for writers and readers of novels and short stories into the 1930s. One of the classics of the genre from the early thirties is Reşat Nuri [Güntekin's] *Yaprak Dökümü* (Falling Leaves) (1930), the story of weakened patriarchal authority and the sexual and moral depravity of daughters.

The cultural world of gender relations and roles, the symbolic meanings underlying the basic conjugal and filial structures of Ottoman and early Republican societies appeared to be shaken, and 'nature' to be reversed. In *Kadın Erkekleşince* we learn that, 'Women have become like men so as not to be repressed'. But, Gürpınar asks, 'Is it possible to change the roles that nature has assigned to the two sexes?'[17] The fear that the basic (what appeared within the perspective of the time to be the 'natural') gender order of the society would be threatened provided a major source of the sense of crisis perceived by many during this period of great change and turmoil. As we have seen, however, domestic gender roles probably did not change very radically during the period, even though many women appeared more modern and had begun to lead more liberated and freer ways of life in the public world. Istanbul society was able to impose its order on this semi-illusory chaos, but the price in the end was a somewhat

[17] *Kadın Erkekleşince*, 78.

more independent-minded woman, freer marriage choice and more companionate conjugal relations than had ever before existed.

What was happening was, as we have observed, referred to by people at the time and in the immediately following years as a 'family crisis'. We would now call such a phenomenon a cultural crisis. Cultural crises concern perceptions, mentalities and radical changes in fundamental values and meanings. Though in the early years of our period only a small minority of Muslim families were affected, by the 1920s and 1930s the changes had become quite wide-spread, many of them receiving the official and unofficial sanction of the new Republican government. The major focal points of the cultural crisis were, as we noted earlier, the family, the place of women in society and sexual morality. More than almost anything else, the position of women touched the jugular vein of Ottoman society, where their modesty was one of the most cherished and deeply rooted social institutions. Another major focal point of change that touched funda-mental values and customs concerned domestic rituals and manners.

The 'crisis' proportions that the family situation took on after the 1910s was no doubt reinforced and exacerbated by other cataclysmic events in society. The extraordinary inflation and plummeting of real wages, beginning during the First World War and continuing until the end of the decade, shook to their roots large segments of Istanbul society by then existing on a fixed wage or salary. Following a period of relative prosperity and security, this was an especially severe blow, particularly to the bureaucratic backbone of Ottoman society. Such economic conditions, and the absence of large numbers of males at the front, sent many women out to work for the first time – itself a great novelty in urban Ottoman society. During the war period many women could be seen on the streets engaged in various trades that had been the sole prerogative of males until then. While those on fixed salaries and wages suffered, many in commerce prospered from the war. A new and, as we have seen, often despised, social type emerged during those years – the 'war rich'. Great shortages, a thriv-ing black market and pitifully low salaries brought with them a great deal of corruption and graft, which further undermined the moral fabric of the society.

This was in many ways the end of an era for the old bureaucratic elite, articulated in the novels and in our interviews as the 'end of *konak* life'. The demise of *konak* life is seen as a great watershed by old Istanbul residents when they look back into their past. Something was lost for them that could never again be regained – something both material and social. Difficult economic circumstances during and after the war forced many of these people to sell or subdivide into apartment flats the large, often magnificent wooden homes that had not only been their residences, but which had been symbols of their superior status in society. For the elite, the demise of their homes was the core of the 'family crisis'. Many of the large multiple families which had occupied them split up at that time, though often later reunited as separate residents of adjacent modern apartment flats. The catastrophes of the war years had brought about a certain levelling of Istanbul society, which helped set the social and emotional foundation for the Kemalist Revolution and the Republican reforms.

Besides the economic deprivation experienced, many people's confidence in the state – in society in general – was shaken. One must remember that it was during this period that Ottoman society experienced three major wars, with the chaos, deprivations and great population losses and personal tragedies that these brought, as well as the demise of their Empire. The Balkan Wars resulted in the losses of significant parts of Ottoman territories in the Balkans and a great influx of refugees to the city. The First World War brought enormous population losses, the humiliation of defeat and the military occupation of Istanbul by the Allies. The War of Liberation and the end of the Empire involved further agonies and deprivations, and finally, a cathartic end to the trauma of the past. But this was only the first step towards what Ahmet Hamdi Tanpınar referred to as the difficult 'acceptance of a civilization whose doorstep we had been occupying, scratching our heads, for a hundred years'.[18] Throughout the years of economic, political and social crisis, the residents of Istanbul more than any other place in the Empire had lived through the throes of a cultural crisis of major proportions. This crisis culminated in the early Republican decade of the 1920s and into the 1930s in a radical transformation in manners, dress, speech, the written script, the civil code, the place of religion in society and many other basic social elements that touched the everyday lives of people in the city. That there was some sort of 'family crisis' in the midst of all of this is hardly surprising.

Family reconstruction

There is no doubt that the Turkish family will be modernized by the introduction of new conceptions from European civilization. But the Turkish family will neither be a copy of the French or English nor of the German family.[19]

---

[18] *Beş Şehir*, 146.
[19] Ziya Gökalp 'The foundations of the Turkish family' in N. Berkes, ed., *Turkish Nationalism and Western Civilization* (New York, 1959), 252.

It is just not the case that Europe is right next to us; it is virtually an integral part of us.[20]

Europeanization

The model of the European family which Ottomans began to possess in the nineteenth and twentieth centuries was part and parcel of a larger material and symbolic world which they had been acquiring with a passion since the early 1800s.[21] It is not possible to separate the images and aspirations they held for their families, their spouses or potential spouses and their children from the totality of the domestic and social environment in which such cultural elements were set. The accoutrements of a European family life-style began to penetrate the homes of significant numbers of Ottomans, particularly during the last three decades of the nineteenth century. Many familiar objects of everyday use disappeared and were quickly replaced with alien alternatives. Many ordinary rituals and routines of everyday family life began to change quite significantly. Domestic life in Istanbul came to contain a significant collection of symbolic markers of European origin which would begin to set it clearly apart from its traditional Islamic past. Even the increasingly Europeanized physical appearance of the individual family members served to remind them that they were different from their ascendants. The end result was a significant change of direction in the symbolic environment of the homes of many people in Istanbul.

Beginning first in the imperial palace during the reign of Mahmud II (1808-39) such changes, which we lump together as Europeanization, gradually began to have an impact on elite households. In the 1840s European theatre troops came to visit Istanbul on a regular basis, and the non-Muslim minorities and elite Ottoman Muslims in European garb were quick to attend and present themselves publicly.[22] Sultan Abdülmecid I (ruled 1839-61) in many ways set the pace. He spoke some French, played the piano, liked western music and theatre and even read illustrated magazines in French.[23] Western manners, dress and numerous material items had begun to take over imperial circles.

---

[20] Ahmed Midhat, *Avrupa Âdab-ı Muaşereti - yahut Alafranga* (European Manners - or *Alafranga*) (Istanbul, 1312/1894), 3.
[21] For a description of the early stages of this process, see Fatma Müge Göçek, *East Encounters West: France and the Ottoman Empire in the Eighteenth Century* (New York, 1987).
[22] Ahmet Hamdi Tanpınar, *19uncu Asır Türk Edebiyatı Tarihi* (The History of Turkish Literature in the Nineteenth Century) (Istanbul, 1982), 131-2.
[23] *Ibid.*, 132-3.

It was during the later years of the century that such developments began to move from the palace circles to the upper and then middle ranks of ordinary Istanbul society. The Crimean War was a turning-point, bringing a great influx of Europeans into the city, followed in the 1860s by large numbers of Europeanized Turks from Egypt, whose styles of consumption came to be emulated by affluent Istanbul Turks.[24] A large European and increasingly non-Muslim Ottoman presence in the city from then on brought European styles, manners and products close to home. Often it was the non-Muslim Ottoman community, first to be influenced by the Europeans, which had the most direct impact on the Muslims. In the 1860s and 1870s, news-papers, magazines and novels began to describe European styles and ways of doing things. Advertisements in the papers brought European objects and consumer fashions closer to the once closed Ottoman Mus-lim home. Non-Muslim merchants began displaying European con-sumer goods in their shops. By the 1910s and 1920s European ways had penetrated many middle-class homes and even had a degree of impact on the lower classes in the city. Since, as we shall see, the lower classes were largely of non-Istanbul origin they carried with them older, often rural, traditions of eating and comportment which slowed down, but did not impede, their eventual urbanization and some degree of Europeanization.

In newspapers and magazines a self-conscious and deliberate com-parison was made between the modern European family and families from other parts of the world; in the novels and stories such compari-son was more implicit. In either case, as with the transformation of the nineteenth-century family in Europe itself, writers on the subject played an important part, 'in establishing the social codes which informed middle-class propriety for many generations'.[25] Sir Edwin Pears, a long-time resident of Istanbul, had the following to say about such developments in early twentieth-century Istanbul:

The influence of Western thought on the status of women is having a valuable effect on home life in Turkey. English, American and French teaching, the study of English literature, even the reading of the ordinary French novel – not a very elevating study in general – all are exerting a useful influence in stimulating thought, and especially in indicating what family life is.[26]

A transformation of something as fundamental as family life was not, as might be expected, a simple matter. Perhaps its most funda-

---

[24] *Ibid.*, 133.
[25] Leonore Davidoff and Catherine Hall, *Family Fortunes: Men and Women of the English Middle Class 1780–1850* (Chicago, 1987), 155.
[26] *Turkey and Its People* (London, 1911), 74.

Plate 7.1 A rare photograph of an Ottoman Istanbul Muslim family at home, 1908. They are reading several of the popular newspapers of the time.

mental feature was the juxtaposition of the old and the new, the Ottoman and the European, and the strange and unusual mixes of the two. Ahmet Hamdi Tanpınar captures that dualism in nineteenth-century elite households; alongside all the changes he says:

Even the most westernized life-style was still very local in its depths. All the *konak*s set tables for the end of the Ramadan fast, the harem still existed, concubines were still being sold, the Palace was sending women out to be apprenticed, alongside the aide-de-camp was the black eunuch, next to the piano teacher *alaturka* music still reigned strong. No doubt, in the end, the society will have reached a new synthesis following a process of elimination and purification. The important thing, however, is the dualism in institutions and in the moral person.[27]

This dualism was, as we have seen, categorized as *alaturka* versus *alafranga*, and it was one of the major subjects of the novels of the period, particularly during the period up to the First World War. Such dualisms still exist in the most westernized Turkish homes, though they have now been moderated and perhaps diluted by decades of western living. Nevertheless, they can be sensed when one knows

---

[27] *19uncu Asır*, 137.

ازدواج
شرائط صحیه و اجتماعیه‌سی

Plate 7.2 The cover of the third edition of Nusret Fuad's *İzdivaç: Şerait-i Sıhhiye ve İçtimaiyesi* (The Hygienic and Social Conditions of Marriage) (1920–1), featuring a blissful European family as the ideal model.

the intimate workings of the Turkish family, and it is highly unlikely that it could be otherwise.

Despite the dualism and the perdurance of older Turkish ways, one must not, however, think of the changes in material conditions of the home and in manners as a kind of veneer pasted upon a fundamentally eastern way of life. This stratigraphic view of culture, to use a phrase of Clifford Geertz,[28] does not do justice to the way in which culture is holistic, to the way in which objects relate to meanings symbolically attributed to them, and to the way in which such meanings are shaped by the complex array of contexts within which human beings operate. A fork derives its meaning from western culture, and symbolizes a certain way of relating in addition to its practical use. Within an Ottoman home the fork carries that imported meaning as well as the local meanings attributed to it by Ottoman society in general, by a particular stratum of the society, and within the specifics of a particular home at a particular time. As a result, the entry into the Ottoman home of every object, or each new manner or way of doing things, must be seen as a complex symbolic act laden with various layers of meaning.[29]

The Europeanization of dining habits, furnishings and dress was a constant reminder to Ottomans that their families were different from those of their parents. A children's reader of 1909 describes the home furnishings of an Istanbul household.[30] It is difficult to know whether such entirely European furnishings were shown because they were so commonly used at that time and, therefore, taken for granted, or because they were the ideal. Most likely the actual situation was a combination of the two. In any case, eclectic as it may have been, we now know that Istanbul households were crossing a cultural bridge.[31] Perhaps this was driven home most persuasively in the everyday ritual confrontation of family eating.

In the traditional Ottoman home of the nineteenth century, regardless of class, the family dined crouching around a large tray (*sini*) set in the centre of what was, at least for those of other than the elite, a multi-functional room. In upper-echelon families men and women might dine separately. There was no dining room, nor was there a dining table; hands or spoons rather than knives and forks were the eating implements, and food was eaten directly from the dishes in which it was served. There was, of course, an etiquette to the eating. It began with *besmele* (grace), and often ended with a short prayer or an expression of thanks to God. It was not considered

[28] 'The impact of the concept of culture on the concept of man', in Clifford Geertz, *The Interpretation of Cultures* (New York, 1973), 37.
[29] In reference to changes in upper-class eating habits, Mardin ('Super westernization', 430), observes that: 'Togetherness simply cannot be obtained with a menu which reads "Potage aux pointes d'asperges – Homard à la Bordelaise – Volaille demi-deuil and Boeuf froid en gelée".'
[30] Ahmed Cevat, *Kıraat-ı Nafia* (Useful Readings) (Istanbul, 1327/1909), 102.
[31] See Göçek, *East Encounters West*, 38–44, for a discussion of earlier stages of this process.

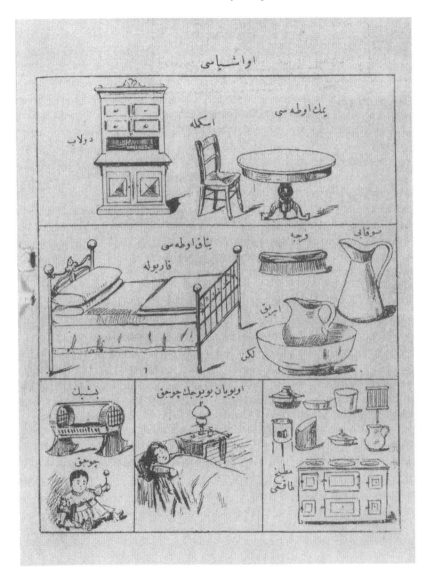

Plate 7.3 'Home furnishings' as portrayed in a children's reader, 1909. The furnishings are almost entirely European. The heading above the table reads, 'Dining room'.

proper to eat without a fez or shawl covering the head. There was also a correct way of eating with the hands, utilizing only two or three fingers as a kind of pincer. This was especially so for girls from good families. In reaching for food from the centre of the tray, they had to be careful not to intrude on the air space of those sitting next to them and not to spill or drip anything on the tray.[32] Small wetted napkins with a rose-water fragrance were provided by the more comfortable families for wiping the face and hands after a meal.[33]

Şerif Mardin comments: 'Introducing knives, forks, and plates to replace the traditional crouching around a tray and eating with a spoon upsets the entire family ... Meeting for meals is not an anticipated pleasure any more, but a torture to be gotten over quickly.'[34] This is, at least, the way it must have been at first, because European and Turkish eating habits could not have been more different.[35] The transformation of European eating habits which took place in the seventeenth and eighteenth centuries, though quite radical in many ways, was moderate compared with what the Ottomans went through.[36] Eating in the *alafranga* style involved an entirely new set of rules which brought with them a considerable degree of distancing, individuation and even some formality among family members previously used to the continual reaching and dipping into communal bowls of food. This was symbolized by the significance of separate plates, separate eating utensils and the distancing of the food from all parts of the body but the mouth. Perhaps even more of a culture shock was the move up from crouching on the floor to sitting on chairs around a table. Soon, the *alaturka* style of eating began to appear repulsive to those initiated into the European way, as one of the many turn-of-the-century descriptions of proper European table manners makes clear to its readers: 'The concern of *alafranga* style eating is not only cleanliness; its purpose is also not to repulse those next to one.'[37] People, of course, had to learn to be repulsed by the ways of eating they had been following for centuries.

During the Hamidian years, 'Tables, chairs, forks, plates and separate glasses for each person make their appearance. But for small and

---

[32] Halid, *Üç Nesil*, 53.
[33] Ayverdi, *İbrahim Efendi Konağı*, 19.
[34] 'Super westernization', 430.
[35] Göçek, *East Encounters West*, 37–44.
[36] See, for example, Fernand Braudel, *The Structures of Everyday Life: Civilization and Capitalism 15th–18th Century* (New York, 1981), I, 206; or Norbert Elias, *The History of Manners* (Oxford, 1983).
[37] Hüseyin Hilmi, 'Alafranga usul-u ta'am' (European-style eating), *Çocuklara Mahsus Gazete*, 216 (4 Muharrem 1317/15 May 1899), 4–6.

مائده باشنده

Plate 7.4 'At the table' as portrayed in a children's reader, 1909. Though the family is not eating, it is very likely that the table is also used for dining.

middle level families this begins slowly and in the simplest way.'[38] This process did not hit the middle classes until the early twentieth century. In the 1909 children's reader we described earlier, the family is portrayed sitting around a table, not crouching on the floor.[39] For Semih Bey, born in 1912 into a middle-level bureaucratic family, the change took place during his childhood. They ate at a table most of the time, but sometimes used a *sini*. 'We always ate with a fork, never with our hands', he said. For Zülfü Bey, born in 1906 to a lower-middle class imam's family, the change began when he was five or six years of age (and at his insistence, he tells us). The lower-class family of Kâzım Bey always ate on the floor at a *sini* in what he called their 'sitting room'. *Alafranga* table manners first began with the Christians and Jews, and were common with their lower classes when still

[38] Halid, *Üç Nesil*, 54.
[39] Ahmed Cevat, *Kıraat*, 28.

rare with upper-class Muslims.[40] However, they seem to have caught on easily: 'The most admired thing we have acquired from Europe is without doubt their manner of dining.'[41] Popular writers of the late nineteenth and early twentieth centuries were quick to spread the word. Ahmed Midhat Efendi, for example, published his *Avrupa Âdab-ı Muaşereti* (European Manners) in 1894, but only after it had already been serialized in the popular newspaper *İkdam*. The tradition of popular guides to manners (*âdab-ı muaşeret*) continued into the Republican years.

The Europeanization of eating habits also had its impact on the timing of the ritual and on family relations. Until the nineteenth century there was no set, regular mealtime, the timing usually being left to the elders of the family and possibly varying from day to day.[42] More regular dining hours became the fashion under the new rules. Elder males had always received priority in being served under the older Ottoman system; under the new system people were advised that 'one should not serve the males until all the women have been served'.[43]

By the early 1940s Refik Halid could insist that, 'The inner face of family manners is revealed around the dining table.'[44] Early Republican writers of books of manners, such as Abdullah Cevdet, certainly saw it that way, hoping that the Europeanization of such family routines would be an important step towards the Europeanization of society.[45] The self-image of the Istanbul family (and of society) was being reconstructed in such minute ways.

The domestic set-up emulated at the time was the small, child-centred, companionate nuclear family found in western Europe. The Istanbul Muslim version of the European family model would, however, include a distinctively different relationship between generations. Even when separated residentially, which was as we have seen quite common, parents and married children maintained (and even to this day, maintain) very close social, economic and emotional ties.[46] Nevertheless, there was a clear turning inward of the affective

[40] Halid, *Üç Nesil*, 50.

[41] Ahmed Midhat, *Yer Yüzünde Bir Melek* (An Angel on Earth) (Istanbul, 1292/1875), 1100.

[42] Ekrem Işın, 'Abdullah Cevdet'in *Cumhuriyet Âdab-ı Muaşereti*' (Abdullah Cevdet's Republican Manners), *Tarih ve Toplum*, 48 (December, 1987), 17.

[43] 'Usûl-u-âdab-ı aile: sofrada' (Family behaviour and manners: at the table), *Çocuklara Mahsus Gazete*, 1 (9 Mayıs 1312/21 May 1896), 6.

[44] *Üç Nesil*, 58.

[45] Işın, 'Abdullah Cevdet', 17.

[46] See Duben, 'The significance of family', 73–99.

strengths of the conjugal couple, an increasingly common purpose attributed to its interests at the ideological level, and a shifting of the focal point of the family towards its children. As a female writer phrased this on the eve of the First World War: 'For a family to be happy, husband and wife must share a common spirit, they must think in common.'[47] By the 1920s there was even talk of the limitations placed upon family size by the relatively small dimensions of the new apartment flats then being built.[48]

What is important here is not, in any case, the numbers of families living in this or that way, but the emergence and occasional articulation of a new conception of the family household. It is of great symbolic significance that even the word used for 'family' during the period of this study changed. Beginning in the late nineteenth century it became commonplace for Muslims in Istanbul to use the word *familya*, of Italian origin (*famiglia*), rather than *aile*, the age-old Arabic origin word for the same concept. By the post-Second World War period this usage had ceased with a return to the use of *aile*. Perhaps that was so because the important changes had already occurred by then, and the heightened self-consciousness that the word *familya* brought with it seemed excessive. The way of life associated with modern families was referred to variously as the *alafranga*, the *avrupaî* (European) or the *medenî* (civilized) way of living. Often specific reference was made to the English, French or American families in particular as ideal types. Even where a European family type is not clearly specified, there is no doubt that Europe was the model. One clearly reads the European aspirations on the faces and costumes of the subjects of the family photographs of the period; such photographs often being a clearer sign of ideals than of the complex reality to which Tanpınar alluded.[49]

The period during which such European influence was becoming particularly rife amongst Istanbul families was also a time of growing Turkish nationalist self-consciousness. In his attempt to give an indigenous legitimacy to the developments in the late Ottoman family and link it to his scheme for a new Turkish society, Gökalp relied, in those heady days of early Turkish nationalism, on a semi-mythic Turkic past. While Turks would and should, he felt, adopt elements of European civilization on their path to progress, they should be careful

[47] Seniye Ata, 'Türk kadınlarına: aile – 2' (For Turkish women: family), *Kadınlar Dünyası*, 72 (14 Haziran 1329/27 June 1913), 2–4.

[48] 'Ev hayatı' (Home life), [*Türk*] *Kadın Yolu*, 1 (16 Temmuz 1341/16 July 1925), 4–5.

[49] Sarah Graham-Brown, *Images of Women: The Portrayal of Women in Photography in the Middle East, 1860–1950* (London, 1988), 95.

to maintain the basic elements of their own culture, and the family was a local cultural (in contrast to cross-cultural, civilizational) element in his scheme. Exactly which elements of the family were to be local cultural and which influenced by European civilization was not clearly specified. Gökalp could not have known that his '*konak* type' multiple family household was itself a rather illusory thing in Ottoman Istanbul. As we have seen, only a small percentage of all households was of that type during his time. The modal type when he was writing, and throughout even the late years of the nineteenth century, was precisely the small nuclear family that he believed would develop as both the child of, and the building-block for, a more democratic Turkish society following the Young Turk Revolution.

Gökalp formulated a scheme which attempted to provide an ideological underpinning for what he believed to be the emergent modern Turkish family, and which he referred to as the 'national' (*millî*) or 'new' family, and sometimes as the '*yuva*' or nest. The 'national' family type was in fact a variant on the European companionate, conjugal (*izdivacî*) family, as he himself indicates.[50] Nuclear in structure, based on a proported equality between the sexes and on the so-called indigenous Turkish moral values, Gökalp argued that this family type would hark back to early Turkic traditions which had been subverted by centuries of Persian and Arab influence. In this sense the 'national' conjugal family was viewed as being a cornerstone of Turkish culture, following its own autochthonous evolutionary path, though functionally interconnected with larger social institutions such as the state.[51] As Toprak indicates: 'The "national family" idea put forward by the [Young Turks] was conceived of as a panacea for the salvation of Ottoman society.'[52] Young Turk 'intellectuals in search of national identity relied upon the family as the germ-cell of the nation-state and family morality as the source of national solidarity.'[53]

Like many Turks of his day, Gökalp very much believed in legalistic solutions to social problems. He was the spearhead of a movement which took shape in the Young Turk years to construct a modern

---

[50] Ziya Gökalp, 'Türk ailesi' (The Turkish family) in Şevket Beysanoğlu, ed., *Ziya Gökalp: Makaleler IX* (Istanbul, 1980), 120–4; 'Aile enmuzecleri' (Family types) in M. Abdülhak Çay, ed., *Ziya Gökalp: Makaleler VII* (Ankara, 1982), 245–52. Zafer Toprak, 'The family, feminism and the state during the Young Turk period, 1908–1918', in Edhem Eldem, ed., *Première Rencontre internationale sur l'Empire Ottoman et la Turquie moderne*, Institut National de Langues et Civilisations Orientales, Maison des Sciences de l'Homme (Istanbul, 1990), 441–52.

[51] *Türk Ahlâkı*, 157.

[52] 'The family', 451.

[53] *Ibid.*

Ottoman civil code, which would provide the legal foundation for the egalitarian conjugal family system he was advocating. In his conceptualization the state would have to play a primary role in this project. He believed that: 'In Europe it was the modern family codes produced by modern states which made possible the development of the "conjugal family" among the European peoples.'[54] He argued, following such logic, that a modern civil code in Turkey would provide the formal legitimation for what he put forward as ancient Turkish egalitarian family traditions, and would lead the way to 'progress' for the Turkish family.

The Family Law of 1917 (*Hukuk-u Aile Kararnamesi*) was the culmination of such effort and marks, as we have observed, the first significant effort of an Islamic state to wrest marriage and family law from the religious establishments, be they Muslim or non-Muslim. While not based on the secular jurisprudence that some modernists would have preferred, it nevertheless took several steps in that direction, with provisions for state sanctioning of marriages and more liberal regulations for divorce and polygyny. In the end, neither the Muslim nor the Christian communities were satisfied with the law, and, following the occupation of Istanbul by the Allies in 1919, it ceased to have any real effect on family life in the city.[55] Its major historic significance is as a precursor for the Republican Civil Code of 1926.

During the early Republican years the state was to take a direct role in trying to remould the Turkish family under the influence of Gökalpian thinking. The most important move in this direction was, without doubt, the Civil Code of 1926, and it is ironic that the nationalists should have chosen the Swiss Civil Code of 1912 as the basis for such a task. The goal of the 1926 Code was clearly Europeanization of Turkish institutions, and in particular family and personal life. As Mahmut Esat, then Minister of Justice, put it, with this law Turkey will, 'close the doors on an old civilization, and will have entered into a contemporary [here read, European] civilization'.[56] This was a revolutionary move in an Islamic country. The new Civil Code superseded the religious *sharia* code and the centuries of Islamic provisions for marriage and divorce, entrusting these entirely to the secular modern state. Though Istanbul families were in many of their practices already quite Europeanized by the mid-1920s, the symbolic value of the Code was very great, as it put the official stamp of legitimization

[54] 'Türk ailesi', 124.
[55] 'Aile Kararnamesi: karilerin mütalâası' (The Family Law: readers' opinions), *Vakit*, 1046 (6 Teşrin-i sâni 1920/6 November 1920), 3; Cin, *Evlenme*, 292–310.
[56] Berkes, *Development*, 470.

on the direction family life had been taking over the previous fifty years or so.[57] This direction was once again reinforced in the 1934 Law of Family Names, requiring Turks to adopt surnames as was the practice in Europe and in other parts of the world.

Wives and husbands

The position of women in Turkish society was changing, and the pace of change stepped up considerably after the Young Turk Revolution. In many respects the tensions and conflict that we witness in the novels – and in the families – of the period are an inevitable outcome of those important changes. It was, as we have seen, during the reign of Sultan Abdülmecit in particular that westernization with its foreign manners, fashions and culture had begun to become entrenched in the domestic life of the palace. The Sultan himself was especially open to these developments, as were members of the imperial family, including some of its women.[58]

The impact of western ideas on Muslim women and men began to be felt outside immediate palace circles after the 1860s. In the late 1860s, the newly founded newspaper *Terakkî* (Progress) directed some of its articles to a female readership, taking up the issue of women's rights for the first time in Ottoman society. By the First World War more than fifteen women's magazines had commenced publication in Istanbul and continued for various lengths of time, some with female contributors. After the war a few more were added to the list and these journals were read by an increasingly literate female population. Among the many issues they raised were veiling, the education and upbringing of children, European family life and the fashions, customs and manners of European women. Such newspapers and journals were a supplement to the novels and short stories that young girls and women were devouring with an increasing voraciousness throughout the period.

If one were to look at the objective indices that are often used to measure the status of women, such as late or increasing marriage age, greater choice in spouse selection, rights of divorce, participation

---

[57] The Code was much in advance of marriage practices in rural Anatolia, and it was viewed by the Kemalist elite as one of the many tools for modernization of social life in the countryside. This penetration of the legal arm of the state was, however, a more complicated process than they had envisaged and it took many decades for the new regulations to change the marriage practices of the average rural family.

[58] Tanpınar, *19uncu Asır*, 129–36.

in the labour force and levels of education,[59] there is little doubt that the women of Istanbul in the 1930s had made considerable progress as compared to their Ottoman sisters. They had moved a great distance in each of these areas. They were marrying at least three or four years later than women in the late nineteenth century, they had an increasingly greater say in the choice of a marriage partner, polygyny was no longer legal, they had the right to apply for a divorce, they were using contraceptives and abortion to limit their family size, greater numbers of them than ever before were in the labour force, and they were participating in the school system in considerable numbers. Significant changes were also beginning to take place in their dress and public comportment. By the 1910s a few courageous Muslim women had even ventured onto the streets of Istanbul, Salonica and Izmir unveiled. Some also attended social occasions with their families or husbands. The feminist ideology of the Kemalist years enthusiastically supported such developments; but does this mean that women's roles and status at home had also changed? The issue of women's roles and status at home is more complicated and certainly much more difficult to assay than the objective indices that are often connected with the public world.

Kemalist feminist ideology rests on developments beginning in the late nineteenth century at a time when both western modernist, reform-minded Islamicist and Turkish nationalist thinking coincided in advocating a new role for women in society. Although by the First World War years certain radical feminists were advocating a greater role for women in politics and in public work life, the overwhelming thrust of thinking in the women's movement of the time was in support of a more sophisticated domestic role for women as modern mothers, and called for their education. Though he advocated a place for women in the public world of work, Gökalp, the ideologue of the movement, placed the greatest emphasis on maternal duties and on socializing children, which were elevated by him to major roles for building the modern Turkish nation of the future. In this sense, the enhancement of women's position in society would not have been primarily of benefit to women themselves, but would have served

---

[59] See, for example, Mason, *The Status of Women*; C. Safilios-Rothschild, *Socioeconomic Indicators of Women's Status in Developing Countries, 1970–1980* (New York, 1986); Christine Oppong and Katherine Abu, *A Handbook for Data Collection and Analysis on Seven Roles of Women* (Geneva, 1985); Gloria Javillonar et al., *Rural Development, Women's Roles and Fertility in Developing Countries: Review of the Literature* (Durham, NC, 1979).

to produce a more sophisticated generation of males to take their public places in society.[60]

How much education should women receive in these new terms? The earlier and more conservative position was, 'only to such a level that would not detract from the responsibilities of a woman [*vezaif-i nisvaniye*]', which meant child-rearing and basic household tasks, and 'an ability to understand the conversations of one's husband and children',[61] or, somewhat later, to 'socialize our children so as to be of service to the nation'.[62] The later and more radical position was, 'as much as is necessary to participate equally with men in public life'. For most Istanbul families, the answer most likely lay somewhere in between.

The education of Istanbul women moved ahead by leaps and bounds, particularly in the early twentieth century. By the 1870s schools for Muslim girls began to appear, many for practical training (such as for midwives), and some for a more general education. By 1906 there were over fifteen middle schools (*rüşdiye*) open to Muslim girls in the city. In 1911 Istanbul high schools accepted females, and by 1916 the university had opened its doors to women. By the 1929–30 school year approximately 75 per cent of all girls aged seven to eleven attended primary school in Istanbul, almost the same percentage as for boys.[63] One can appreciate this rather extraordinary situation when one learns that, nationwide, only 26 per cent of girls and 51 per cent of boys were enrolled in primary school that year. Though there were great advances made in female participation at the secondary and university levels during the early Republican years, males still maintained the overwhelming advantage as they moved up in the system.

Nevertheless, it was a great accomplishment to have women constitute 10 per cent of all university graduates between the years 1920 and 1938. A woman who was a university student during that period recalled the highly charged atmosphere of the time: 'We had removed the veil; we had opened our faces to the world. We had become some sort of European (*avrupalı bir şey olmuşuz*). We could think of nothing but advancing our education.'

---

[60] Ayşe Durakbaşa, 'Cumhuriyet döneminde Kemalist kadın kimliğinin oluşumu' (The development of Kemalist female identity in the Republican period), *Tarih ve Toplum*, 51 (March 1988), 40.

[61] 'Kızların tahsili hakkında bir mütalâa – 3' (Observations on the education of girls), *Hanımlara Mahsus Gazete*, 22 (Teşrin-i sâni 1311/November 1895).

[62] 'Vezaif-i nisvan' (Women's duties), *Kadınlar Dünyası*, 27 (30 Nisan 1329/13 May 1913), 1.

[63] Frederic C. Shorter, 'The population of Turkey after the war of independence', *International Journal of Middle East Studies*, 17 (1985), 417–41.

Plate 7.5 Children, pre-First World War period. The book in the girl's hand points symbolically to her education.

As early as 1895 in *Hanımlara Mahsus Gazete*, one of the first Ottoman women's magazines, the author of a series on the family tells his readers that: 'The family should be characterized by a most sincere, most affectionate atmosphere. Just as it is desirable that husband and wife be close to each other in age, they should also have an intellectual

Plate 7.6 Pupils and teachers at a girls' middle school, Istanbul, 1926.

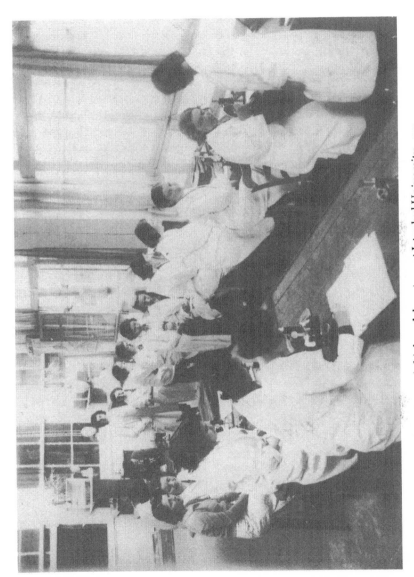

Plate 7.7 Women's biology laboratory at Istanbul University, 1933.

and emotional relationship.'[64] While, no doubt, such ideas were in advance of their time, they were portentous of the changes that became more widespread during the post-First World War years. On the eve of the war, *Kadınlar Dünyası* elaborates on the theme of companionate relationships, adding its own egalitarian prescriptions: 'Neither should the male be the ruler, nor the female the ruled. A man is a woman's life-long companion.'[65] By 1926 the popular family magazine *Sevimli Ay* evaluates developments in this direction in an article entitled 'Ailede demokrasi' (Democracy in the family), as follows: 'Whereas in the past a man married to build a family, today he does so to achieve happiness.'[66] Just as in western Europe, personal fulfilment and a satisfactory conjugal relationship began to move into the forefront of marital needs.[67]

Despite these developments, support for the traditional sexual division of labour was repeatedly featured in the family magazines and newspapers of the period: the husband being responsible for 'external affairs' (*umur-u hariciye*), which basically meant providing an income for the family, and the wife for 'ordinary domestic affairs' (*umur-u adiye-i beytiye*), which meant running the house and raising children.[68] What changed were the emphases, not the cultural definitions or actualities of the gender-based realms and responsibilities. During the late nineteenth century the emphasis was more equally divided between a woman's responsibility for running the house and her role in child-rearing. As the century drew to a close an increasing emphasis was placed on the child-rearing role and, as a result, on the necessity for training more sophisticated mothers. This position, perhaps the dominant one for most Istanbul women throughout the period, was articulated as follows by a woman writing in 1908 in *Demet*, a popular women's magazine:

I am not in favour of men and women being equal in all respects. I am not in favour of women becoming civil servants, MPs, judges, frequenting pubs or sitting in the Taksim tea gardens. I would feel pity for those who take such a position. However, women should go to school and be educated,

[64] Mehmed Hilmi, 'Hayat-ı aile' – 2–3.
[65] 'Müsavat-ı hukuk' (Equality of rights), *Kadınlar Dünyası*, 30 (3 Mayıs 1329/16 May 1913), 1.
[66] 'Ailede demokrasi' (Democracy in the family), *Sevimli Ay*, 3 (Mayıs 1926/May 1926).
[67] Barbara Brookes, 'Women and reproduction' in Jane Lewis, ed., *Labour and Love: Women's Experience of Home and Family 1850–1940* (Oxford, 1986), 150.
[68] 'Kadınlara mâlûmat: tefrik-i vezaif' (Information for women: various duties), *Sabah*, 1822 (6 Rebiyülevvel 1312/7 September 1894), 3–4.

should be capable of producing ideas and have the ability to make judgements.[69]

During the growing nationalism of the Young Turk and First World War period the child-rearing role of women was, in the hands of Gökalp and others, linked to the needs of the Turkish nation and combined with the idea that women could be, or rather should be, companions of men. 'Women are not just responsible for raising children', Gökalp writes to his daughter Seniha. 'They also have a duty to educate the nation, to set men on the right path.'[70] Motherhood came to be seen as a patriotic duty. Celâl Nuri, a well-known supporter of women's rights, perhaps one of the best known during the Young Turk period, emphasized the same roles: 'At this time we do not really need female politicians or technicians ... What we primarily need are mothers, wives, governesses, that is, women to bring up future generations.'[71]

At a time when larger numbers of women were entering the labour force to replace men at the fronts, there was also much more discussion of the importance of women in the work-force, a theme picked up and developed by the Kemalists in the twenties and thirties, when there was an increase of women's employment in factories, in white-collar occupations and in the professions.[72] Perhaps, as Shorter argues, low urban fertility favoured the employment of women outside the home.[73] However, there must have been other factors, because in 1927 26 per cent of all factory production workers were women, whereas by 1975 it was only 18 per cent.[74] Atatürk himself called for women to, 'take their place in the general economic division of labour', in a speech delivered in 1923.[75] And this call was repeated, multiplied and taken very seriously, particularly by elite urban men and women in the late twenties and thirties. Yet there was a contradiction in this Kemalist feminism, because, as Mustafa Kemal himself said in the same 1923 speech, 'a woman's highest duty is motherhood'.[76] The Republican Civil Code of 1926, a revolutionary document from an Islamic point of view, gives the legal sanction of the modernists to the traditional gender division of labour. The Code assigns

[69] Atıfet Celal, 'Terbiye-i nisvaniye' (Female socialization), *Demet*, 2 (24 Eylül 1324/7 October 1908), 27–8.
[70] *Limni ve Malta*, 322.
[71] *Kadınlarımız* (Our Women) (Istanbul, 1331/1913), 119ff.
[72] Shorter, 'Population of Turkey', 431.
[73] *Ibid.*
[74] *Ibid.*, 433–4.
[75] E. Z. Karal, *Atatürk'ten Düşünceler* (Some Thoughts of Atatürk) (Ankara, 1956), 55.
[76] *Ibid.*, 56.

the headship and the provision of family income to the husband and the following role to the wife: 'The wife . . . is the assistant and advisor of the husband. She is responsible for the housework.'[77]

Abdullah Cevdet, the well-known author of a book of etiquette targeted at elite westernized Republican families and published one year after the promulgation of the Civil Code, echoes the law and what were very likely the sentiments of most people. 'The primary duties of a woman are to look after her home',[78] and properly socialize her children, he says. The prime justification for women's education and entry into the work-force put forth by the major feminist magazine of the pre-Republican years, *Kadınlar Dünyası*, was in terms of their role as mothers and child-rearers.[79]

Şirin Tekeli observes that the Kemalist women who took all of these contradictory messages seriously led a kind of schizophrenic existence. They believed in the egalitarian and female professional rhetoric of the day, held professional jobs, yet continued to do all the traditional domestic tasks, their husbands being sanctified as the head of the household under Turkish law.[80] The advances of women in the public world and the enthusiastic discussions of the equality of the sexes in the context of the modernizing Turkish nation – a kind of 'state feminism' in Tekeli's words – were not paralleled by significant changes in the ordinary domestic world of men and women, where traditional gender responsibilities and sexual morality persisted.[81]

Such a traditional sexual division of labour was by no means unique to Turkey. It was also found in England, the homeland of the feminist movement, during that period, though without the same degree of restrictive gender-based morality and codes of comportment that accompanied it in Turkey.[82] Such gender relations were, indeed, the cornerstone of the modern western nuclear family as it emerged in the nineteenth and early twentieth centuries.[83] With very few exceptions, a similar sexual division of labour still exists today in homes in Istanbul and in other major Turkish cities. A recent sociological

---

[77] H. V. Velidedeoğlu, *Türk Medeni Kanunu* (The Turkish Civil Code) (Ankara, 1970), 81.

[78] Işın, 'Abdullah Cevdet', 17.

[79] 'Çalışmak hakkımızdır' (We have the right to work), *Kadınlar Dünyası*, 19 (22 Nisan 1329/5 May 1913), 1.

[80] 'The meaning and the limits of feminist ideology in Turkey' in F. Özbay, ed., *The Study of Women in Turkey* (Istanbul, 1986), 180.

[81] Işın, 'Abdullah Cevdet', 20; Durakbaşa, 'Cumhuriyet dönemi', 151–3.

[82] Jane Lewis, 'Introduction: reconstructing women's experience of home and family' in J. Lewis, ed., *Labour and Love: Women's Experience of Home and Family* (Oxford, 1986), 1.

[83] Eli Zaretsky, *Capitalism, the Family, and Personal Life* (New York, 1973).

study of contemporary Turkish women indicates that, 'employment does not bring women more power in their marital relations', and that, 'certain areas of marital interaction and resources are still tabu and under male control regardless of social class, such as women's physical mobility, their employment decisions, autonomy in birth control or family planning, and sexuality'.[84]

While it is very difficult to know about the intimacies of conjugal relationships with any precision, it appears that although inegalitarianism in the family division of tasks was very slow to change, if it did so at all, the move towards a companionate relationship between husband and wife went beyond the modernist rhetoric of the time. By the 1920s and 1930s the *haremlik–selâmlık* (female–male) divisions of space in the homes of the better-off had already become a thing of the past, thrusting husbands and wives upon each other on a more regular and routine basis. The Istanbul poor had never had such separations anyway, though the 'inescapable' physical intimacy of their relationships did not appear to bring egalitarianism or a companionate relationship with it. We also know, for example, from our interviews, that by the 1920s and 1930s it was quite common for husbands and wives from middle-class and even lower middle-class families to socialize as couples. Semih Bey, the child of a middle-class bureaucratic family, tells us that his parents played music together, played cards with each other and with their friends, 'and always went out together as a couple ... They loved to socialize'. This trend presumably had begun during, perhaps even before the war, since some of our informants tell us about such visiting practices at earlier dates. One of these, whose father was an imam, says that his parents and other religious personnel at a naval post in the lower-class neighbourhood of Kasımpaşa in the middle of the city, visited each other with their wives during the evenings in those years. For most of the lower strata of the city, however, it is very likely that men and women did not socialize together. The parents of Kâzım Bey, from a lower-class family, did not socialize as a couple. His father would regularly visit the neighbourhood café in the evenings; his mother might visit neighbours but 'the men did not usually go visiting'.

A number of important demographic changes during the late nineteenth and early twentieth centuries moved parallel to and provided an underpinning for the ideational developments that eventually led toward greater companionship between husbands and wives. Perhaps

---

[84] Nilüfer Kuyaş, 'Female labor power relations in the urban Turkish family' in Ç. Kâğıtçıbaşı, *Sex Roles, Family and Community in Turkey* (Bloomington, Ind., 1982).

Plate 7.8 Husband and wife, early 1920s. They stand like equals side by side.

the most important of these was the steady increase in the age at which women married, combined with a relative stability in male marriage age. As we have seen, at the turn of the century the age gap between husband and wife was nearly ten years; by the mid-1930s it was around six years. While a small age gap between husband and wife is not necessarily a sign of a companionate relationship – as was clearly not the case in rural Anatolia, where both men and women married quite young – it certainly is a common prerequisite. Also, of course, an older bride is presumably a somewhat more mature wife and future mother – as many Ottoman writers advocating later marriage were quick to point out.

Given the great importance placed on seniority in the traditional Istanbul Turkish household, a relatively large age gap would quite naturally bring with it forms of deference and a kind of distance that would have been inimicable to a relationship of companions. In the traditional pre-First World War Istanbul conjugal relationship, a husband addressed his wife by her name or the term 'wife' (*hanım*), usually using the familiar verb form '*sen*' (*tu*). The wife never addressed her husband by name, always using '*bey*' (Mr) or '*efendi*' (Sir) and the formal '*siz*' (*vous*). In referring to him, *Kadınlar Dünyası* tells us that: 'It is improper to repeat one's husband's name and so one refers to him as "our man" or "father of such-and-such child".'[85] Some women were aware of and critical of the implications of such usages. One such writer in *Kadınlar Dünyası* reminds her readers that: 'Our women address their husbands as "*efendi*". Whereas that is a term of address used by a slave towards a master. That means that we are just so many slaves.'[86]

Such usages are part of a larger age- and gender-based system of deference. In some families even siblings with significant age differences would follow an almost identical pattern, using '*ağabey*'(elder brother) or '*abla*' (elder sister) with the '*sen/siz*' (*tu/vous*) differentiation. Emine Foat Tugay, a woman who grew up in an elite family of that period, tells us in her memoirs that: 'The Turkish family of my time was sharply divided into seniors and juniors. Regardless of sex, all juniors owed deference to elders.'[87] Gender distinctions added greater differentiation and complexity to such relationships. Distinctions in forms of address between siblings generally became less pronounced as one moved down the urban social scale.

By the 1920s and 1930s forms of address used between husbands and wives had begun to change quite radically amongst the middle and upper classes. Such couples marrying during those years were much more egalitarian in this respect, often addressing each other by name, using the familiar form of address reciprocally, as would

[85] Sacide, 'Kızlarımızın çehizi ne olmalı? Yine terbiye-i fikriye' (What should our daughters' trousseaux/dowries be? More intellectual training), *Kadınlar Dünyası*, 97 (9 Temmuz 1329/22 July 1913), 3.

[86] Nesrin Salih, 'Türk kızları' (Turkish girls), *Kadınlar Dünyası*, 47 (20 Mayıs 1329/2 June 1913), 2–3.

[87] *Three Centuries: Family Chronicles of Turkey and Egypt* (London, 1963), 233.

their children amongst themselves, regardless of age. In the 1930s, one of our informants named Nimet ordinarily addressed her husband by his first name, Tahir, except in the presence of her more traditional-minded mother-in-law, when she would use the more formal 'Tahir Bey'.

Later female marriage age, combined with an earlier end to child-bearing years, meant that by her early thirties the average woman in Istanbul was free of the immobility that frequent pregnancies and immediate postnatal responsibilities often demanded. Since women brought only two or perhaps three children into the world, they were also not burdened with large families to look after. Given the ease with which most Istanbul mothers could find familial or paid help in looking after their children, they would have had more time to devote to themselves and to their husbands, and in certain instances, to work outside the home.

We recall that three-quarters of male household heads in their prime marriageable years (thirty to thirty-four) were heading households that were either nuclear (51 per cent) or extended (22 per cent). In most cases the extension resulted from the presence of a mother or, less likely, a mother-in-law. In other words half of newly married couples were living independently, residentially isolated from extended families. When a widowed mother or mother-in-law joined the married couple as a resident in their home in about a quarter of all cases, her traditional role as child-rearer and babysitter allowed them a considerable amount of time to be on their own, to socialize together outside the home and entertain their friends at home. In any case, the elderly mother would have been subordinate to the young married couple who were the master and mistress of the household.

Parents and children

The evidence we have examined leads us to believe that there were significant changes in the attitudes of many people in Istanbul towards children from the mid to late nineteenth century, and particularly in the early twentieth century. These changes in attitude had their roots, among other things, in the reformist policies of the state in the nineteenth century at a time when formal education had begun to move into the forefront of the Ottoman programme for the improvement of the nation. Like so many of the social changes of the time, much of the direction was influenced by ideas and practices found in Europe as transmitted to Ottoman society by the elite literati who were the first to be exposed to European ways.

Plate 7.9 A dervish grandfather with his modern-looking granddaughters, 1897.

Plate 7.10 A father and his children, turn of the century.

The changes typically began at the top of society and moved down as they diffused. The Ottomans eagerly followed the social and intellectual life of Europeans and constantly compared themselves to them, in some respects negatively, in others favourably. Mardin tells us that: 'The whole Tanzimat, is suffused by [a] new interest in children as persons to whom society is going to be entrusted.'[88] This new

---

[88] 'Ideology', 9.

Plate 7.11 Children from a well-to-do family, 1911.

perspective on children as the trustees of the future of the Empire,[89]
quite naturally went hand in hand with a great interest in child-rearing
and in education, informed by current European ideas on the subjects,
which in turn intensified the attention upon children and childhood

[89] *Ibid.*, 19.

as such. As Mardin notes: 'In the past ... guardianship had indeed been part of the ideology of the ruling class, but in this ideology, the steward of state interests was the Grand Vizier or the bureaucracy.' And he continues: 'Any implication that youth had something to contribute as compared with experience would have met with raised eyebrows.'[90] While childhood and youth clearly came into focus as stages of life during the period, we have no knowledge of their place in the life-cycle categorizations commonly used in previous periods in Ottoman history. A history of Ottoman childhood has yet to be written.

Following a European tradition that in modern times dates back to the Enlightenment and which received impetus from the social movements of the eighteenth and nineteenth centuries,[91] nineteenth-century Ottomans began to make connections between child-rearing, education and social reform and turned to the betterment of children's health, character and knowledge as the road to the betterment of society at large. The influence of the then new secular approaches to primary education in Europe, particularly that of Lancaster in England, was felt quite directly in Istanbul in the 1830s with the founding of primary schools, first for Greeks and Armenians by missionaries with Lancastrian ideas in mind, and later, after the intervention of the reformist Sultan Mahmud II, for Turkish children. This was the first time in Turkish history that primary education was to take place outside the traditional religious establishment.[92] Even as early as 1824 Mahmud had, as part of his effort to 'deliver the Muslims from worldly and other-worldly misfortunes', issued a decree in which he required that, 'no man henceforth shall prevent his children from attending school until they have reached the age of adulthood'.[93] These developments did not, however, have a major impact on the Muslim primary school system until the late years of the Empire. But they do seem to have been among the first steps in a change of mentality which eventually led to a new attitude towards the place of children in society, which in turn affected fertility and family relations. These events were part of the impetus lying behind the reform of the Ottoman school system by the early twentieth century.

By the last decade of the nineteenth century, intellectuals and writers had seized upon and developed the theme of children and their place in society. Perhaps the most influential role in this respect was played

[90] *Ibid.*
[91] Davidoff and Hall, *Family Fortunes*, 343.
[92] Berkes, *Development*, 103–4.
[93] *Ibid.*, 101.

by Ahmed Midhat Efendi, one of the first to take up the theme of children and childhood *per se* in a number of books prepared for primary-school children, as well as in his many writings on child-rearing and child health prepared for parents, thus beginning a tradition which continued and flourished throughout the period. Following his return from travels in Europe in the late 1890s, where he was a most enthusiastic observer of the minutiae of that civilization, Ahmed Midhat Efendi began to publish a number of books with titles such as, *Çocuk Melekât-ı Uzviye ve Ruhiyesi* (The Physical and Mental Faculties of Children), *Hikmet-i Peder* (The Wisdom of a Father), *İstidâd-i Etfâl* (Children's Aptitude), *Babalar ve Oğullar* (Fathers and Sons), *Peder Olmak Sanatı* (The Art of Being a Father) and *Ana ve Babanın Evlâd Üzerinde Hukuk ve Vezaifi* (The Rights and Duties of Parents in Relation to Children).[94] In the latter, he praises the French for the efforts they have made in the training of children, efforts which he connects with the progress of Europe over the previous 300 or 400 years. This theme was picked up by many other late nineteenth-century intellectuals and seems to have been the subject of considerable discussion. In an entry in her diary dated 18 August 1889, the poetess Nigâr writes: 'If one wishes to improve the world, to make it possible for man to live in peace and security, it is necessary to concern oneself with child-rearing ... in order for a child to be a person of value he must have an education and proper training.'[95] These ideas, beginning in the elite segments of society, gradually began to have a widespread impact with the broadening of the educational base, particularly in Istanbul. As we now know, by the late 1920s three-quarters of the children in the city were indeed completing a primary education.

By the turn of the century Hüseyin Cahit [Yalçın] issued the following rather severe injunction in the first of his novels: 'It is a fitting end for mothers who have not given sufficient care to the education of their children to be excoriated by human society, for in the final analysis the burden of this neglect will be borne by society.'[96] In the growing nationalism of the Young Turk years, child-rearing was seen by some to be a political duty, with the family, nation and children more than ever equated with each other. 'Family means nation, nation means family', *Kadınlar Dünyası* tells its readership in the year before the First World War.[97] This message is repeated again and again in the popular literature of the time. A rather melodramatic play,

[94] Okay, *Batı*, 244.
[95] *Hayatımın Hikâyesi* (The Story of My Life) (Istanbul, 1959), 33–4.
[96] As quoted in Mardin 'Ideology', 9.
[97] Aliye Cevad 'Aile – 1' (Family) 37 (10 Mayıs 1329/23 May 1913), 2.

published during the war years by the popular writer Hüseyin Rahmi [Gürpinar], draws to a close with the authorial voice of moderation, in the form of the lead character, telling the audience something that they had no doubt been hearing quite frequently – that child-rearing 'is one of the most important duties toward the nation'.[98]

This is the theme that Gökalp reiterates in his sociological and ideological writings during the same years, later to be picked up as a cornerstone of Kemalist ideology in the twenties and thirties. *Gürbüz Türk Çocuğu* (Robust Turkish Child) the popular magazine of the Society for the Protection of Children, is replete with feature stories on healthy Turkish children (including numerous photographs of chubby babies breastfed by devoted mothers), whom one can presume are being groomed at infancy to be loyal state bureaucrats. The extent to which Istanbul mothers were motivated by such nationalist goals is uncertain. In the intense chauvinistic spirit of the times it is likely that some probably were. But there were also many mothers whose attitudes towards their children and whose practices of child-rearing were more a response to their own personal, less societal, perhaps even selfish, aspirations. A number of the women we interviewed evinced such attitudes.

All, or most, of the signs of a child-oriented society were present by the late nineteenth and early twentieth centuries in Istanbul. To begin with, the economic utility of children was no doubt lower than it had been in the past, this being the result of changes in the economic structure of the city beginning during the early *Tanzimat* years. The expansion of the civil bureaucracy, particularly during the Hamidian period, was also paralleled by an increase in the non-domestic industrial base of the city as the urban economy modernized. From at least the 1880s on, the modernized bureaucracy de-emphasized in-house training as an apprentice, which had been the fashion in the Ottoman past, and placed great importance on formal education as the stepping-stone to a bureaucratic career.[99] Increasing factory production and the opening up of more wage work in general in the city meant the application of somewhat more formal criteria for job recruitment, alongside the traditional ones, and an increasing emphasis on educational qualifications. This was also a period of rapid social mobility as immigrants from the old Ottoman provinces made their way up

---

[98] Gürpınar, *Kadın Erkekleşince*, 80.
[99] Findley, *Bureaucratic Reform*.

the rather open social ladder of the time.[100] Education played an important role in this movement, which in turn increased the opportunity costs of having children for families.

There was a great concern for child health and survival during the period. A flurry of articles about the subject began to appear in the popular press beginning in the late 1800s.[101] Numerous guides to child health and nutrition were published and there were serious efforts made by both the Ottoman and Republican governments, as well as by various public associations, to encourage the use of modern methods in these respects.[102] Refik Halid is quite emphatic about the changes in his ethnographic vignettes of the time: 'There is no doubt that child care entered a new phase during this [Hamidian] period.'[103] There was, as we have seen, also a great interest in various methods of child-rearing, influenced in particular by current trends in French sociology, psychology and paediatrics of the period, which Ottoman intellectuals followed and often translated into Turkish.[104] After the

---

[100] Shaw and Shaw, *History of the Ottoman Empire*, II, 172ff; Mardin, 'Ideology'; 'Modernization'; 'Turkey: the transformation of an economic code' in Ergun Özbudun and Aydın Ulusan, eds., *The Political Economy of Income Distribution in Turkey* (New York, 1980); Bernard Lewis, *The Emergence of Modern Turkey* (London, 1961).

[101] The following are examples of this literature: 'Çocuk bakmak' (Child care), *Terakkî'i Muhadderat*, 15 (21 Eylül 1285/3 October 1869), 7-8; 'Hıfz-ı sıhhat-ı etfal' (Health care for children), *Çocuklara Mahsus Gazete*, 37 (26 Kânun-ı evvel 1312/7 January 1897), 3-4; 'Kadınlara mâlûmat: çocukların beslenmesi (Information for women: children's nutrition)', *Sabah*, 1840 (24 Rebiyülevvel 1312/25 September 1894), 3-4; 'Hıfz-ı sıhhat-ı beden: velâdetten 2 yaşına kadar' (Physical health: from birth to two years of age), *Sabah*, 6068 (1 Recep 1324/21 August 1906), 3; 'Himaye-i etfal: 3 – çocuk doğduktan sonra çocuğu kendi validesi emzirmeli' (Child care: after birth a child should be breastfed by its own mother), *Vakit*, 785 (12 Kânun-ı sâni 1920/12 January 1920), 3; 'Gürbüz çocuk nasıl meydana gelir?' (How does one get a robust child?) *Gürbüz Türk Çocuğu*, 2 (Teşrin-i sâni 1926/November 1926), 8-9; Dr Ali Vahit, 'Bebek nasıl beslenir' (How to feed a baby), *Gürbüz Türk Çocuğu*, 54 (Mart 1931/March 1931), 12-13; Dr Besim Ömer [Akalın], *Nüfus Meselesi ve Küçük Çocuklarda Vefiyyat* (The Population Problem and Infant Mortality) (Istanbul, 1339/1921).

[102] During the early Republican years, for example, the *Himaye-i Etfal Cemiyeti* (Society for the Protection of Children), implementing government policies, was very active in promoting the necessity for proper child care, and in connecting the neglect of this with what were felt to be serious problems of child morbidity and mortality. Among other things, it published a child-care magazine called *Gürbüz Türk Çocuğu* (Robust Turkish Child).

[103] *Üç Nesil*, 15.

[104] See, for example, 'Terbiye-i etfal' (Child-rearing), *Terakkî-i Muhadderat*, 18 (12 Teşrin-i evvel 1285/24 October 1869), 1-2; 'Kadınlara mâlûmat: terbiyede mekteb ve aile' (Information for women: school and family in child-rearing), *Sabah*, 1687 (23 Şaban 1312/19 February 1895), 3: 'Çocuk terbiyesi' (Child-rearing), *Demet*, 1 (17 Eylül 1324/30 September 1908), 12-13; 'Çocuğunuzun zekâsı gıdasına bağlıdır' (The intelligence of your child depends upon what he eats), *Gürbüz Türk Çocuğu*, 34 (Temmuz 1929/July 1929), 10-11.

turn of the century Ottoman doctors were quick to join in the publication of child-health and child-rearing manuals. The first paediatric specialists in the Empire emerge during the Hamidian era.[105]

Parents were concentrating their limited resources on fewer children, as our fertility data clearly indicate, and they were more concerned than ever about their future. When asked why they did not have more children than the few they had, our informants from all classes and with few exceptions, said that they were concerned to bring them up well. As one middle-class woman put it:

Perhaps we were overly concerned [about our children] because we wanted to bring them up properly, and so we didn't want many of them ... No one was keen on having a lot of children. It was a matter of raising them properly. That's a great responsibility.

An upper middle-class father tells us that, 'we were quite well-off, but still we never thought about having a third child'. The reason was that, 'though we could easily have fed it, our goal was to bring up our children [in this case two daughters] very well'. He recalled the difficulties his father had had in bringing up his sister and himself, especially during the years following the First World War. He reiterated that families had a special interest in the education of children during the first years of the Republic.

Were Istanbul parents more child-centred because they were having fewer and fewer children, or did they have fewer children because they were becoming more child-centred? Having fewer children certainly meant that mothers could spend a greater proportion of their years rearing, rather than bearing their children, and of course, have more time to spend with fewer children. The mean age at the birth of the last child of wives of those in elite, civil-service and wage-earning occupations was about twenty-nine in 1907. It was thirty-one for shopkeepers and artisans. The burdens and risks of childbirth were over for the average woman before she reached the age of thirty, after which she could spend more time with the children to whom she had already given birth. But perhaps such women had fewer children because they wanted to be able to devote more time and effort to those they had and because they were ambitious for them. That is the distinct impression we get from the women we have interviewed. They knew about and regularly used various birth-control methods. They had no moral or religious compunctions about doing so. Many even chose to use abortion, about which they seem to have

---

[105] Halid, *Üç Nesil*, 15.

taken a very pragmatic position; abortion was illegal and could be dangerous, but was not, as we have seen, immoral in their minds. The danger was their primary concern.

It was not just women who were involved in child-rearing, though the traditional division of labour at home allotted them that task. It became increasingly fashionable for men, elite men at first, to take a special interest in the upbringing of their children – even their daughters. Reflected as an ideal in the novels and stories of the late nineteenth and early twentieth centuries, it soon became a more commonplace reality by the twenties and thirties.[106] In the turn-of-the-century novel, *Aşk-ı Memnu*, perhaps the best-known work of literature of the period, the author is not hesitant to portray Adnan Bey, the protagonist and a rich widower as intimately involved in his children's affairs, their education, and discussing the details of these with their nanny. Adnan Bey is not at all aloof or patriarchal. He reads Turkish literature to his daughter Nihal and they enjoy chatting with each other.[107] In the novel *Handan* (1912), another father, Refik Cemal, says this about his son Nazım and wife Neriman:

Right now in the whole wide world there is just blue-eyed blond little Nazım and my dear Neriman. At last I have found my role ... to be a slave to little Nazım, to wash him and play with him, to feel in my arms this tiny soft thing that the spirits of Neriman and I have united to produce.[108]

The symbolic association with the West of blond hair and blue eyes should not be missed. This is a far cry from the following description of an ideal paternal role in the then progressive paper, *Terakkî-i Muhadderat* in 1869:

When a father is speaking to his child he should never let go of his awesome power, and a mother should always frighten her child with the threat of the father.[109]

Remote, authoritarian and foreboding as the father-figure was presented, it is interesting that such subjects, featured in a series of articles called 'Terbiye-i etfal' (Child-rearing), were even the subject of concern at that time.

In contrast, after the turn of the century there is Ziya Gökalp, the prototypically engaged father of the period, who wrote a series of letters to his daughters, Türkân and Hürriyet, from Malta where he

---

[106] See, for example, the discussion of the father–daughter relationship in Ayşe Durakbaşa, 'The formation of ''Kemalist female identity'': a historical-cultural perspective', MA thesis, Boğaziçi University (Istanbul, 1987), 124–33.
[107] Uşaklıgil *Aşk-ı Memnu*, 42, 70.
[108] *Ibid.*, 76.
[109] 'Terbiye-i etfal', 1–2.

was incarcerated by the Allies after the First World War, in which he gives them detailed advice about their upbringing and education. His letters are full of love and paternal intimacies. On 8 September 1919 he wrote to his younger daughter Türkân:

Little Bitty Türkân, my dearest daughter,
I just received that little bitty letter that you wrote with your tiny hands. I read it with great pleasure. I delighted in the photograph of you. Your fingers were in your mouth. Most certainly to send me a kiss. You are just a little girl, but you are aware of everything. Do comfort your mother; when you smile at her it soothes her heart. And don't be jealous that she wrote a poem to Hürriyet. Here's one for you.[110]

Gökalp was by no means typical. There were, no doubt, many traditional-minded, remote, authoritarian fathers even amongst the elite. But they were increasingly to become a phenomenon of the past and to be looked upon with disfavour. Gökalp represented the wave of the future, and was in many respects the precursor of the ideal Republican fathers of the twenties and thirties. Family photographs of those decades often display such modern-minded fathers and children in very intimate, very affectionate poses. It is difficult to use photographs of the more conservative elements of society or of an earlier period as a contrast, because traditional-minded families did not have their photographs taken at all, and middle-class families did not do so before the First World War years. Only elite families did so then, and they were set in very formal poses which usually excluded women.

We know much less about the way in which ordinary Istanbul parents related to and raised their children than we do about the children of the literate middle and upper classes, who either left records of their attitudes and actions or were the subject of the novels and stories of the period. In addition to their lower levels of literacy and their lesser exposure to modern ideas, working-class, artisan, shopkeeping Istanbul men were less exposed to the traditions of the metropolis. Whereas approximately 60 per cent of those in the elite and white-collar professions were born in Istanbul, only 18 per cent of artisan-shopkeepers and 10 per cent of wage-earners were born there. These figures are for the 1907 census, at a time when the population of the city was perhaps most stable of all the years in the period. As today, the Muslim blue-collar classes of Istanbul of the early years of this century were largely not native to the city and therefore carried with them traditions, often rural, from elsewhere. It is difficult to know precisely what sort of parental role or roles they followed, or to what

[110] *Limni ve Malta*, 31.

Plate 7.12 Father and daughter, 1924. A very modern-looking man places his daughter in the forefront of attention.

extent city life affected the traditions which they brought with them. The few informants of those classes we were able to locate, looking back on their childhood years, reflect upon a considerable variety in ways of relating to one's children at the turn of the century, much as there is today. That is hardly surprising among classes of people exposed to such rapid and radical change.

Conclusion: civilizational shift

The years between 1880 and 1940 were especially important ones for Muslim families and households in Istanbul, and perhaps in the other major urban centres in the Ottoman Empire. The powerful social forces which transformed a great Islamic empire into a secular republic also reverberated in the rhythms of ordinary family life. The family, marriage, women, children and the mundane, taken-for-granted routines of daily domestic life became focal points in the great drama of political and cultural transformation then taking place. Though the 'big stakes' were to be played out in the political arena, it was at home that the revolution was to be lived in all its prosaic glory. The changes and crises felt in the family were, in this sense, microcosms of the larger crisis of civilizational metamorphosis.

Late Ottoman and early Republican families in Istanbul lived through great changes in their daily domestic lives, changes which could easily be called revolutionary. At the same time, however, as is true with all revolutions, familial or political, much was carried forward from the past, and there were many instances when continuities and changes met and combined in unexpected and imperspicuous ways. The full picture is complex and far from clearly understood. This is perhaps because the basic elements of a social and cultural history of late Ottoman Turkey have yet to be written.

Our inquiries into Ottoman family life began with an examination of certain striking demographic patterns visible in the 1920s and 1930s. Demographic patterns are, as Ariès has emphasized,[1] often signs of what has been happening below the surface of society, in the way of hidden collective attitudes. The substrata of demographic forces moving through late nineteenth- and early twentieth-century Istanbul

---

[1] 'Two successive motivations.'

were both a precursor and a marker of other changes to come in the social and cultural spheres; at the same time, they were part and parcel of those very same socio-cultural events. Age at marriage, fertility, mortality, even household size and composition can be viewed in one sense as 'demographic' phenomena, and their impact on social and cultural events can be examined as such. They are, however, equally integral parts of those very same socio-cultural systems. The marriage age of women can affect fertility; but both the age at which women marry and their fertility are the products of a complex array of social and cultural phenomena. Demographic 'facts' like all other 'facts' are a matter of interpretation, and as a result can be seen in a different light by different people at different times, using different perspectives.

Fertility was quite low even at the beginning of the period, and women and men were clearly practising some forms of birth control or abortion, as they no doubt had been doing for some time, though it has proved difficult, if not impossible, to discover a precise timing either for the fall of fertility or for the inception of changes in nuptiality or marriage patterns. Our data nevertheless point to a quite early start in the process of transition from high to low fertility among Istanbul Muslim women. In trying to document the fertility decline in Istanbul in the first four decades of this century we have, at each step, come across bits of evidence leading us to the idea of a much earlier start in the fall of the indices used. The process of fertility decline seems to have been contemporaneous to that in many parts of western or northern Europe, that is during the last quarter of the nineteenth century.

The Islamic religion does not forbid birth control and there were a great variety of age-old methods known to ordinary people in Istanbul. Given the exigencies of social and economic life in a huge city like Istanbul, it is unlikely that parents would have needed or wanted large numbers of children as did their rural compatriots. What is interesting is that after the 1880s they clearly wanted fewer and fewer children as time went on, and that by the 1930s they were basically only just reproducing themselves in number – at a time when rural Turks were eagerly producing large families to make up for the population losses of the long years of war and revolution.

Child limitation took place in two ways: one which must have been quite conscious and deliberate, and the other which was the end result of other social processes quite unrelated to children. Husbands and wives used various forms of birth control to deliberately limit the number of children they had. We know this because of the information we have collected on methods used, but most importantly because of the statistical record we have of the ages at which mothers had their last child, which is on a continuous downward slope throughout the period. The fertility decline started in Istanbul at a time when none of the so-called 'modern' methods of family planning were as yet available. The process, like that in most parts of Europe, was one of progressive 'democratization' of traditional methods such as withdrawal, douche and abortion. Potential parents also limited the number of children they would have by marrying increasingly late as the years went by. But they did not marry late to limit the number of children they would bring into the world. They did so for other quite unrelated reasons.

It is not entirely clear why people married at the ages that they did during the period. Women in Istanbul added a year a decade from the turn of the century on to the age they married and by the 1930s this age was, on average, twenty-three. We can only surmise why that was so, based on the logic of indirect evidence. The evidence concerns the changes which took place in the status and position of women in Istanbul society during that time. Here we refer to the many 'objective indices' of increasing female status such as education, entry into the work-force, the late Ottoman and early Republican movements and other efforts to improve the position of women in society, the growing antipathy felt towards polygyny and concubinage, the increasing degree of choice involved in marriage and the influence of western models on all of these things. We do not know, however, how the total package of influences came together to affect the decisions made by or for particular women during that period. We do, nonetheless, know that the rise in female marriage age was one of the major factors in the decline of fertility in Istanbul.

The age at which men marry does not have a direct impact on fertility, though it does have important implications for the timing of household formation. Men married consistently late throughout the years of this study, with a slight rise during the war years. We have attributed this to the financial difficulties of setting up a household, and to cultural concepts governing the age men are considered to be mature enough to get married. Though these are interrelated phenomena, one cannot be reduced to the other.

Though much has changed over the past 100 years in relation to the institution of marriage in Istanbul, little is different about its frequency. Marriage was, and still is, considered an inevitable stage in the life-course of individuals in the city, as it is throughout Turkey. The low and declining total fertility rate in Istanbul during our period is even more striking in view of the near universality of marriage. Although set in a dense web of extended family relationships, marriage increasingly came to be seen as a conjugal rather than a familial matter in the years after the turn of the century. Whereas child-rearing and social reproduction were always major purposes of marriage, the emphasis, even in the late nineteenth century, was never on the quantity of children. We do not know what people thought – or did – about this in the more distant past. No doubt better public health conditions and what was most likely to have been declining infant mortality in the late nineteenth century made having few children less of a risk for parents than it had been in the past. Polygyny, while a major social issue for reformist Ottomans and a subject of great fascination for foreigners, was in fact a practice limited to a small minority of people in Istanbul, and even for them was often only a stage in the course of marital life.

By the early years of the twentieth century the quality of the children brought into the world, their health, proper socialization and education, became a major focus of the attention of parents. Though child care and child-rearing were increasingly articulated in nationalistic terms, especially during the war years and during the first decades of the Republic, it is more likely that the decisions of most people in this regard merely coincided with the purposes of the ideologues, but in actuality followed the dictates of domestic necessity and, for many, the aspirations for a modern – read 'European' – way of life, of which the small conjugal family with healthy and properly educated children was one important component.

The Muslim population of Istanbul appears, to the best of our knowledge, to have been the first sizeable Muslim group to have systematically and extensively practised family planning. Our analyses of marriage, fertility, household formation, reproduction systems and demographic behaviour add support to the view held by some that Istanbul held a rather unique status within the mosaic of peoples, countries and ethnic groups that made up the Ottoman Empire. It is clear, for example, that the prevalence of parity-based family limitation, combined with a family formation system fostering universal though rather late male and female marriage, set Istanbul apart from any discernible 'Muslim' or 'Middle Eastern' pattern.

In no other Middle Eastern or Muslim city do we know of a parallel to these historical trends, nor does there seem to be any other where fertility started to decline so early, so efficiently, and on such a wide scale. As we have shown, the decline of fertility in Istanbul was due in part to the rise in female marriage age and partly to the adoption of birth-control methods. The former had little to do with limiting births in the minds of people; the latter was part of a complex, and still not clearly understood, array of economic necessities, aspirations for one's children, and emerging, though not clearly articulated, conceptions of how modern or – in the terms of the Turks of that period – 'civilized' families should be composed. Istanbul Muslims stood apart from their coreligionists in the Middle East as pioneers in many areas: in marriage age and household formation, in polygyny, in family-planning practices, in fertility trends and in attitudes towards the family in general. There is some evidence available to suggest that a more or less similar marriage and household formation system also characterized the city of Beirut in the 1930s and 1940s.

Despite much popular and scholarly opinion to the contrary, we now know that the late Ottoman Muslim household in Istanbul was, on the average, small in size. It is likely that this was not a new phenomenon in the late nineteenth century when we enter the scene, but that it was a long-term feature of the metropolitan social economy. Future studies will, perhaps, shed more light on this important issue. The Istanbul household was not only small, it was also, for the great majority, not very complex. Only slightly over 10 per cent of all households were of the multiple family type, and these were more likely than not to be the households of the upper echelons of the society. The median type was the simple family household, though it was common at certain stages of the domestic cycle for other relatives, particularly widowed mothers, to join the single conjugal unit.

Given the late age at which men married and the difficulties of setting up a household, most couples began their marital life charged with their own survival, not jointly with one set of parents. For the majority of Muslim residents of Istanbul there was, then, no question of a major shift from complex to simple family households during our period. Though there are no studies available for the latter part of the period that allow us to compare over time, the starting-point in the 1880s is, as we have seen, sufficient evidence for this. Perhaps there was some decline in the percentage of multiple family households following the demise of *konak* life for elite Istanbul families in the years during and after the First World War. The widespread belief that household structures changed radically during this period is most likely due to this. To a large extent such misconceptions may stem from the fact that what we know about families in the past is a monopoly of information passed on orally or in written form by the members of the upper strata. The poorer segments of society have hardly left any evidence of the way they lived. It is also likely that the percent-

ages of solitaries and no family households declined – and that, correspondingly, simple family households increased – as the Muslim population of the city stabilized in the twenties and thirties. Given the
absence of statistical data on households for that period, systematic
retrospective interviews appear to be the only way of obtaining the
data necessary to answer such questions.

Despite the absence of large percentages of complex family households in Istanbul during our period, the strength of extended family
ties does not seem to have greatly waned. This is, of course, very
difficult to measure. We know that family members from neighbouring
households shared many tasks and pleasures together in the past,
that relatives would frequently stay with their kin in households other
than their own for long periods of time, and that the boundaries
between households were rather fluid. We also know that to this
day extended family ties, even amongst the middle and upper classes,
are very strong in Istanbul and other major cities, though the boundaries between them are perhaps a bit more impermeable and long-term
visits are uncommon. Nevertheless, the generations are connected
in a dense array of practical and emotional relationships in a way
that they are not in western Europe or North America. We do not
know this with great certainty, however, for there are very few studies
available of middle- and upper-class urban families in Turkey.[2] We
surely know very little about what took place during the long interven-
ing years between the census of 1907 and the present, other than
what we have been able to glean from the press and a few retrospective
interviews.

Something about the social and cultural configuration in Istanbul
allowed, perhaps fostered, the unique confluence of demographic and
cultural events that set the city apart even from its most immediate
Anatolian hinterlands. Istanbul does not seem to easily fit any of the
known socio-geographic categories. Built upon a rather segmentary
structure of local neighbourhood communities (*mahalles*) which ostensibly bore the centuries-old characteristics of the ideal Islamic urban
molecule, the sum total of Istanbul bore little resemblance to such
eastern social patterns. As early as the 1880s the demographic and
household structures of the city had set the stage for the social and
cultural restructuring that would make its impact with greater force
after the turn of the new century. Perhaps their etiologies had little
connection with those of the social and cultural revolution that was
to follow, but they provided the patterns required for modern family

---

[2] Duben, 'The significance of family'.

life. Certainly we need to know much more about how and why Istanbul was what it was, and how it compared to other cosmopolitan cities in the Empire such as Izmir, Salonica or even Bursa, if we are to disentangle the various causes and effects from each other. Part of this story will no doubt also lie in a better understanding of the significance of the influences of the non-Muslim segments of the city population on Muslim life.

The world of work, conceived in its broadest sense, also increasingly came to differentiate Istanbul from Anatolia, and provided more of the requisites of the changes which were to come in family life and fertility. It was particularly during the extended reign of Abdülhamid II that the long-run processes of differentiation of work from home which had begun to be felt since the beginning of the century, took extensive root. Nineteenth-century reforms of the state bureaucracy, bringing it closer in line with European institutions, led to a much more marked separation of affairs of state and households than had been the case in the Ottoman past. The increasing commercialization of life, especially after the Crimean War, and nascent industrialization led greater numbers of people in the city into jobs away from their families. By the turn of the century, a significant proportion of the population was working outside the home and dependent upon the vagaries of a salary or wage for a living.

This dependency hit home during the First World War years when inflation and irregular payments wrecked the steady prosperity that had previously been enjoyed by the working people of the city. Traumatized by runaway inflation, war, and the demise of their centuries-old imperial way of life, Istanbul families were made more receptive to the processes of westernization which had already been undermining and rebuilding their daily habits and their values for several decades. It was during the war years that women went to work outside the home for the first time in significant numbers. Such women in the market-place and office – and featured in the press – were very 'visible' (much more so than their numbers could reflect), and were, no doubt, one of the factors instrumental in facilitating the changing status of women in the society.

Western products had begun to attract better-off Turks at least since the 1860s when European consumer goods became more readily available in Istanbul shops and were regularly advertised in its popular press. The press not only brought goods to the public eye, but regularly bombarded families with news about European ways of life, European institutions, values and political and social movements. In other words, a revolution in communications had taken place. The growing array of newspapers and magazines also brought novels and stories in serial form to their avid readers. Reformist in nature, most of this fiction took issue with traditional family arrangements and with the place of women in home and public life. Non-fiction also took up these issues in addition to problems of education, health, child care and child-rearing practices. Though an attempt was made to preserve traditional Islamic or Turkish values in the midst of this cultural on-slaught, the weakness of the Ottoman state, the great attractiveness of European institutions and the predilections of many Istanbul Turks ultimately made this a rather futile cause. Indigenous values and ways of living did not, of course, totally disappear. They persisted in particu-lar at two extremes: either in the nominal form of the labels chosen for changing institutions, such as in the so-called 'national' family of Gökalp, or in deep and often imperceptible ways of thinking, relat-ing and doing things which survived in the midst of and as a uniquely Turkish part of the process of the westernization of family life.

There is an almost natural tendency to dichotomize when reflecting on one's social surroundings, and the Istanbul Ottomans were no exception to this. Old and new, *alaturka* and *alafranga*, were the terms in which the changes were mentally separated and comprehended. The reality, as Tanpınar has noted, was often more complex. In most people's lives the old and new were mixed in various proportions depending on social class background, social status and occupation, length of residence in the city and exposure to western influences, among other things. While it seems quite certain that westernization penetrated the literate middle and upper classes more deeply than it did the traditional lower classes in the city, we must not forget that there was not a great difference in marriage and fertility patterns between the classes during our period. The connection between west-ernization, social class and the demographic phenomena of concern to us remains unresolved.

Much to-do was made, for example, of the so-called move from arranged to love marriages. Yet, these pure forms were in all likelihood only pure in the minds of people, not in their actualization. Some sort of love relationship under the guidance and sponsorship of fami-lies was the more common, certainly the increasingly predominating arrangement, while the *idea* of love carried an implicit threat to family and social order.

Though the authority of senior over junior generations was not broken to the extent portrayed in writings of the period, the greater self-consciousness that the debate about generational conflict brought forth played a part in the gradual process of differentiation of generational roles and responsibilities that accompanied the western simple family ideal. There was a clear inward turning of family focus. But, at the same time, though residentially separate, the members of the various generations of families did not, as we observed, stop playing crucial roles in each others lives, roles that continue even to this day in Istanbul society. Though nuclear families live separately from each other in most cases, Turkey – even Istanbul – can still easily be called a familistic as opposed to an individualistic society.

Part and parcel of the critique of the authority of the senior generation was a radical deconstruction of the institution of the family, beginning as early as the 1860s. This conceptual dissection and analysis opened the door to a questioning of age-old ways of relating and thinking which culminated in Istanbul Muslims viewing their families in a state of 'crisis'. It also made the acceptance of alternatives that much easier. Life in Istanbul really was in crisis, as major political and social institutions were questioned, undermined and eventually rejected in favour of various western alternatives. More companionate relations between husbands and wives and more egalitarian and intimate relations between parents and children, especially fathers and children, were among the prominent sociological signs of these changes in family life – in addition to all the changes of great symbolic import in manners and the physical setting of the home. While there were many defenders of traditional Turkish family values – and these were preserved, in particular in the high degree of emotional and practical engagement maintained between generations and between siblings – it was the western family model that was the dominant, though often unarticulated, force underlying the domestic changes in Istanbul during those years.

Istanbul in the late nineteenth and early twentieth centuries was an extraordinary city. It was an amalgam of diverse influences from western Europe, the Balkans and Asia. It was a meeting place of civilizations. As one made one's way through the streets of Istanbul, a person was continually possessed by the juxtaposition of cultures in the various Islamic and European visages and vistas that confronted the eye. We have come to see, however, that the special features of Istanbul were in fact much more than a surface impression, and that in many instances they were beyond the awareness of its residents. This unique confluence of cultures was even felt in the intimate details of family life and in the demographic patterns of the city.

To hold that Istanbul was unique in many aspects of its social and cultural life does not, however, mean that what happened in Istanbul during the years of our study was peripheral to the developments in Turkish society. On the contrary, it was quite central. As the capital of the Ottoman Empire and its major cultural centre, Istanbul came to be the crucible for the complex chemistry of cultural and social change that would reshape the identity of the entire society. While the identity and directionality of contemporary Turkish society are complex and perhaps still to be determined in the future confrontation of East and West, what happened in Istanbul during the transition from Empire to Republic continues to provide the largely unspoken paradigm for a western way of life.

Glossary

Glossary of Ottoman-Turkish terms
(applicable for the period 1880–1940)

âdab-ı muaşeret: rules of good manners, etiquette
ağa: term of reference and address often used in the urban context following the name of an illiterate person, villager, manual labourer
ağabey: elder brother
ağırlık: marriage payment, Turkish language term for *mehr-i muaccel*
aile: family, kin; used in both reference to non-residential and coresidential units and relationships
alafranga: in the European ('frankish') style
alaturka: in the Ottoman or Turkish style
asrî: contemporary, modern
aşifte: whore, whorish, loose (woman), harlot-like
avrupaî: European
azat: free, not enslaved, emancipated
azil: *coitus interruptus*, withdrawal
başlık: bridewealth (in rural areas)
bekâr: single (male)
bekârodaları: hostels or rooms used in Ottoman Istanbul for housing single men temporarily resident in the city, usually as labourers
bey: mister, sir; term of reference and address used following the name of an urban gentleman
cami: mosque
cariye: concubine, female servant, slave
cihaz: trousseau, dowry
çapkınlık: debauchery, rakishness
çeyiz: same as *cihaz*
damat: daughter's husband
devletlû: term of reference used in the Ottoman period for officials of the first and highest class in the state bureaucracy
efendi: mister, sir; term of reference and address used in the Ottoman period following the name of a literate person, one of moderate to high status
esas nüfus kayıt defteri or *esas defter*: original main population roster
familya: term of Italian origin (*famiglia*) used during the late Ottoman and early Republican periods for family; equivalent to the Turkish term, *aile*
ferman: imperial rescript
fevkânî: (house) with two storeys
fitil: vaginal pessary
gelin: bride, daughter-in-law
hacı: someone who has made the pilgrimage (*hajj*) to Mecca
hafız: someone who has memorized the entire Koran
hamam: Turkish bath
hammal: street porter
hane: household, coresidential group

hanım: lady, woman, Mrs, Miss; term of reference or address used following the name of a woman of moderate to high status

harem, haremlik: women's or private family quarters in a house or palace

hodgâmlık: egotism, selfishness

hul: divorce by mutual consent according to Islamic law

hürriyet-i şahsiye: individual or personal freedom or liberty

hürriyet-i tabiiye: natural freedom or liberty

iç güvey: uxorilocal son-in-law (especially in rural areas, where the term carries a negative connotation)

iddet: a period of time prescribed by Islamic law during which a divorced woman cannot remarry

ihanet: treason, unfaithfulness

ilân-ı aşk: proclamation of love

ilân-ı hürriyet: literally, 'proclamation of freedom'; a term used by the Ottomans to refer to the Young Turk Revolution of 1908 and the resulting freedom from oppression

irade: imperial decree

iskat-ı cenin: abortion

izdivaç: marriage

izinname: licence (to marry)

kadı: judge of Islamic law

kalfa: supervisor of female servants, stewardess; term of reference or address used following the name of a stewardess in an Ottoman household

kefaet: homogamy

kefil: guarantor (in a contract)

konak: urban mansion; luxurious house

loğusa: woman after childbirth; a period of confinement (usually forty days) for women after childbirth

mahalle: neighbourhood community

medenî: civilized

mehr: a payment (or promise of payment), in accordance with Islamic law, which devolves from the groom's family to the bride upon marriage

mehr-i misl: the amount of *mehr* as dictated by the *kadı* in cases where mention of it was omitted from the marriage contract

mehr-i muaccel: urgent or premarital *mehr*; the first part of the *mehr* payment paid at the drawing up of the marriage contract

mehr-i müeccel: deferred *mehr*; the second part of the *mehr* payment; usually a promise to pay a specified amount at a future date, especially in the case of separation or divorce

mehr-i müsemma: the amount of *mehr* as specified in the marriage contract

millet: a nation, people, religious community

molla: Turkish for mullah

muhabbet: companionship, affection, friendship, love

muhacir: immigrant, refugee; especially used in reference to Muslim Turks who emigrated to the central Ottoman lands as the Empire began to lose its territories

muhalâa: divorce by mutual consent according to Islamic law

muhalâa hücceti: an Islamic court ruling for a case of divorce by mutual consent

muhtar: headman or administrative official in a *mahalle*

mükellef: luxurious (house)

mutavassıt: average, ordinary

nafaka: alimony payment

nafaka-yı iddet: alimony paid during the period of time when a divorced woman cannot, according to Islamic law, remarry

namus: honour, particularly as stemming from the proper behaviour of female members of a family or kin group

nüfus tezkeresi: a combination of birth certificate and identification card introduced in Ottoman society at the time of the census of 1885

paşa: Turkish spelling for pasha

rüşdiye: Ottoman middle school

sahilhane: literally, a house on the shore (especially of the Bosphorus or Sea of Marmara); waterfront mansion

selâmlık: that part of an Ottoman house reserved for males

sen: you (familiar form)

seyyibe: no longer a virgin, evermarried

siz: you (formal form)

sofa: vestibule or hall, an atrium-like space connecting rooms in an Ottoman home

süflî: inferior (house)

şart: condition (in a contract or other legal document)

şerif: a descendant of the Prophet Muhammad

şeriye sicilleri: records of the Islamic courts

şeyh: Turkish for shaikh

tahrir: register, registration

tahrir-i nüfus: population census

Tanzimat: the period of westernizing reforms in the Ottoman Empire beginning in 1839

tatlik hükmü: a ruling by an Islamic court for a case of spousal repudiation

teehhül: marriage

tekke: dervish convent

ümmet: Turkish spelling for the Arabic, *umma*, community of the faithful

vukuat defteri: register for vital events

yabancı defteri: population register for non-permanent Istanbul residents

yuva: nest, home

Sources and bibliography

ARCHIVAL SOURCES

Population rosters (Nüfus kayıt defterleri) (by roster number)
Beşiktaş Directorate of Population (*Beşiktaş Nüfus Müdürlüğü*)
For the 1885 census: 133, 135, 152, 154, 155, 166, 175, 176 (*Şenlikdede*).
For the 1907 census: 1 (*Kaptan İbrahim Ağa*), 1 (*Muhacir*), 1 (*Mübadil*), 2 (*Muha-cir*), 2/2, 2/3, 2/4, 2/5, 8, 9, 10, 11, 12, 19, 20, 22, 23, 25, 25/1, 26, 26/2, 27, 28, 29 (*Şenlikdede*), 30, 33, 34/1, 34/2, 34/3, 35, 38, 39, 40, 43, 45, 47, 49.
Eminönü Directorate of Population (*Eminönü Nüfus Müdürlüğü*)
For the 1885 census: 1, 4, 7, 8, 10, 14, 15, 16, 17, 18, 19, 21, 33.
For the 1907 census: 7, 8, 11, 7/2, 17, 17/1, 29 (*Müsvedde*), 30, 32 (*Müsvedde*), 35, 40 (*Müsvedde*), 44, 44B, 44/1, 45 (*Müsvedde*), 49, 56, 70, 72, 72A, 73, 74, 75, 76, 77, 78, 80, 81, 82, 85, 90, 92, 93, 96.
Fatih Directorate of Population (*Fatih Nüfus Müdürlüğü*)
1885 census rosters not available.
For the 1907 census: 1(*Emin Nurettin*), 1 (*Manisalı Mehmet Paşa*), 2 (*Manisalı Mehmet Paşa*), 2 (*Akseki*), 2 (*Oruç Gazi*), 2A 3 (*Manisalı Mehmet Paşa*), 4(*Har-aççı Muhittin*), 5(*Haraççı Muhittin*), 6(*Haraççı Muhittin*), 9/2 (*Kazasker-i esbak Mehmed Efendi*), 10(*Sinan Ağa*), 13/1(*Koğacı Dede, Kızıl Minare*), 15(*Hasan Halife*), 15/1(*İskender Paşa*), 16/1, 17/1, 17/2, 17/3, 21/1, 21/1A, 21/2, 21/2A, 22, 23, 25, 29, 30, 31, 37, 38, 49, 50, 50A, 54, 59, 60, 61, 62, 63, 64, 66.
Şişli Directorate of Population (*Şişli Nüfus Müdürlüğü*)
For the 1885 census: 163, 164, 165, 166, 168.
For the 1907 census: 5, 6, 7, 8, 27, 49.
Üsküdar Directorate of Population (*Üsküdar Nüfus Müdürlüğü*)
For the 1885 census: 432, 433, 435, 436, 437, 438, 439, 441, 442, 443, 444, 445, 446, 447, 449, 450, 451, 452, 454, 455, 456.
For the 1907 census: 1(*Arakiyeci Hacı Mehmet*), 1(*Kazasker Ahmet*), 1(*Selimiye*), 1(*Hamza Fakih*), 1(*Selman Ağa*), 1(*Tabaklar*), 1(*Hayrettin Çavuş*), 1(*Çakıcı Hasan Paşa*), 1(*Rumî Mehmet Paşa*), 1(*Murat Reis*), 1(*Sinan Paşa*), 1(*Gülfem Hatun*), 1(*Ayazma*), 1(*Hacı Hesna Hatun*), 2(*Tavaşi Hasan Ağa*), 2(*Selimiye*), 2(*Selman Ağa*), 2(*Rumi Mehmet Paşa*), 2(*Tabaklar*), 7(*İnkilâp*), 8(*Tenbel Hacı Mehmet*), 9(*Evliya Hoca*), 17/1(*Pazarbaşı*), 17/2(*Pazarbaşı*), 18(*Solak Sinan*), 18/1(*Solak Sinan*), 27(*Selamî Ali*), 27A(*Selamî Ali, Toygar Hamza*), 27B(*Toygar Hamza*), 27/1(*Toygar Hamza*), 28/1(*İhsaniye*), 28/2(*İhsaniye*), 28/3(*İhsaniye*), 29(*Durbalî*), 41(*Müteferrik*), 42(*Müteferrik*), 43(*Müteferrik*), 43/1, 45(*Müteferrik*), 45/1.

Istanbul marriage registers (İstanbul evlenme vukuat defterleri)
For districts of Beşiktaş, Eminönü, Fatih, Şişli and Üsküdar, 1905–40

Archive of the Istanbul Religious Courts (İstanbul Müftülüğü Şeriye Sicilleri Arşivi)
Court of Istanbul (*İstanbul Mahkemesi*): 1/254, 1/255, 1/256, 1/257, 1/258, 1/259, 1/260, 1/261, 1/262, 1/263, 1/264, 1/267, 1/289, 1/295, 1/298, 1/301, 1/304, 1/307, 1/310, 1/313, 1/316, 1/319, 1/325, 1/328, 1/331.
Court of Üsküdar (*Üsküdar Mahkemesi*): 6/726, 6/729, 6/731, 6/736, 6/780, 6/781, 6/782, 6/784, 6/785, 6/786, 6/787, 6/788, 6/789, 6/790, 6/791, 6/792, 6/793, 6/794, 6/796, 6/797, 6/798, 6/799.
Treasury Inheritance Court (*Maliye Beytülmal Kassamlığı Mahkemesi*): 27/65, 27/70, 27/71, 27/73, 27/75, 27/76, 27/77, 27/78, 27/81, 27/82, 27/86, 27/95, 27/96, 27/97, 27/92, 27/93.
Former Districts Inheritance Court (*Mülga Beledî Kassamlığı Mahkemesi*): 16/155.

Notebooks of the imam of Kasab İlyas Mosque
Leatherbound notebook, forty pages (42cm by 17cm), containing 281 marriage recordings (from 1281/1864 to 1302/1885).

Unbound notebook, eighty-nine pages (20cm by 27cm), containing sixty-three marriage recordings (from 1304/1887 to 1308/1891), as well as various other entries.

Clothbound notebook, 136 pages (24cm by 33cm), containing 310 marriage recordings (from 1308/1891 to 1324/1906), as well as various other entries.

LATE OTTOMAN AND EARLY REPUBLICAN NEWSPAPERS AND
PERIODICALS

Newspapers	Period covered
Terakkî-i Muhadderat	1869–70
Sabah and *Peyam-ı Sabah*	1889–1914
Terakkî	1897–9
Vakit	1917–29
Cumhuriyet	1928–35

Periodicals	
Aile	1880
Şükûfezar	1883–4
Çocuklara Mahsus Gazete	1896–1901
Hanımlara Mahsus Gazete	1895–1909
Demet	1908–9
Kadın (Salonica)	1908–10
Mehasin	1908–10
Şehbal	1908–13
Erkekler Dünyası	1913–14
Musavver Mâlûmat-ı Nafia	1913–14
Kadınlar Dünyası	1913–15
Çocuk Dostu	1914–15
Yeni Mecmua	1917–18
Türk Kadını	1918–19

İnci	1918–22
Ev Hocası	1923
Süs	1923–4
Resimli Ay	1924–5
Türk Kadın Yolu	1925–6
Resimli Perşembe	1925–8
Sevimli Ay	1926
Gürbüz Türk Çocuğu	1926–8

PUBLISHED SOURCES (*c.* 1846–1940)

Works are listed in this section of the bibliography by their original date of publication or by the date written if they were not published soon after that time. Anonymous articles are listed alphabetically. Turkish authors are listed according to their first name if they did not live until 1934 (when Turks were first required by law to adopt a surname), and by their surname if they lived to adopt one, regardless of when the work cited was published or written. (In cases where the author adopted a surname, it is given in square brackets in the text if the work referred to was written before 1934.) Some Ottomans used only one name and they are listed as such.

Abalıoğlu, Yunus Nadi. 'Bekârlık vergisi' (Bachelors' tax). *Cumhuriyet*, 1757 (31 Mart 1929/31 March 1929), 1.

Adıvar, Halide Edip. *The Memoirs of Halide Edip*. London, 1926.
   Sinekli Bakkal (published in English as *The Clown and his Daughter*. London, 1935). Istanbul, 1980 [1935].

Ahmed Cevat. *Kıraat-ı Nafia* (Useful Readings). Istanbul, 1327/1909.

Ahmed Midhat. *Felâtun Bey ile Râkım Efendi* (Felâtun Bey and Râkım Efendi). Istanbul, n.d. [1875].
   Yer Yüzünde Bir Melek (An Angel on Earth). Istanbul, 1292/1875.
   Bahtiyarlık (Happiness) in *Letaif-i Rivayat* (Finest Tales). Istanbul, 1302/1885.
   Avrupa Âdab-ı Muaşereti – yahut Alafranga (European Manners – or *Alafranga*). Istanbul, 1312/1894.
   'Teehhül' (Marriage) in *Musahebat-ı Leyliye* (Nightly Conversations). Istanbul, 1304/1887.

'Aile Kararnamesi: karilerin mütalâası' (The Family Law: readers' opinions), *Vakit*, 1046 (6 Teşrin-i sâni 1920/6 November 1920), 3.

'Ailede demokrasi' (Democracy in the family). *Sevimli Ay*, 3 (Mayıs 1926/May 1926).

Akalın, Besim Ömer, Dr. *Nüfus Meselesi ve Küçük Çocuklarda Vefiyyat* (The Population Problem and Infant Mortality). Istanbul. 1339/1921.

Ali Vahit, Dr, 'Bebek nasıl beslenir' (How to feed a baby). *Gürbüz Türk Çocuğu*, 54 (Mart 1931/March 1931), 12–13.

Aliye Cevad. 'Aile – 1' (Family). *Kadınlar Dünyası*, 37 (10 Mayıs 1329/23 May 1913), 2.
   'Aile – 2'. *Kadınlar Dünyası*, 40 (13 Mayıs 1329/26 May 1913), 3–4.
   'Aile – 4'. *Kadınlar Dünyası*, 46 (19 Mayıs 1329/1 June 1913), 2–3.

Atıfet Celâl. 'Terbiye-i nisvaniye' (Female socialization). *Demet*, 2 (24 Eylül 1324/7 October 1908), 27–8.

Aziz Haydar. 'İçtimaî dertlerimizden: izdivaç, kadınlık' (Some of our social troubles: marriage, femininity). *Kadınlar Dünyası*, 82 (24 Haziran 1329/7 July 1913), 1-2.

'Bana sorarsanız: 1930 kızı annesinden daha mesut mu?' (If you ask me: is the girl of 1930 happier than her mother?). *Cumhuriyet*, 2150 (1 Mayıs 1930/1 May 1930), 2.

'Bana sorarsanız: anne baba reşit olan kıza karışmalı mı?' (If you ask me: should parents tell a mature daughter what to do?). *Cumhuriyet*, 2222 (19 Temmuz 1930/19 July 1930), 2.

'Bekârlık' (Being single). *Cumhuriyet*, 1751 (24 Mart 1929/24 March 1929), 3.

'Bekârlık vergisi: çok çocukluları da dinleyelim' (Bachelors' tax: let's also listen to those with many children). *Cumhuriyet*, 1749 (22 Mart 1929/22 March 1929), 4

'Bizde hayat-ı aile' (Our family life). *Kadınlar Dünyası*, 27 (30 Nisan 1329/13 May 1913), 2.

'Bugünkü Türk kadınları' (Turkish women today). *Resimli Ay*, 2 (Mart 1340/ March 1924).

Celâl Nuri. *Kadınlarımız* (Our Women). İstanbul, 1331/1913.

'Çalışmak hakkımızdır' (We have the right to work). *Kadınlar Dünyası*, 19 (22 Nisan 1329/5 May 1913), 1.

'Çocuğunuzun zekâsı gıdasına bağlıdır' (The intelligence of your child depends upon what he eats). *Gürbüz Türk Çocuğu*, 34 (Temmuz 1929/July 1929), 10-11.

'Çocuk bakmak' (Child care). *Terakkî-i Muhadderat*, 15 (21 Eylül 1285/3 October 1869), 7-8.

'Çocuk büyütmek: memeden kesme' (Child care; weaning). *Hanımlara Mahsus Gazete*, 2 (27 Zilhicce 1320/27 March 1903), 30-2.

'Çocuk düşürenlere ibret' (An exemplary case for abortionists). *Hanımlara Mahsus Gazete*, 27 (5 Receb 1322/15 September 1904), 422-3.

'Çocuklarımız' (Our children). *Kadınlar Dünyası*, 29 (2 Mayıs 1329/15 May 1913), 1.

'Çocuk terbiyesi' (Child-rearing). *Demet*, 1 (17 Eylül 1324/30 September 1908), 12-13.

'Erkekler yeni bir hayat kuracakları zaman hangi kızları ararlar? (What sort of women do men look for when they decide to set up a new life for themselves?). *Resimli Perşembe*, 71 (Eylül 1926/September, 1926), 2.

'Ev hayatı' (Home life). [*Türk*] *Kadın Yolu*, 1 (16 Temmuz 1341/16 July 1925), 4-5.

Fatma Aliye. *Nisvan-ı İslam* (Muslim Women). İstanbul, 1309/1891.

Fatma Bedia, 'Kadınlık Şu'unu' (Women's affairs). *Türk Kadını*, 7 (15 Ağustos 1334/15 August 1918), 111-12.

Feridun Necdet. 'Bir erkek karısından neler bekler?' (What does a man expect from his wife?). *Sevimli Ay*, 3 (Mayıs 1926/May 1926).

Fuad, Dr. *Gebe Kalmamak İçin Ne Yapmalı?* (What Should One Do to Avoid Pregnancy?). İstanbul, 1927.

Galib Ata. 'Kaç yaşında evlenmeli' (At what age should one marry?). *Vakit*, 854 (2 Receb 1338/22 March 1920), 3.

Garnett, Lucy M. J. *Home Life in Turkey*. New York, 1909.

Gökalp, Ziya. *Limni ve Malta Mektupları* (Letters from Limni and Malta). Ankara, 1965 [written 1919-21].

Türk Ahlâkı (Turkish Morality). Istanbul, 1975 [essays used first published 1917].

'The foundations of the Turkish family' in N. Berkes, ed. *Turkish Nationalism and Western Civilization*. New York, 1959 [article first published in 1917].

'Türk ailesi' (The Turkish family) in Şevket Beysanoğlu, ed., *Ziya Gökalp: Makaleler IX*. Istanbul, 1980 [article first published in 1923].

'Aile enmuzecleri' (Family types) in M. Abdülhak Çay, ed., *Ziya Gökalp: Makaleler VII*. Ankara, 1982 [article first published in 1923].

'Aile ahlâkı- 1' (Family morality). *Yeni Mecmua*, 10 (13 Eylül 1917/13 September 1917)., 181–5.

'Aile ahlâkı- 3.' *Yeni Mecmua*, 17 (1 Teşrin-i sâni 1917/1 November 1917), 321–4.

'Aile ahlâkı- 4.' *Yeni Mecmua*, 18 (8 Teşrin-i sâni 1917/8 November 1917). 341–3.

Güntekin, Reşat Nuri. *Yaprak Dökümü* (Falling Leaves). Istanbul, 1978 [1930].

'Gürbüz çocuk nasıl meydana gelir?' (How does one get a robust child?). *Gürbüz Türk Çocuğu*, 2 (Teşrin-i sâni 1926/November 1926), 8–9.

Gürpınar, Hüseyin Rahmi. *Mutallâka* (The Divorcee). Istanbul, 1971 [1898].

Şıpsevdi. Istanbul, 1971 [1911].

Kadın Erkekleşince (When a Woman Becomes Like a Man). Istanbul, 1974 [1916].

'Hıfz-ı sıhhat-ı beden: velâdetten 2 yaşına kadar' (Physical health: from birth to two years of age). *Sabah*, 6068 (1 Recep 1324/21 August 1906), 3.

'Hıfz-ı sıhhat-ı etfal' (Health care for children). *Çocuklara Mahsus Gazete*, 37 (26 Kânun-ı evvel 1312/7 January 1897), 3–4.

'Himaye-i etfal: 3- çocuk doğduktan sonra çocuğu kendi validesi emzirmeli' (Child care: after birth a child should be breastfed by its own mother). *Vakit*, 785 (12 Kânun-ı sâni 1920/12 January 1920), 3.

Hüseyin Hilmi. 'Alafranga usul-u ta'am' (European-style dining). *Çocuklara Mahsus Gazete*, 216 (4 Muharrem 1317/15 May 1899), 4–6.

Hüseyin Mazhar. 'Aile' (Family). *Çocuklara Mahsus Gazete*, 41 (9 Kânun-ı sâni 1312/21 January 1897). 2–3.

'İlk İzdivaç talibleri' (First marriage advertisements). *Vakit*, 151 (21 Mart 1918/21 March 1918), 1.

'İskat-ı cenin' (Abortion). *Sabah*, 349 (3 Muharrem 1307/30 August 1889), 2.

'İskat-ı cenin muhakemesi' (A court case concerning abortion). *Sabah*, 500 (6 Cemaziyülahir 1307/28 January 1890), 3.

İstanbul Şehri Rehberi (Guide to Istanbul). Istanbul, 1934.

'İzdivaç' (Marriage). *Hanımlara Mahsus Gazete*, 70, 72, 73, 75 (Safer–Rebiyülevvel 1314/July–August 1896).

'İzdivaç anketi' (Marriage survey). *Resimli Perşembe*, 58 (1 Temmuz 1926/1 July 1926), 7.

'İzdivaç dünyanın en emin sigortasıdır' (Marriage is the world's best insurance). *Resimli Ay*, 4 (Mayıs 1341/May 1925), 23.

'İzdivaç için en iyi çağ hangisidir' (What is the best age for getting married?). *Resimli Perşembe*, 134 (14 Cemaziyülahir 1346/9 December 1927), 2.

'İzdivaç talibleri' (Marriage advertisements). *Sabah*, 10209 (6 Receb 1336/17 April 1918), 2.

'İzdivaç ve talâk' (Marriage and divorce). *İnci*, 1 (1 Şubat 1919/1 February 1919), 1.

'İzinnamesiz nikâh kılma davası' (The case of an unlicensed marriage). Peyam, 10 (15 Şevval 1340/11 June 1922), 3.

Jenkins, Hester. Beyond Turkish Lattices: The Story of a Turkish Woman's Life. Philadelphia, Pa., 1911.

Johnson, C. R. Constantinople To-day; or, The Pathfinder Survey of Constantinople. New York, 1922.

'Kaç yaşında izdivaç etmeli' (What is the proper age for marriage?). Hanımlara Mahsus Gazete, 138 (13 Teşrin-i sâni 1313/16 November 1897), 4–5.

'Kaç yaşında evlenmeli' (What is the proper age for getting married?). Vakit, 854 (3 Receb 1336/14 April 1918), 3.

'Kadınlara mâlûmat: çocukların beslenmesi' (Information for women: childrens' nutrition). Sabah, 1840 (24 Rebiyülevvel 1312/25 September 1894), 3–4.

'Kadınlara mâlûmat: izdivaç' (Information for women: marriage). Sabah, 1889 (13 Cemaziyülevvel 1312/November 1894), 3–4.

'Kadınlara mâlûmat: tefrik -i vezaif' (Information for women: various duties). Sabah, 1822 (6 Rebiyülevvel 1312/7 September 1894), 3–4.

'Kadınlara mâlûmat: terbiyede mekteb ve aile' (Information for women: school and family in child-rearing). Sabah, 1687 (23 Şaban 1312/19 February 1895), 3.

'Kadınları çalıştırma teşebbüsü' (The attempt at employing women). Vakit, 111 (9 Şubat 1918/9 February 1918), 1.

Karaosmanoğlu, Yakup Kadri. Kiralık Konak (A Mansion for Rent). Istanbul, 1981 [1922].

Sodom ve Gomore (Sodom and Gomorrah). Istanbul, 1981 [1928].

'Kızların tahsili hakkında bir mütalâa - 3' (Observations on the education of girls). Hanımlara Mahsus Gazete, 22 (Teşrin-i sâni 1311/November 1895).

'Mahalle mıntıka ve daire teşkilâtı' (Neighbourhood, district and borough organization). Şehremaneti Mecmuası, 43, 45, 48, 49 and 51 (Mart/March, Mayıs/May, Ağustos/August, Eylül/September and Teşrin-i sâni/November 1928).

Mehmed Hilmi. 'Sin-i İzdivaç' (Age at marriage). Hanımlara Mahsus Gazete, 99 (30 Kânun-ı sâni 1312 /11 February 1897), 2–3.

'Hayat-ı aile -5' (Family life). Hanımlara Mahsus Gazete, 117 (19 Haziran 1313/1 July 1897), 2–3.

Memâlik-i Osmaniyenin 1330 Senesi Nüfus İstatistiği (Ottoman Population Statistics from the Year 1330/1914). Istanbul, 1330/1914.

'Memâlik-i Osmaniye'de tezayüd ve tenâkıs-ı nüfus' (Population increase and decrease in Ottoman lands). Sabah, 346 (1 Muharrem 1307/28 August 1889), 2–3.

Monroe, W. S. Turkey and the Turks. London, 1908.

'Müsavat-ı hukuk' (Equality of rights). Kadınlar Dünyası, 30 (3 Mayıs 1329/16 May 1913), 1.

Namık Kemal. 'Aile' (Family) in A. H. Tanpınar, ed., Namık Kemal Antolojisi (A Namık Kemal Anthology). Istanbul, 1942. (Originally in İbret, 56, 1872.)

Nesrin Salih. 'Türk kızları' (Turkish girls). Kadınlar Dünyası, 47 (20 Mayıs 1329/2 June 1913), 2–3.

Nigâr. Hayatımın Hikâyesi (The Story of My Life). Istanbul, 1959 [written 1879–1918].

Nusret Fuad, Dr. *İzdivaç: Şerait-i Sıhhi٬ ve İçtimaiyesi* (The Hygienic and Social Conditions of Marriage). 3rd ed٬, Istanbul, 1338–9/1920–1.

'Oğlum, tahsil-i ilm et, yoksa ham٬ ٬al olursun' (Study hard, my son, or else you will be a street porter), *İnci* NS 8 (Mart 1923/March 1923), 2.

Pears, Edwin. *Turkey and its People*. London, 1911.

Rıfat, Dr. 'Yeni doğan çocuklara mahsus hıfzıssıhha' (Health care for nursing infants). *Türk Kadın Yolu*, 4 (6 Ağustos 1341/24 August 1922), 5–6.

Rusçuklu Hakkı, Dr. 'Elvah-ı hayat: 1 – izdivaca dair' (Tablets of life – 1: on marriage). *Sabah*, 4038 (16 Şevval 1318/8 February 1902), 3–4.

'Elvah-ı hayat: 2 – izdivaca dair' (Tablets of life – 2: on marriage). *Sabah*, 4047 (25 Şevval 1318/15 February 1901), 3–4.

Safa, Peyamî. *Cânân*. Istanbul, 1980 [1925].

Sacide, 'Kızlarımızın çehizi ne olmalıdır? Yine terbiye-i fikriye' (What should our daughters' trousseaux/dowries be like? More intellectual training). *Kadınlar Dünyası*, 97 (9 Temmuz 1329/22 July 1913), 3.

Sami Paşazade Sezai. *Sergüzeşt* (Adventure). Istanbul, 1978 [1889].

Seniye Ata. 'Türk kadınlarına: aile – 1' (For Turkish women: family). *Kadınlar Dünyası*, 70 (12 Haziran 1329/25 June 1913), 3–4.

'Türk kadınlarına: aile – 2' (For Turkish women: family). *Kadınlar Dünyası*, (14 Haziran 1329/27 June 1913), 2–4.

Sicill-i Nüfus Kanunu (The Population Registration Law). Istanbul, 1332/1914.

Sicill-i Nüfus Nizamnamesi (Regulations for Population Registration). Istanbul, 1300/1883.

Sicill-i Nüfus Nizamnamesi (Regulations for Population Registration). Istanbul, 1320/1902.

'Sin-i teehhül' (Age at marriage). *Sabah*, 1966 (3 Şaban 1312/30 January 1895), 3–4.

'Süt emen çocuklar' (Breastfeeding babies). *Terakkî-i Muhadderat*, 3 (28 Haziran 1285/19 July 1869), 7.

Şinasi. *Şair Evlenmesi* (The Marriage of a Poet). Istanbul, 1982 [1860].

'Teehhül' (Marriage). *Terakkî-i Muhadderat*, 10 (17 Ağustos 1285/29 August 1869), 1–2.

'Teehhül' (Marriage). *Terakkî-i Muhadderat*, 13 (16 Teşrin-i sâni 1285/28 November 1869), 1–2.

'Teehhül' (Marriage). *Sabah*, 355 (9 Muharrem 1307/5 September 1889), 2–4.

'Terbiye-i etfal' (Child-rearing). *Terakkî-i Muhadderat*, 18 (12 Teşrin-i evvel 1285/6 October 1869), 1–2.

Tevfik Nuri. 'İzdivaç hakkında evlenmesinden evvel çocuklarıma nasihatlerim' (Advice to my children about marriage before matrimony). *Resimli Ay*, 6 (Temmuz 1341/July 1925), 40.

Twain, Mark. *The Innocents Abroad or the New Pilgrim's Progress*. New York, 1911.

Uşaklıgil, Halid Ziya. *Aşk-ı Memnu* (Forbidden Love), Istanbul, 1978 [1900].

'Usûl-u âdab-ı aile: sofrada' (Family behaviour and manners: at the table). *Çocuklara Mahsus Gazete*, 1 (9 Mayıs 1312/21 May 1896), 6.

'Vezaif-i nisvan' (Women's duties). *Kadınlar Dünyası*, 27 (30 Nisan 1329/13 May 1913), 1.

'Vilayette izdivaç, nahiye naibleri, köy muhtarları' (Marriage in cities, district judges, village headmen). *Sabah*, 4263 (5 Cemaziyülahir 1319/19 September 1901), 2.

White, Charles. *Three Years in Constantinople; or Domestic Manners of the Turks in 1844.* London, 1846, III.

Yahya Halid. 'Zorla nikâh' (Mandatory marriage). *Vakit*, 1898 (24 Mart 1924/24 March 1924), 3.

Yalçın, Hüseyin Cahit. *Edebî Hatıralar* (Literary Reminiscences). Istanbul, 1935.

Yalman, Ahmet Emin. *Turkey in the World War.* New Haven, Conn., 1930.

'İzdivaç ve maişet' (Marriage and subsistence). *Vakit*, 828 (26 Şubat 1920/26 February 1920), 1.

'Yeni anketimiz; Taaddüt-ü zevcata taraftar mısınız' (Our new survey: are you in favour of polygyny?) *Vakit*, 2195 (25 Şubat 1340/25 February 1925), 4.

PUBLISHED SOURCES (*c.* 1941–89)

Ahmad, Feroz. 'Vanguard of a nascent bourgeoisie: the social and economic policy of the Young Turks, 1908–1918' in O. Okyar and H. İnalcik, eds., *Social and Economic History of Turkey (1071–1920).* Ankara, 1980.

'War and society in the Young Turk period.' *Review*, 11 (1988), 265–86.

Alkan, Türker. *Kadın-Erkek Eşitsizliği Sorunu* (The Question of Inequality between Men and Women). Ankara, 1981.

Amani, M. 'La population de l'Iran.' *Population*, 27 (1972), 411–19.

Andorka, Rudolph, and Faragó, Tamás. 'Pre-industrial household structure in Hungary' in Richard Wall, ed., in collaboration with Jean Robin and Peter Laslett, *Family Forms in Historic Europe.* Cambridge, 1983.

Ariès, Philippe. *Centuries of Childhood.* New York, 1962.

'Two successive motivations for the declining birth rate in the West.' *Population and Development Review*, 6 (1980), 645–50.

Aydın, M. Akif. *İslam-Osmanlı Aile Hukuku* (Islamic-Ottoman Marriage Law). Istanbul, 1985.

Ayverdi, Sâmiha. *İbrahim Efendi Konağı* (The Mansion of İbrahim Efendi). Istanbul, 1982.

Banks, J. A. *Prosperity and Parenthood.* London, 1954.

Bayındır, Abdülaziz. *İslâm Muhakeme Hukuku: Osmanlı Devri Uygulaması* (Islamic Court Law: Its Implementation during the Ottoman Period). Istanbul, 1986.

Bayrı, Mehmet Halit. *İstanbul Folkloru* (Istanbul Folklore). Istanbul, 1972.

Behar Cem. 'Les tables de mortalité de la Turquie' in *Colloque national du CNRS sur l'analyse demographique et ses applications.* Paris, 1976.

'Nuptiality and marriage patterns in Istanbul (1885–1940).' *Boğaziçi University Research Papers.* Istanbul, 1985.

'The 1300 and 1322 *tahrirs* as sources of Ottoman historical demography.' *Boğaziçi University Research Papers.* Istanbul, 1985.

Belge, M. 'Türk romanında tip' (Character in the Turkish novel). *Yeni Dergi*, 4 (1968), 33–6.

Benedict, Peter, 'Hukuk reformu açısından başlık parası ve mehr' (Bridewealth and *mehr* from the perspective of legal reform). in A. Güriz and P. Benedict, eds., *Türk Hukuku ve Toplumu Üzerine İncelemeler.* Ankara, 1974.

Berkes, Niyazi. *Bazı Ankara Köyleri Üzerine Bir Araştırma* (Research on Some Ankara Villages). Ankara, 1942.

The Development of Secularism in Turkey. Montreal, 1964.

Berksan, Samira. 'Marriage patterns and the effect on fertility in Turkey' in F. C. Shorter and B. Güvenç, eds., *Turkish Demography. Proceedings of a Conference*. Ankara, 1969.

Bongaarts, John. 'A framework for analyzing the proximate determinants of fertility.' *Population and Development Review*, 4 (1978), 105–32.

Boratav, K., Ökçün, A. G., and Pamuk, Ş. 'Ottoman wages and the world economy, 1839–1913.' *Review*, 8 (1985), 379–406.

Brass, William. *Methods for Estimating Fertility and Mortality from Limited and Defective Data*. Chapel Hill, NC, 1975.

Braudel, Fernand. *The Structures of Everyday Life: Civilization and Capitalism 15th–18th Century*. New York, 1981, I.

Brookes, Barbara. 'Women and reproduction' in Jane Lewis, ed., *Labour and Love: Women's Experience of Home and Family 1850–1940*. Oxford, 1986.

Bulatao, Rodolfo A., and Lee, Ronald D., eds. *Determinants of Fertility in Developing Countries*. New York, 1983, I, II.

Caldwell, J. C. *Theory of Fertility Decline*, New York, 1982.

'Direct economic costs and benefits of children' in R. A. Bulatao and R. D. Lee eds., *Determinants of Fertility in Developing Countries*. New York, 1983, I.

Cassells, Manuel. *The Urban Question: A Marxist Approach*. London, 1977.

Chamie, Joseph. 'Polygyny Among Arabs.' *Population Studies*, 40 (1986), 55–66.

Cin, Halil. *İslâm ve Osmanlı Hukukunda Evlenme* (Marriage in Islamic and Ottoman Law). Ankara, 1974.

Coale, Ansley J. 'The decline of fertility in Europe since the eighteenth century as a chapter in human demographic history' in Ansley, J. Coale, and Susan Cotts Watkins, eds., *The Decline of Fertility in Europe*. Princeton, NJ, 1986.

'Age patterns of marriage.' *Population Studies*, 25 (1971), 193–214.

Coale, Ansley J., and Demeny, Paul. *Regional Model Life Tables and Stable Populations*. Princeton, NJ, 1966.

Coale, Ansley J., and Treadway, Roy. 'A summary of the changing distribution of overall fertility, marital fertility, and the proportion married in the provinces of Europe' in Ansley J. Coale and Susan Cotts Watkins, *The Decline of Fertility in Europe*. Princeton, NJ, 1986.

Coale, Ansley J., and Trussell, James. 'Model fertility schedules.' *Population Index*, 40 (1974), 185–258.

Coale, Ansley J., and Trussell, James. 'Technical note: finding the two parameters that specify a model schedule of marital fertility.' *Population Index*, 44 (1978), 203–13.

Coale, Ansley J., and Watkins, Susan Cotts, eds. *The Decline of Fertility in Europe*. Princeton, NJ, 1986.

Çelik, Zeynep. *The Remaking of Istanbul: Portrait of an Ottoman City in the Nineteenth Century*. Seattle, Wash., 1986.

Davidoff, Leonore, and Hall, Catherine. *Family Fortunes: Men and Women of the English Middle Class 1780–1850*. Chicago, Ill., 1987.

Davis, Fanny. *The Ottoman Lady: A Social History from 1718 to 1918*. New York, 1986.

Demeny, Paul, and Shorter, Frederic C. *Estimating Turkish Mortality, Fertility and Age Structure*. Istanbul, 1968.

Denel, Serim. *Batılılaşma Sürecinde İstanbul'da Tasarım ve Dış Mekanlarda Değişim ve Nedenleri* (Urban Design, Changes in External Space and their Causes in Istanbul during the Process of Westernization). Ankara, 1982.

Dirks, Sabine. *La Famille Musulmane Turque*. Paris, 1969.

Dixon, R. 'Explaining cross cultural variations in age at marriage.' *Population Studies*, 25 (1971).

Duben, Alan. 'The significance of family and kinship in urban Turkey' in Ç. Kâğıtçıbaşı, ed., *Sex Roles, Family and Community in Turkey*. Bloomington, Ind., 1982.

'Turkish families and households in historical perspective.' *Journal of Family History*, 10 (1985), 75–97.

Dumont, Paul and Georgeon, François. 'Un bourgeois d'Istanbul au début du XXe siècle.' *Turcica*, 17 (1985), 127–88.

Dupâquier, J. *et al.*, eds. *Marriage and Remarriage in Populations of the Past*. London, 1981.

Durakbaşa, Ayşe. 'The formation of ''Kemalist female identity'': a historical-cultural perspective.' MA thesis. Boğaziçi University, Istanbul, 1987.

'Cumhuriyet döneminde Kemalist kadın kimliğinin oluşumu' (The development of Kemalist female identity in the Republican period). *Tarih ve Toplum*, 51 (March 1988), 39–43.

Eldem, Vedat. *Osmanlı İmparatorluğunun İktisadî Şartları Hakkında bir Tetkik* (A Study of the Economic Conditions of the Ottoman Empire). Istanbul, 1977.

Elias, Norbert. *The History of Manners*. Oxford, 1983.

The Estimation of Recent Trends in Fertility and Mortality in Egypt. Washington DC., 1982.

Erder, Leila. 'The women of Turkey: A demographic overview' in N. Abadan-Unat, ed., *Women in Turkish Society*. Leiden, 1981.

Ergin, F. 'Birinci dünya savaşında ve Atatürk döneminde fiyatlar ve gelirler' (Prices and incomes in the First World War and in Atatürk's time). *Atatürk Araştırma Merkezi Dergisi*, 3 (1986), 59–84.

Evin, Ahmet Ö. *Origins and Development of the Turkish Novel*. Minneapolis, Minn., 1983.

Eyüboğlu, İsmet Zeki. *Anadolu Büyüleri* (Anatolian Magic). Istanbul, 1978.

Fındıkoğlu, Z. F. *Essai sur la Transformation du Code Familial en Turquie*. Paris, 1936.

'Tanzimatta içtimaî hayat' (Social life during the *Tanzimat*) in *Tanzimat*. Istanbul, 1940.

Findley, Carter Vaughn. *Bureaucratic Reform in the Ottoman Empire: the Sublime Porte, 1789–1922*. Princeton, NJ, 1980.

'Patrimonial household organization and factional activity in the Ottoman ruling class' in O. Okyar and H. İnalcık, eds., *Social and Economic History of Turkey (1071–1920)*. Ankara, 1980.

'Economic bases of revolution and repression in the late Ottoman Empire.' *Comparative Studies in Society and History*, 28, (1987), 81–106.

Finlay, Roger P. *Population and Metropolis: The Demography of London, 1580–1650*. Cambridge, 1981.

Finn, Robert P. *The Early Turkish Novel*. Istanbul, 1984.

Gaskin, K. 'Age at first marriage in Europe before 1850: a summary of family reconstitution data'. *Journal of Family History*, 3 (1978), 23–36.

Gay, Peter. *The Bourgeois Experience, Victoria to Freud. Education of the Senses*, New York, 1984, I.

Geertz, Clifford. *Islam Observed*. New Haven, Conn., 1968.

'The impact of the concept of culture on the concept of man' in Clifford Geertz, *The Interpretation of Cultures*. New York, 1973.

Georgeon, François. 'XX. yüzyıl başlarında bir Osmanlı ailesinin bütçesi üzerine notlar' (Notes on the budget of an Ottoman family at the beginning of the twentieth century). *Tarih ve Toplum*, 23 (1985), 43–6.

Gerber, Haim. 'Social and economic position of women in an Ottoman city, Bursa, 1600–1700.' *International Journal of Middle East Studies*, 12 (1980), 231–44.

Göçek, Fatma Müge. *East Encounters West: France and the Ottoman Empire in the Eighteenth Century*. New York, 1987.

Goode, William J. *World Revolution and Family Patterns*. New York, 1963.

Göyünç, Nejat. ' "Hane" deyimi hakkında' (On the term 'household') *Tarih Dergisi*, 32 (1979), 331–48.

Graham-Brown, Sarah. *Images of Women: The Portrayal of Women in Photography in the Middle East, 1860–1950*. London, 1988.

Hajnal, John. 'European marriage patterns in perspective' in D. V. Glass and E. C. Eversley, eds., *Population in History*. London, 1965.

'Two kinds of preindustrial household formation system.' *Population and Development Review*, 8 (1982). Also in Richard Wall, ed. in collaboration with Jean Robin and Peter Laslett, *Family Forms in Historic Europe*. Cambridge, 1983.

'Births, marriages and reproductivity in England and Wales, 1938–1947.' *Papers of the Royal Commission on Population Section A*. London, 1950.

'Age at marriage and proportions marrying.' *Population Studies*, 7 (1953), 111–32.

Halid, Refik. *Üç Nesil Üç Hayat* (Three Generations, Three Lives). Istanbul, 1943.

Halsband, Robert, ed. *The Complete Letters of Lady Mary Wortley Montagu*. Oxford, 1965, I.

Henry, Louis. 'Perturbations de la nuptialité résultant de la guerre 1914–1918.' *Population*, 2 (1966), 273–333.

Herlihy, David, and Klapsich-Zuber, Christiane. *Tuscans and their Families: A Study of the Florentine Catasto of 1427*. New Haven, Conn., 1985.

Himes, Norman E. *Medical History of Contraception*. New York, 1936 (reprinted 1963).

Huzayyin, Soliman A. 'Marriage and remarriage in Islam' in J. Dupâquier et al., *Marriage and Remarriage in Populations of the Past*. London, 1981.

Işın, Ekrem. 'Abdullah Cevdet' in *Cumhuriyet Âdab-ı Muaşereti'* (Abdullah Cevdet's Republican Manners). *Tarih ve Toplum*, 48 (1987), 13–20.

Issawi, Charles. *The Economic History of Turkey: 1800–1914*. Chicago, Ill., 1980.

Javillonar, Gloria, et al., *Rural Development, Women's Roles and Fertility in Developing Countries: Review of the Literature*. Durham, NC, 1979.

Jennings, Ronald. 'Women in early 17th century Ottoman judicial records: the Sharia court of Anatolian Kayseri.' *Journal of the Economic and Social History of the Orient*, 18 (1975), 53–414.

'Sakaltutan four centuries ago.' *International Journal of Middle East Studies*, 9 (1978), 89–98.

'Divorce in the Ottoman Sharia court of Cyprus, 1580–1640.' Paper presented at the Workshop on Turkish Family and Household Organization. City University of New York, New York, 23–5 April 1986.

Kâğıtçıbaşı, Çiğdem. *Çocuğun Değeri: Türkiye'de Değerler ve Doğurganlık* (The Value of Children: Values and Fertility in Turkey). Istanbul, 1981.

Karal, E. Z. *Atatürk'ten Düşünceler* (Some Thoughts of Atatürk). Ankara, 1956.

Karpat, Kemal H. *Ottoman Population 1830–1914: Demographic and Social Characteristics*. Madison, Wisc., 1985.

'Population movements in the Ottoman state in the nineteenth century: an outline' in J. L. Bacqué-Grammont and P. Dumont, eds., *Contributions à l'histoire économique et sociale de l'Empire Ottoman*. Paris, 1983.

'Ottoman population records and census of 1881/82–1893.' *International Journal of Middle East Studies*, 9 (1978), 237–74.

Kertzer, David I. *Family Life in Central Italy, 1880–1910: Sharecropping, Wage Labor and Coresidence*. New Brunswick, NJ, 1984.

Keyder, Ç. 'The political economy of Turkish democracy.' *New Left Review*, 115 (1979), 3–44.

Khadduri, Majid and Liebesny, Herbert J. *Law in the Middle East*. Washington, DC, 1955.

Koçu, Reşat Ekrem. 'Aksaray yangınları' (The fires of Aksaray). In *İstanbul Ansiklopedisi*. Istanbul, 1958, I.

Kongar, Emre. *İzmir'de Kentsel Aile* (The Urban Family in Izmir). Ankara, 1972.

Kuyaş, Nilüfer. 'Female labor power relations in the urban Turkish family' in Ç. Kâğıtçıbaşı, ed., *Sex Roles, Family and Community in Turkey*. Bloomington, Ind., 1982.

Laslett, Peter. 'Characteristics of the western family considered over time' in P. Laslett, ed., *Family Life and Illicit Love in Earlier Generations*. London, 1977.

'Family and household as work group and kin group: areas of traditional Europe compared' in Richard Wall, ed., in collaboration with Jean Robin and Peter Laslett, *Family Forms in Historic Europe*. Cambridge, 1983.

Laslett, Peter, ed., assisted by Richard Wall. *Household and Family in Past Time*. Cambridge, 1972.

Lewis, Bernard. *The Emergence of Modern Turkey*. London, 1961.

Lewis, Jane. 'Introduction: reconstructing women's experience of home and family' in J. Lewis, ed., *Labour and Love: Women's Experience of Home and Family*. Oxford, 1986.

Linant de Bellefonds. Y. *Traité de droit Musulman comparé*. Paris, 1965.

Livi-Bacci, Massimo. *A History of Italian Fertility during the Last Two Centuries*. Princeton, NJ, 1977.

'Social group forerunners of fertility control in Europe' in Ansley J. Coale and Susan Cotts Watkins, eds., *The Decline of Fertility in Europe*. Princeton, NJ, 1986.

Löfgren, Ovar. 'Family and household, images and reality: cultural change in Swedish society' in Robert McC. Netting *et al.*, eds., *Households: Comparative and Historical Studies of the Domestic Group*. Berkeley, Calif., 1984.

Logue, Larry, 'Tabernacles for waiting spirits: monogamous and polygynous fertility in a Mormon town.' *Journal of Family History*, 10 (1985), 60–74.

Macfarlane, Alan. *Marriage and Love in England, 1300–1840*. Oxford, 1986.

'Modes of reproduction' in G. Hawthorn, ed., *Population and Development.* London, 1978.

Mantran, Robert. 17. *Yüzyılın İkinci Yarısında İstanbul* (Originally published in French as *Istanbul dans la seconde moitié du XVIIe siècle; essai d'histoire institutionnelle, économique et sociale.* Paris, 1962). Istanbul, 1986, I.

Manual IV – Methods of Estimating Basic Demographic Measures from Incomplete Data, United Nations, Department of Economic and Social Affairs, publication no. 42. New York, 1967.

Mardin, Şerif. *The Genesis of Young Ottoman Thought.* Princeton, NJ, 1962.

'Super westernization in the Ottoman Empire in the last quarter of the nineteenth century' in P. Benedict *et al.,* eds., *Turkey: Geographic and Social Perspectives.* Leiden, 1974.

'The modernization of social communication' in G. Laswell, D. Lerner and H. Speier, eds., *Propaganda and Communications in World History.* Honolulu, 1979.

'Turkey: the transformation of an economic code' in Ergun Özbudun and Aydın Ulusan, eds., *The Political Economy of Income Distribution in Turkey.* New York, 1980.

'Ideology, student identity, and professional role.' Mimeographed, 1972.

Mason, Karen O. *The Status of Women: A Review of Its Relationships to Fertility and Mortality.* New York, 1984.

McCarthy, Justin. 'Age, family and migration in nineteenth century Black Sea provinces of the Ottoman Empire.' *International Journal of Middle East Studies,* 10 (1979), 309–23.

McLaren, Angus. *Reproductive Rituals. The Perception of Fertility in England from the Sixteenth to the Nineteenth Century.* London, 1984.

Meeker, Michael. 'Meaning and society in the Near East: examples from the Black Sea Turks and the Levantine Arabs (II).' *International Journal of Middle East Studies,* 7 (1976), 382–422.

Mitterauer, Michael, and Sieder, Reinhard. *The European Family.* Oxford, 1982.

Monroe, W. S. *Turkey and the Turks,* London, 1908.

Moran, Berna. *Türk Romanına Eleştirel Bir Bakış* (A Critical Look at the Turkish Novel). Istanbul, 1983.

'Tanzimat'tan Cumhuriyet'e roman' (The novel from the *Tanzimat* to the Republic) in *Tanzimat'tan Cumhuriyet'e Türkiye Ansiklopedisi.* Istanbul, 1985, I.

Murdock, G. P. *Social Structure.* New York, 1949.

Musallam, B. F. *Sex and Society in Islam.* Cambridge, 1983.

Netting, Robert McC. 'Introduction' in Robert McC. Netting *et al.,* eds., *Households: Comparative and Historical Studies of the Domestic Group.* Berkeley, Calif., 1984.

Okay, Orhan. *Batı Medeniyeti Karşısında Ahmed Midhat Efendi* (Ahmed Midhat Efendi Confronting Western Civilization). Ankara, 1975.

Oppong, Christine and Abu, Katharine. *A Handbook for Data Collection and Analysis on Seven Roles of Women.* Geneva, 1985.

Orga, Irfan. *Portrait of a Turkish Family.* New York, 1957.

Ortaylı, İlber. *Tanzimattan Cumhuriyete Yerel Yönetim Geleneği.* (The Tradition of Local Administration from the *Tanzimat* to the Republic). Istanbul, 1985.

İstanbul'dan Sayfalar (Pages from Istanbul). Istanbul, 1986.

'Anadolu'da 16. yüzyılda evlilik ilişkileri üzerine bazı gözlemler' (Some observations on marriage relations in Anatolia during the sixteenth century). *The Journal of Ottoman Studies*, 1 (1980), 33–40.

Pahl, R. E. 'Urban social theory and research' in R. E. Pahl, *Whose City? and Further Essays on Urban Society*. London, 1975.

Pamuk, Şevket. *Osmanlı Ekonomisi ve Dünya Kapitalizmi, 1820–1913*. (The Ottoman Economy and World Capitalism, 1820–1913). Ankara, 1984.

Osmanlı-Türkiye İktisadi Tarihi, 1500–1914 (An Economic History of Ottoman Turkey, 1500–1914). Istanbul, 1988.

Parla, Taha. *The Social and Political Thought of Ziya Gökalp, 1876–1924*. Leiden, 1985.

lakans, Andrejs. *Kinship in the Past: an Anthropology of European Family Life, 1500–1900*. London, 1984.

Prothro, E. T., and Diab, L. N. *Changing Family Patterns in the Arab East*. Beirut, 1974.

Quataert, D. 'Ottoman households, Ottoman manufacturing and international markets.' Paper presented at the Workshop on the Turkish Family and Household Organization, City University of New York, New York, 23–5 April 1986.

Reher, D. S. 'Old issues and new perspectives: household and family within an urban context in nineteenth century Spain.' *Continuity and Change*, 2 (1987), 103–43.

Research on the Practice of Family Planning in Turkey. Ankara, 1961.

Rosenthal, Steven T. *The Politics of Dependency: Urban Reform in Istanbul*. Westport, Conn., 1980.

Rotber, Robert, and Rapp, Theodore, K., eds. *Marriage and Fertility: Studies in Interdisciplinary History*. Princeton, NJ, 1980.

Sa, Sophie. 'Marriage among the Taiwanese of pre-1945 Taipei' in S. B. Hanley, and A. P. Wolf, eds., *Family and Population in East Asian History*. Stanford, Calif., 1985.

Safilios-Rothschild, C. *Socioeconomic Indicators of Women's Status in Developing Countries, 1970–1980*. New York, 1986.

Samman, M. L. 'La situation démographique de la Syrie.' *Population*, 31 (1976), 1253–89.

Seklani, M. 'La fécondité dans les pays Arabes: données numériques, attitudes et comportements.' *Population*, 15 (1960), 831–56.

Schneider, Jane, and Schneider, Peter. 'Demographic transitions in a Sicilian town.' *Journal of Family History*, 9 (1984), 245–72.

Sharlin, Allan. 'Urban-rural differences in fertility in Europe during the demographic transition' in Ansley J. Coale and Susan Cott Watkins, eds., *The Decline of Fertility in Europe*. Princeton, NJ, 1986.

Shaw, Stanford J. 'The Ottoman census system and population, 1831–1914.' *International Journal of Middle East Studies*, 9 (1978), 325–38.

Shaw, Stanford J., and Shaw, Ezel K. *History of the Ottoman Empire and Modern Turkey*. London, 1977, II.

Shorter, Edward. *The Making of the Modern Family*. New York, 1975.

Shorter, Frederic C. 'The population of Turkey after the war of independence.' *International Journal of Middle East Studies*, 17 (1985), 417–41.

Shorter, Frederic C., and Macura, Miroslav. *Trends in Fertility and Mortality in Turkey, 1935–1975*. Washington, DC. 1982.

Smith, D. 'Age at first marriage.' World Fertility Survey Comparative Studies, 7 (1980).

Smith, James, E., and Kunz, Philip R. 'Polygyny and fertility in 19th century America.' Population Studies, 30 (1976), 465–80.

Smith, Richard. 'Fertility, economy, and household formation in England over three centuries.' Population and Development Review, 7 (1981), 595–622.

'The people of Tuscany and their families in the fifteenth century: medieval or Mediterranean.' Journal of Family History, 6 (1981), 107–28.

Stirling, Paul. Turkish Village. New York, 1965.

Stone, Lawrence. The Family, Sex and Marriage in England, 1500–1800. London, 1977.

Tanpınar, Ahmet Hamdi. Beş Şehir (Five Cities). Istanbul, 1969.

19uncu Asır Türk Edebiyatı Tarihi (The History of Turkish Literature in the Nineteenth Century). Istanbul, 1982.

Teitelbaum, Michael S., and Winter, J.M. The Fear of Population Decline. New York, 1985.

Tekeli, Şirin. 'The meaning and the limits of feminist ideology in Turkey' in F. Özbay, ed., The Study of Women in Turkey. Istanbul, 1986.

Tietze, Andreas. 'The study of literature as the cultural manifestation of socio-economic changes: achievements and potential of the study of Ottoman literature.' International Journal of Turkish Studies, 2 (1981), 44–56.

Tilly, Charles, ed. Historical Studies of Changing Fertility. Princeton, NJ, 1978.

Timur, Serim. Türkiye'de Aile Yapısı (Family Structure in Turkey). Ankara, 1972.

'Socioeconomic determinants of differential fertility in Turkey' in J. Allman, ed., Women's Status and Fertility in the Muslim World. New York, 1978.

Todd, Emmanuel. The Explanation of Ideology: Family Structures and Social Systems. Oxford, 1985.

Todorova, Maria. 'Population structure, marriage patterns, family and household (according to Ottoman documentary material from north-eastern Bulgaria in the 60s of the 19th century).' Etudes Balkaniques, 1 (1983), 59–72.

'Marriage and nuptiality in Bulgaria during the nineteenth century.' Mimeographed, n.d.

Toprak, Zafer. Türkiye'de Millî İktisat, 1908–1918 (Nationalist Economics in Turkey, 1908–18). Ankara, 1982.

'La population d'Istanbul dans les premiéres années de la République' in Travaux et Recherches en Turquie 1982. Louvain, 1983.

'The family, feminism and the state during the Young Turk period, 1908–1918' in Edhem Eldem, ed., Première Rencontre internationale sur l'Empire Ottoman et la Turquie moderne, Institut National de Langues et Civilisations Orientales; Maison des Sciences de l'Homme. Istanbul, 1990.

Trumbach, Randolph. The Rise of the Egalitarian Family: Aristocratic Kinship and Domestic Relations in Eighteenth-Century England. New York, 1978.

Tucker, Judith. 'Marriage and family in Nablus: 1720–1856: toward a history of Arab marriage.' Journal of Family History, 13 (1988), 165–81.

Tugay, Emine Foat. Three Centuries: Family Chronicles of Turkey and Egypt. London, 1963.

Turkey: Report of Mission on Needs Assessment for Population Activities. New York, 1980.

Turkish Population and Health Survey (1983). Ankara, 1987.
Türkiye İktisat Kongresi – İzmir 1923: Haberler, Belgeler, Yorumlar (The Turkish Economics Congress – Izmir 1923: News, Documents, Interpretations). Ankara, 1968.
Unat, F. R. *Hicrî Tarihleri Milâdî Tarihlere Çevirme Kilavuzu* (A Guide to Coverting Hegirian to Gregorian Dates). Ankara, 1974.
Uşaklıgil, Halid Ziya. *Kırk Yıl* (Forty Years). Istanbul, 1969.
Vallin, J. 'La nuptialité en Tunisie.' *Population*, Special issue (1971), 150–4.
'Facteurs socio-économiques de l'âge au mariage de la femme Algérienne. *Population*, 28 (1973), 1172–7.
Velidedeoğlu, H. V. *Türk Medenî Kanunu* (The Turkish Civil Code). Ankara, 1970.
Vital Statistics from the Turkish Demographic Survey. Ankara, 1970.
Wall, Richard. 'Introduction' in Richard Wall, ed., in collaboration with Jean Robin and Peter Laslett, *Family Forms in Historic Europe*. Cambridge, 1983.
Wolf, Arthur P. and Hanley, Susan B. 'Introduction' in S. B. Hanley and A. P. Wolf, eds., *Family and Population in East Asian History*. Stanford, Calif., 1985.
World Bank. *World Development Report (1984)*. Oxford, 1984.
Wrigley, E. A. 'Population history in the 1980s.' *Journal of Interdisciplinary History*, 12 (1981), 208–26.
Wrigley, E. A. and Schofield, R. *The Population History of England, 1541–1871*. London, 1981.
Yalman, Ahmet Emin. *Turkey in My Time*. Norman, Okla., 1956.
Yamagisako, S. J. 'Family and household: the analysis of domestic groups' in *Annual Review of Anthropology*, 8. Palo Alto, Calif., 1979.
Zaretsky, Eli. *Capitalism, the Family, and Personal Life*. New York, 1973.
Zeldin, Theodore. *France 1848–1945: Ambition and Love*. Oxford, 1979.
Zurayk, H., and Armenian, H. K. eds. *Beirut 1984: A Population and Health Profile*. Beirut, 1985.
Zurayk, Huda and Shorter, Frederic C. 'The social composition of households in Arab cities and settlements: Cairo, Beirut, Amman.' Cairo, 1988.

Index

Cambridge Studies in Population, Economy and
Society in Past Time 15

Titles available in paperback are marked with an asterisk

Made in the USA
Columbia, SC
09 September 2019